Protection and Competition in International Trade

Essays in Honor of W. M. Corden

Protection and Competition in International Trade

Essays in Honor of W. M. Corden

Edited by
HENRYK KIERZKOWSKI

Basil Blackwell

First published 1987

Basil Blackwell Ltd
108 Cowley Road, Oxford OX4 1JF, UK

Basil Blackwell Inc.
432 Park Avenue South, Suite 1503
New York, NY 10016, USA

British Library Cataloguing in Publication Data

Protection and competition in international
trade: essays in honour of W. M. Corden.
1. Commerce
I. Kierzkowski, Henryk II. Corden, W. M.
382 HF1008

ISBN 0-631-15004-8

Library of Congress Cataloging in Publication Data

Protection and competition in international trade.

Includes index.
1. Commercial policy. 2. Free trade and protection.
3. Competition, International. 4. Corden, W. M.
(Warner Max) I. Corden, W. M. (Warner Max)
II. Kierzkowski, Henryk.
HF1411.P697 1987 382′.3 86-29915
ISBN 0-631-15004-8

Phototypeset in 10 on 11½ pt Times Roman
by Dobbie Typesetting Service, Plymouth, Devon
Printed in Great Britain by Billing & Sons Ltd, Worcester

Contents

Contributors vii

1 Introduction
Henryk Kierzkowski 1

2 Protection Policy and the Assignment Rule
Peter J. Lloyd 4

3 Safeguards Policy and the Conservative Social Welfare Function
Alan V. Deardorff 22

4 Voluntary Export Restrictions versus Import Restrictions: A Welfare-theoretic Comparison
Richard A. Brecher and Jagdish N. Bhagwati 41

5 Factor Shadow Prices in Distorted Open Economies
Alasdair Smith 54

6 Industrial Policy and Trade Policy: The Connections
Richard E. Caves 68

7 International Capital Mobility and the Dutch Disease
Ronald W. Jones, J. Peter Neary and Frances P. Ruane 86

8 Bundled International Factor Mobility
Wilfred J. Ethier 99

9 Tariffs and Subsidies under Oligopoly: The Case of the US Automobile Industry
Avinash Dixit 112

10 Market Access and Competition in High Technology Industries: A Simulation Exercise
Paul Krugman 128

11 Product Quality, Intra-industry Trade and (Im)perfect Competition
Rodney E. Falvey and Henryk Kierzkowski 143

12 Intermediate Goods, Export Taxation and Resource-based Industrialization
Ronald Findlay 162

13 The Importance of Economic Policy in Development: Contrasts between Korea and Turkey
Anne O. Krueger 172

14 GATT Reform: Selected Issues
Robert E. Baldwin 204

15 The Importance of Frontier Barriers
Richard H. Snape 215

Index 233

List of Contributors

Robert E. Baldwin
University of Wisconsin

Jagdish N. Bhagwati
Columbia University

Richard A. Brecher
Carleton University, Ottawa

Richard E. Caves
Harvard University

Alan V. Deardorff
University of Michigan

Avinash Dixit
Princeton University

Wilfred J. Ethier
University of Pennsylvania

Rodney E. Falvey
Australian National University

Ronald Findlay
Columbia University

Ronald W. Jones
University of Rochester

Henryk Kierzkowski
Graduate Institute of International Studies, Geneva

Anne O. Krueger
World Bank

Paul Krugman
Massachusetts Institute of Technology

Peter J. Lloyd
University of Melbourne

J. Peter Neary
University College, Dublin

Frances P. Ruane
Trinity College, Dublin

Alasdair Smith
University of Sussex

Richard H. Snape
Monash University

1
Introduction

Henryk Kierzkowski

This volume is in honor of Max Corden on the occasion of his sixtieth birthday, and is intended to express an appreciation of Max's work by the profession.

Anyone truly deserving a festschrift must have made a lasting mark on the development of his field. His work must have captured the attention of others, resolved some important issues and stimulated new research. Max Corden's contributions to the theory of international trade, and especially the theory of tariffs, the effective rate of protection, growth and trade and the theory of customs unions, are well established and are known not only among a narrow group of specialists but also across the economics profession and among policy-makers. Rather than dwell here on his numerous works, I intend to reveal a few 'snapshots' from the professional life of the man we are honoring.

Several years ago Max invited me to make an extended research visit to the Australian National University. We talked almost daily through the summer of 1983. It was always very informal and spontaneous; we would chat in his office at the university, go for a long walk in the hills surrounding Canberra or have dinner at his house. Our conversations would inevitably revolve around economics, but there were also recurring remarks about Max's academic career and life. It was then that I realized that, in spite of his youthfulness, Max was nearing 60; and it was then and there that I decided to undertake preparation of the present festschrift.

Max Corden was educated at Melbourne Boys' High School, continued at the University of Melbourne, before leaving Australia for the London School of Economics. The passage to England in 1953 and his subsequent stay there was of crucial importance in Corden's life. The London School of Economics was at that time one of the world's centers of excellence in economics. Max went to the LSE to learn the gospel, but even before leaving Australia he knew that he wanted to work on the effects of labor inflow in an open economy. His interest in problems of factor accumulation and trade goes back to his undergraduate years and had been clearly stimulated by the Australian experience with labor migration in the 1940s and 1950s. This pattern was to recur time and again in the future: Corden's research interests and his academic work tend toward the theoretical, but they are almost always rooted in real-life phenomena.

Max's mentor at the LSE was James Meade, for whom he developed a lasting admiration and respect. The LSE, however, comprised not only great teachers, but also great students. The list of Corden's contemporaries there reads like today's *Who's Who* in international economics. At the risk of omitting some, it included Richard Lipsey, Ted Rybczynski, Robert Mundell, Kelvin Lancaster and Richard Cooper. I asked Max if he knew at that time that he was going to make it in a big way. With typical modesty, he judged himself to be below the level of his colleagues and friends. It was only several years later, when James Meade went to Australia to work on internal and external balance and there spoke very highly of his former student's work, that Max got the first inkling of where he stood in the eyes of his teacher.

It was very revealing that Max wanted to go back to Australia after finishing his PhD in 1956. His academic positions, first at the University of Melbourne and later at the Australian National University, gave him a chance to establish himself as a scholar in his own right. Once again, he was motivated by real-life puzzles, namely, the commercial policy of his own country. Some of his most important articles come from that period: 'The Calculation of the Cost of Protection'; 'Monopoly, Tariffs and Subsidies'; 'Recent Developments in the Theory of International Trade' and, of course, 'The Structure of a Tariff System and the Effective Protection Rate.' Written far away from leading centers of economic research, these papers nevertheless quickly attracted international attention.

Harry Johnson in particular followed Max Corden's work very closely, and he obviously thought very highly of it, because when the position of Nuffield Reader in International Economics at Oxford University become available he urged Max to apply for it. This prestigious post had been previously held by Sir Roy Harrod. Max hesitated, not convinced that he deserved such a distinction, but Harry persisted; his letters to Max became more and more impatient, and those who knew Johnson well can imagine what that meant. When Max finally did apply and got the job, Harry was first to break the news. He sent a cable that read: 'The best man won. Congratulations.'

On his way to Oxford, Max passed through Chicago, where he attended a conference organized by Robert Mundell. The conference was also attended by Sir Roy Harrod. Sir Roy did not know at the time who his successor was, and as Max did not see fit to boast about his appointment, Harrod left the conference without knowing that he had just met his successor.

The time spent in Oxford, 1967–76, resulted in many outstanding articles and two very important books: *The Theory of Protection* and *Trade Policy and Economic Welfare*. The true contribution of that period must also include teaching and inspiring a large body of students. Oxford University in the 1960s and 1970s was one of the best places to study international economics, thanks to Max Corden and others, and naturally it attracted brilliant students from all over the world. The value added by Max Corden to the process of human capital formation is today clearly apparent in many countries.

The last decade took Max Corden away from Oxford and back to Canberra, and away from international trade theory and commercial policy and into the macroeconomics of the open economy. Once again, the shift in interest can be readily explained by real-life events, namely, the emergence of unemployment and inflation as the dominant economic problems of the period. In Australia he also became involved in debates on important policy issues such as structural adjustment, trade unions and unemployment and the economic consequences of a booming sector. At the international level he contributed to discussions on international monetary issues through his association with the Group of Thirty. The new themes are best reflected in a highly successful book, *Inflation, Exchange Rates, and the World Economy*.

Although international trade theory does not occupy the dominant position in Corden's current academic work, this need not be a permanent situation. I hope that ten years from now we shall be able to honor him with another trade festschrift.

The present volume could not have been possible without the generous help of Max's friends and colleagues. When I asked various scholars for their contributions, I had anticipated a positive response: I was, however, struck by the enthusiasm of many responses. This fact in itself speaks for the esteem in which Max Corden is held.

2

Protection Policy and the Assignment Rule

Peter J. Lloyd

The debate about protection policy is perennial in virtually all countries. For many years economists have been circumscribing more and more narrowly the set of conditions under which border protection is a policy which is optimal or even welfare-improving. Moreover, in recent years there has been a growing awareness of why legislators are prepared to supply protection in order to promote their selfish political interests. Yet, the profession of international economics has been conspicuously unsuccessful in persuading politicians and the public at large that industries should not generally be assisted by instruments of protection.

This paper reconsiders the issues of protection policy as an assignment problem, that is, as one of choosing the optimal instrument for a policy problem. This is, of course, an old perception, but some recent developments in the theory of international trade make it possible to extend earlier results. Section 1 outlines the model which is used to analyse the demand for protection and the design of optimal policy rules. This is an extension of the specific-factor model of Jones (1971, 1975) to incorporate inter-industry and international flows of intermediate inputs. Section 2 considers the optimal assignment rules for some problems and in particular for problems involving so-called 'non-economic objectives'. These are often used to justify protective policies, and they illustrate well the deficiencies of protection policies. Section 3 puts forward two very general propositions concerning the universal demand for protection. These are couched in terms of the concepts of 'true friends' and 'true enemies', which are alternatives to the Jones–Scheinkman (1977) concepts of 'natural friends' and 'natural enemies'. Finally, Section 4 indicates the ineffectiveness and sometimes the inefficacy of protective policies which are sub-optimal assignments.

1 THE MODEL

The model used throughout this paper is the extension of the Jones model developed by Burgess (1980) and Hosios (1982). In the Jones (1975) model there are n industries, each of which uses one specific input and one mobile or non-specific input, a total of $n+1$ inputs. These two types of inputs are arbitrarily called 'capital' and 'labour', respectively. Thus, the dimensions of the model are $n \times (n+1)$. For the minimum-dimension 2×3 version of this model, Burgess and Hosios independently added the complication that the outputs of each industry can be used for intermediate or final demand. This makes the model considerably richer for the purpose of policy analysis. In this paper I shall generalize the Burgess–Hosios extension to the $n \times (n+1)$ version. This will be called the Jones–Burgess–Hosios (JBH) model.[1]

The technology of each industry is described by a single-output production function:

$$g_i = f^i(v_i, q_i) \tag{1}$$

where $v_i = (K_i, L_i)$ is the vector of the two primary inputs used in the industry, one specific and one non-specific, and

$$q_i = (g_{1i}, \ldots, q_i = (g_{1i}, \ldots, g_{ni})$$

is the vector of intermediate inputs. Intermediate inputs may be produced locally or imported. Some of the elements of q_i may be zero. f^i satisfy regularity properties; in particular, they are linearly homogeneous and strictly quasiconcave for all i. This permits us to assume that the industries are all competitive. The supplies of both the mobile factor and the specific factors are assumed to be fixed and the factor markets to be competitive with flexible prices that clear the markets. The country is assumed to be small. With these assumptions, we can define the net output and the real value added of industry i:

$$y_i = f^i(v_i, q_i) - \sum_j g_{ij} \tag{2}$$

and

$$z_i = f^i(v_i, q_i) - \sum_j (p_j/p_i)\, g_{ji} \tag{3}$$

$$z_i = F^i(v_i, \bar{p}_i) \tag{4}$$

respectively, where $\bar{p}_i$ is the vector of relative prices of intermediate inputs whose jth elements is (p_j/p_i), z_i is the value added in industry i in units of output of this industry, and F^i is the multiple-input–commodity version of the real value added function introduced by Khang (1971).

For such a small open economy, the equilibrium conditions for the production sector are

$$\begin{aligned} p - A(u)u &= 0 \\ a_L(u)g &= L \\ a_{Ki}(u)g_i &= K_i \end{aligned} \tag{5}$$

where p denotes the $n \times 1$ vector of commodity prices, u the $(2n+1) \times 1$ vector of prices for primary and intermediate inputs, A the $n \times (2n+1)$ transpose of the matrix of least-cost input–output coefficients, a_L the vector of labour coefficients, g the vector of gross outputs, a_{Ki} the specific capital coefficient and g_i the gross output of industry i. The equations relate to the n commodities which are produced in strictly positive quantities. (These may be regarded as the solution from a larger system of equations for $s \geqq n$ commodities where some commodities which the economy is capable of producing may not be produced because the profits are strictly negative.) The first equation in (5) represents the zero profit conditions and the remaining equations the factor market conditions. This is the JBH model of dimension $n \times (n+1)$. It will be assumed that the set of produced commodities does not change when commodity prices change.

One variant of the model is obtained by assuming that the factor labour is also industry-specific. In this variant equation (5) separates into n sub-systems:

$$\begin{aligned} p_i - A_i(u_i)u_i &= 0 \\ a_{Li}(u_i)g_i &= L_i \\ a_{Ki}(u_i)g_i &= K_i. \end{aligned} \tag{6}$$

Here, $u_i = (w_i, r_i, p')'$ is the $(n+2) \times 1$ vector of prices of inputs for industry i and A_i is the ith row of A. This gives a $n \times 2n$ model of the economy.

A second variant is obtained by assuming instead that both factors are mobile. This is the $n \times 2$ version of the Heckscher–Ohlin model with intermediate input flows. However, it is well-known that the output vector is indeterminate with these dimensions. One way of overcoming indeterminary is to assume there are n primary inputs. These primary inputs can be considered as types of mobile labour and capital. In this variant the equilibrium conditions become:

$$\begin{aligned} p - A(u)u &= 0 \\ a_k(u)g &= v_k \qquad k = 1, \ldots, n. \end{aligned} \tag{7}$$

Here, u is $2n \times 1$ vector of input prices and A is an $n \times 2n$ matrix. a_k is the vector of inputs of the kth factor into all industries and v_k is the national endowment of factor k. This gives the $n \times n$ version of the Heckscher–Ohlin model with intermediate inputs.

The basic model and its two variants can be arrayed in terms of increasing factor mobility. Hosios (1982) identifies this array with periods of time. The variant with both factors specific is called the Very Short Run, the standard JBH model the Short Run and the third model the Long Run. I shall employ the Short Run and Long Run variants. These give a versatile set of models for analysing issues of movement of factors and real incomes and policies relating to these movements.

2 OPTIMAL ASSIGNMENT RULES

For an economy whose production structure is specified as in the JBH model of section 1, we can now determine optimal policy in any policy situation.

We seek to maximize the utility of one household, say household 1, $U_1(x_{11}, \ldots, x_{1n})$, given the utility levels of other households,

$$\{U_h(x_{h1}, \ldots, x_{hn}) - \mu_h\} = 0 \qquad \text{h} = 2, \ldots, \text{H} \qquad (8)$$

and subject to the constraints. The constraints are the technology (equation (1)) and net imports, defined as the differences between consumption and net output (equation (2)), which can be combined in the set of equations

$$\{\sum_h x_{hi} - f^i(v_i, q_i) - \sum_j g_{ij} - m_i\} = 0 \qquad i = 1, \ldots, n, \qquad (9)$$

the fixed supplies of primary factors,

$$(\sum_i v_{ki} - v_k) = 0 \qquad k = 1, \ldots, \ell, \qquad (10)$$

the balance of payments,

$$(\sum_i p_i^* m_i) = 0 \qquad (11)$$

and any other constraints which may be added. $h = 1, \ldots, H$ indexes the households of the economy. Thus, x_{hi} is the consumption by household h of the commodity i. In equation (10), ℓ is the number of mobile factors. This specification covers both the Short Run and Long Run variants where $\ell = 1$ and n, respectively. $(p_i^*, \ldots, p_n^*)$ is the vector of international prices and $m = (m_\text{i}, \ldots, m_n)$ is the vector of quantities of imports of these commodities. $\lambda_{1\text{h}} = (\lambda_{11}, \ldots, \lambda_{1H})$, $\lambda_2 = (\lambda_{21}, \ldots, \lambda_{2n})$, $\lambda_3 = (\lambda_{31}, \ldots, \lambda_{3\ell})$ and λ_4 are the Lagrange multipliers for these constraints in equations (8), (9), (10) and (11), respectively. This maximization gives the Pareto-efficient allocations for the economy. The choice variables are x_{hi}, v_{ki}, m_i and g_{ji}.

If there are no additional constraints on the economy and the utility functions of all households are strictly quasi-concave, the first-order conditions for Pareto-efficient allocations may be written as:

$$\begin{aligned} \lambda_{1h}\partial U_h/\partial x_{hi} &= \lambda_4 p_i^* & h &= 1, \ldots, H,\ i = 1, \ldots, n \\ \lambda_4 p_i^*\, \partial f^i/\partial v_{ki} &= \lambda_{3k} & k &= 1, \ldots, \ell. \\ p_i^*\, \partial f^i/\partial g_{ji} &= p_j^* & i &= 1, \ldots, n,\ j = 1, \ldots, n \end{aligned} \qquad (12)$$

These equations have a solution which is unique up to a factor of proportionality. $\lambda_4 p^*$ and λ_3 may be interpreted as the vectors of commodity and primary factor prices, respectively. The standard theorem that Pareto efficiency is achieved by a 'free trade' (zero price distortion) competitive economy applies.

If there are other additional constraints because of unremovable price distortions (tariffs, subsidies and so on) or non-economic objectives or other factors, the optimal policy can be determined. J. N. Bhagwati enunciated the following important general principle:

> i. Optimal policy intervention in the presence of distortions involves a tax-cum-subsidy policy addressed directly to offsetting the source of the distortions, when the causes are endogenous or autonomous, policy-imposed [and] ii. When distortions have to be introduced into the economy, because the values of certain variables (e.g. production or employment of a factor in an activity) have to be constrained, the optimal (or least-cost) method of doing this is to choose that policy intervention that creates the distortion affecting directly the constrained variable.
> (Bhagwati, 1971, p. 77)

I shall call this rule the Assignment Rule. It applies to price distortions and non-economic objectives. However, the same principle also applies to other justifications for government intervention in an open economy. For example, when applicable, the infant-industry and the terms-of-trade justification for intervention can be interpreted in the same way. Indeed, any standard market failure justifications for intervention can be interpreted in this way. The elementary but powerful idea is that each optimal policy instrument has to be tailored to the exact source of the problem and that this generally requires an instrument whose base is directly related to the source of the problem.

This rule can be illustrated by the theory of so-called 'non-economic objectives'. (This description is rather inapt, as the 'objectives' are usually treated as constraints and the 'non-economic' constraint is specified in terms of economic variables and derives from economic arguments.) The standard reference is to Bhagwati and Srinivasan (1969). However, the term seems to have been coined by Johnson (1960) and the central idea of ranking policies can be traced to the seminal paper by Corden (1957). This theory has received little attention in recent years except for special cases such as the revenue constraint under uncertainty (for example, Young, 1980), but it is still an accepted part of international economic theory and is commonly cited in the USA, UK and other countries as a justification of protection policies such as 're-industrialization', that is, the promotion of output and/or employment in the manufacturing sectors of these countries. Similar problems of optimal policy determinatión arise with price distortions and other second-best problems.

Consider first that the additional constraint relates to *production*. Corden (1957) introduced this case for a model with a much simpler structure and a single importable commodity. In the JBH model we may constraint the model by assuming that there is a set of importable commodities (α_1) for which the aggregate (real) value added cannot fall below some specified minimum, P. This gives the additional constraint

$$[\sum_{i\epsilon\alpha_1}\{p_i^* f(v_i, q_i) - \sum_j p_j^* g_{ji}\} - P] = 0 \tag{13}$$

whose associated Lagrange multiplier is λ_5. Maximization of the objective function now yields the modified set of first-order conditions.

$$\left.\begin{array}{lll}
\lambda_{1h}\,\partial U_h/\partial x_{hi} & =\lambda_4 p_i^* & i\epsilon(\alpha_1 \cup \alpha_1^c) \\
\lambda_4 p_i^*\,\partial f^i/\partial v_{ki} & =\lambda_{3k} & k=1, \ldots, \ell \\
\lambda_4 p_i^*(1-\lambda_4/\lambda_5)\partial f^i/\partial v_{ki} & =\lambda_{3k} & i\epsilon\alpha_1, k=1, \ldots, \ell \\
p_i^*\,\partial f^i/\partial g_{ji} & =p_j^* & i\epsilon\alpha_1^c, j\epsilon\alpha_1^c \\
p_i^*(1-\lambda_5/\lambda_4)\,\partial f^i/\partial g_{ji} & =p_j^* & i\epsilon\alpha_1, j\epsilon\alpha_1^c \\
p_i^*\,\partial f^i/\partial g_{ji} & =p_j^* & i\epsilon\alpha_1, j\epsilon\alpha_1
\end{array}\right\} \tag{14}$$

where α_1^c is the complement of α_1. This set of equations is satisfied if a uniform *ad valorem* subsidy at the rate $(-\lambda_5/\lambda_4)$ is granted on the gross outputs of the set, including those outputs which are used as inputs in the production of some other commodity or commodities in this set; that is, a subsidy on real value added by these industries. The subsidy rate is positive since $\lambda_5<0$ and $\lambda_4>0$. Equivalently, the system is satisfied by a uniform subsidy at the same rate on all domestic inputs used in the production of this set of commodities. One may note that this solution implies inefficient production since the price to producers of outputs of these α_1 industries which are used as inputs by another industry in this set will differ from the price to producers in industries outside this set. This generalized the results obtained by Corden (1957), Bhagwati and Srinivasan (1969), Tan (1971) and Vandendorpe (1974).

We may instead, following Bhagwati and Srinivasan (1969), add the constraint that the aggregate *employment* of some factor k in some specified set of industries (α_2) must not fall below a critical minimum, V. This gives the constraint:

$$(\sum_{i\epsilon\alpha_2}\lambda_{ki} - V) = 0 \tag{15}$$

whose associated Lagrange multipler is λ_6. This case may be solved in the same way. The optimal policy is a uniform *ad valorem* rate of subsidy at the rate (λ_6/λ_{4k}) on units of this factor employed in the set of industries only. Like the previous case, this results in inefficient production because the policy distorts the relative factor prices across industries.

These two examples suffice to show how the base of the corrective tax subsidy instruments must be modified when the variable entering the additional constraint changes.

The Assignment Rule seems to give admirable guidance to the formulation of policies relating to non-economic objectives. Yet, there are a number of difficulties with this formulation. In the first instance, it is assumed implicitly that the net revenue required (or obtained) from the optimal set of taxes–subsidies can be raised (dispersed) by non-distortionary lump-sum taxes (payments). But the main difficulties relate to the formulation of the policy problems themselves. The constraint is of the fixed target type. (During the 1950s and 1960s fixed target models were frequently used for the assignment of multiple macroeconomic instruments.) Hence the choice of level at which the target variable is fixed is quite arbitrary. However, the basic question concerns the choice of target variable itself. Why should a government seek to constraint the level of output or employment in some set of industries? This state of theory is quite inadequate. We should seek to endogenize the target.[2]

An insight into the problem can be had by applying an equivalence relation from the theory of mathematical programming. Under certain conditions, which are satisfied here because of the concavity restrictions imposed on the technologies and the utility functions, one may interchange one of several constraints in an optimization problem with the objective function and still obtain the same solution. Consider, for example, the problem in which the added constraint is real value added in some industry. Call this problem A. Denote the solution values to this problem obtained from equation (14) as $(x^*_{hi}, v^*_{hi}, m^*_i, g^*_{ji})$. Formulate a second problem by substituting the additional constraint of problem A as the objective function of the new problem and add the objective function of problem A as the added constraint of this problem. Call this problem B. It is

$$\max[\sum_{i\epsilon\beta}\{p^*_i f^i(v_i, q_i) - \sum_j p^*_j g_{ji}\}] \tag{16}$$

subject to the constraints of problem A minus that of equation (13) plus $U_1(x_1) \geqq \mu^*_1$. μ^*_1 is the solution value for U_1 in problem A. It is easy to verify that problem B has the same solution as problem A. Why should any government seek to maximize the value added (or employment) in these industries?

The answer to this question must be, it seems to me, that the choice of constraint (or 'objective') in these problems was ill-conceived. In some cases it may be possible to derive the constraint from a full model in which there is a market failure. Bhagwati and Srinivasan (1976) construct a two-period model in which the possibility of a market-disruption-induced quota on second-period exports is a function of the level of first-period trade. This may justify a restraint on first-period trade. This problem is really very different from an arbitrary initial assumption that trade should be restricted to some level. The level of restriction – and, indeed, whether there should be any restriction – will be a function of the probability of a quota and it should apply only to first-period trade. Furthermore, when the full problem is revealed it raises the possibility that there are other instruments which might rank above a restraint on trade. In particular, it may be that inter-government negotiation or the threat of retaliation will avoid the imposition of the second-period quota and therefore remove the problem. In all cases we must ask for the ultimate cause of any problem and a complete specification of it.

Earlier literature on non-economic objectives tended merely to cite 'ideology' or 'national pride' as a justification of sectoral output or employment targets. Currently, 're-industrialization' is also based on the premise that there is some unidentified additional merit in the production of the manufacturing sector. A more likely explanation is that these policies have been advocated as a form of income support by some factors employed in the industries who advance any supposed public benefit to support their private cause. The next section considers two basic propositions concerning universal rent-seeking.

3 TWO GENERAL PROPOSITIONS

Since the famous article by Stolper and Samuelson (1941), international economists have analysed the relationships between changes in (relative) commodity prices on the one hand and the real incomes of factor owners on the other in terms of the matrix of real income changes measured in terms of wage goods. For the Short Run version of the JBH model, in which only 'labour' is mobile, this $(n+1)\times n$ matrix is

$$U=\begin{bmatrix} \hat{u}_1/\hat{p}_1 & \dots & \hat{u}_1/\hat{p}_n \\ \vdots & & \vdots \\ \hat{u}_{n+1}/\hat{p}_1 & \dots & \hat{u}_{n+1}/\hat{p}_n \end{bmatrix}$$

where $u^*=(w, r_1, \ldots, r_n)$ is the vector of primary input prices, the wage rate and capital rentals. It is understood that each commodity price is varied one at a time and the circumflex denotes the corresponding proportionate rate of change of the variable. The rows of this matrix show the effects on one factor of changes in the price of each commodity while the columns show the effects on each factor of changes in the price of one commodity. For the Long Run variant in which all n primary inputs are mobile, u reduces to an $n\times n$ matrix.

In the context of the $n\times n$ model, Jones and Scheinkman (1977) introduced the useful terminology of 'natural friends' and 'natural enemies'. A commodity i is a natural friend of a factor k if and only if $(\hat{u}_k/\hat{p}_i)>1$, and a commodity i is a natural enemy of factor k if and only if $(\hat{u}_k/\hat{p}_i)<0$. Thus a natural friend is a commodity for which a price increases the real income of the factor in terms of all wage goods and, therefore, unambiguously increases the real income (= utility) of the factor. Similarly, a natural enemy is a commodity for which a price increase lowers the real income of the factor in terms of all wage goods and, therefore, unambiguously lowers the real income of the factor.

It is these concepts which underlie the original Stolper–Samuelson theorem. While they have proven very productive in the context of the 2×2 version of the Heckscher–Ohlin model, they have not proven so useful for the $m\times n$ dimensional generalization of this model. The source of the problem is that elements of the U matrix may lie in the interval [0, 1]. If this occurs, and assuming the jth commodity and at least one other are consumed in strictly positive quantities, the change in real income of the factor is ambiguous on the basis of this information. Nevertheless, using these concepts, Jones and Scheinkman (1977) were able to show that every factor has at least one natural enemy, but concerning natural friends, which are the more interesting property, they were not able to show that every factor must have a natural friend unless further restrictions are imposed on the technology. If restrictions are imposed on the factor intensity pattern, the Stolper–Samuelson pattern generalizes to the $n \times n$ version but the restrictions required are very strict (see Ethier, 1984, section 6.2).

More progress may be made if we revert to the pre-Stolper–Samuelson method of considering real income in the sense of utility. This is best stated in terms of the indirect utility function. For the hth household, this function is $V^h(I^h, p)$ where I^h is the income of the household. Differentiating totally,

$$\hat{V}^h = \hat{I}^h - \sum_i \phi_{hi} \hat{p}_i$$

where ϕ_{hi} is the share of commodity i in the budget of household h[3]. This reduces to

$$\hat{V}^h = \hat{u}_k - \sum_i \phi_{ki} \hat{p}_i \tag{18}$$

if the household earns its income solely from factor k. When each commodity price is varied singly, we obtain the vector of utility changes for the household:

$$\hat{V}^h = (\hat{V}^h / \hat{p}_1, \ldots, \hat{V}^h / \hat{p}_n). \tag{19}$$

If there is another household which earns its income solely from each of the other factors, we can obtain the matrix of real income changes:

$$W = \begin{bmatrix} \hat{u}_1/\hat{p}_1 - \phi_{11} & \ldots & \hat{u}_1/\hat{p}_n - \phi_{1n} \\ \vdots & & \vdots \\ \hat{u}_{n+1}/\hat{p}_1 - \phi_{n+1,1} & \ldots & \hat{u}_{n+1}/\hat{p}_n - \phi_{n+1,n} \end{bmatrix} \tag{20}$$

In this matrix the households $h = 1, \ldots, n+1$ have been numbered in accordance with the factors from which they earn their incomes. Evidently, $W = U - \phi$ where ϕ is the transpose of the matrix of household expenditure shares. For the Long Run variant the corresponding W matrix is $n \times n$.

The element W_{kj} represents the proportionate change in the indirect utility of a household which earns income from factor k with respect to the price of commodity j. The first term of the expression is the effect on the household as an income earner and the second term, the effect as a consumer. If $W_{kj} > 0$ we say that commodity j is a 'true' friend of the household owning factor k, and if $W_{kj} < 0$ we say that commodity j is a 'true' enemy of the household. This terminology is employed because W_{kj} are true quantity indices, that is, indices which index utility, in differential form. $W_{kj}>(<)0$ is the necessary and sufficient condition for commodity j to increase (decrease) utility. Ignoring the borderline case in which the two effects exactly cancel, for every household in the matrix every commodity must be either a true friend or a true enemy. Unlike the natural friend and natural enemy matrix, there can be no ambiguity. The matrix in this form is defined only for households which earn income from only one factor. This is a limitation, but it should be noted that the same limitation applies to the U matrix whose elements have meaning in terms of utility only for a single-factor household. It should also be noted that the element W_{kj} has been defined for a single household owning factor k. In general, preferences and therefore the expenditure shares ϕ_{kh} will differ across households owning a factor. Consequently, the magnitude of the one element and perhaps also the sign will differ among households which earn income solely from the same factor. Perhaps surprisingly, this does not turn out to be a difficulty in deriving the two qualitative propositions below. Finally, it can be noted that a commodity j, which is a natural friend (enemy) of household k, is by definition, a true friend (enemy) of household k, but the converse is not true.[4]

The following two basic propositions hold for the Short Run and Long Run variants of the JBH model.

Proposition 1 Every household which earns its income from the ownership of a single factor has at least one true friend and at least one true enemy.

Proposition 2 When the price of any single commodity chosen arbitrarily increases, it will increase the real income (= utility) of some set of households which derive their income from the ownership of a single factor and decrease the real income of some other set of households which derive their incomes from the ownership of some other factor–provided only that the commodity requires at least one primary input whose nominal income increases and which is used elsewhere in the economy. For the first household(s) the commodity is a true friend, and for the second household(s) it is a true enemy.

Propositions 1 and 2 are proven in the Appendix. The expressions contained in the W matrix were applied in Cassing (1981) for the case of the Hecksher–Ohlin model which is $n \times n$ but has no intermediate flows. He established, in the terminology adopted here, that in this model every factor must have at least one true friend and at least one true enemy. Proposition 2 extends a result obtained by Jones and Scheinkman (1977) for the $n \times n$ Heckscher–Ohlin model. The extensions cover intermediate flows and specific inputs. Thus, in the Jones (1975) model with specific inputs but no intermediate inputs, it is well-known that every specific factor gains from an increase in the price of the industry i in which it is employed and loses from an increase in any other commodity price. That is, its own industry is its true (and natural) friend and every other industry is its true (and natural) enemy. What proposition 2 adds for this model is that the mobile factor labour has a commodity which is a true (but not a natural) friend.

The first proposition states that every row of the *W* matrix must contain at least one positive and at least one negative element. The second proposition states that every column must have at least one positive and at least one negative element, subject to the proviso. These propositions hold for any number of commodities and any pattern of inter-industry input–output relations.

The first of these propositions implies that all such households have an incentive to seek to persuade the state to intervene in the economy to raise the price of their friendly commodity. There is a *universal incentive for rent-seeking*. For tradable commodities this leads to rent-seeking by means of border protection. The second of these propositions implies that, whenever any household or group of households seeks rents by means of changes in relative commodity prices, there exist other households whose real incomes will suffer and who will have, therefore, an incentive to oppose the change. In this sense there is *universal opposition* to the changes. Together, these propositions imply that there is a perpetual conflict between the claims being made on the government administering an economy. These two propositions are the foundations of the political economy of protection.

From proposition 1, if all households earning their incomes from one factor have identical expenditure shares, they will form a natural coalition to lobby for assistance to their friendly commodity. If they have distinct expenditure shares, a commodity which is a true friend to some households earning their incomes from a factor used in the industry may be a true enemy to other households earning their incomes solely from the same factor. In practice, however, we can ignore this aspect since the expenditure shares for the outputs of most other industries will be close to zero.

More importantly, there are many households which earn income from endowments of more than one factor. Diversification of income sources is important since it reduces the benefit to the household from an increase in the price of a particular commodity friend. For a household with more than one source of factor income, the proportionate change in its income when the output price for one industry which employs one of these factors changes is only $b_k \hat{u}_k$, where b_k is the fraction of income earned from this source. A true friend may cease to be a true friend as b_i decreases. Indeed, if all households owned an equal share of the national endowments of all factors, they would all lose from protection in a small open economy.

In the Very Short Run an increase in the price of a single commodity may lower the real income of households owning one specific factor in terms of both commodities, as Hosios (1982, p. 149) noted; that is, it may lower the utility of owners of one factor. If, as seems reasonable to assume, there is zero substitutability between intermediate inputs and primary inputs in the Very Short Run, the price of both primary inputs rises in proportion to the output price. Hence, both factors have their own commodity as their true friend. This result becomes important if factor-owners are myopic.

4 THE INEFFECTIVENESS OF PROTECTIVE POLICIES

Given the universality of incentives for rent-seeking, economists should be sceptical of arguments put forward, at times by other economists, for assistance to particular activities. In the last ten years or so these arguments have shifted away from the traditional grounds of infant industries, terms of trade and non-economic objectives. The arguments used nowadays in most countries to justify increases in industry assistance mostly relate to structural adjustment difficulties in the presence of alleged market failures. If there are distortions in domestic markets arising from, say, rigid or sticky factor prices, markets might fail to take account of the full social costs of adjustment. Or, if firms have less than perfect information, this might cause them in some instances to undervalue existing assets and to close plants and lay off workers prematurely and/or to underestimate the rates of return on prospective developments.

Such arguments too may be evaluated individually, but the Assignment Rule establishes a presumption that an intervention, if any is called for, will be based on variables directly related to the structural adjustment and not on imports. For example, Neary (1982) examined the adjustment process in a Jones-type specific factor model with the added complication of sticky real wages. Adjustments are in general desirable, but they may in some cases call for a temporary subsidy on labour employed in the adjusting activities which is reduced over time to zero. Similarly, Mussa (1982) examined a variant in which industry-specific capital can be converted into capital for the other industry instantaneously but only by the use of labour. If all prices are flexible and expectations are rational, the first-best policy is zero intervention. The government should intervene only to correct distortions which induce privately perceived costs or benefits of adjustment to diverge from the true social costs or benefits. Thus, to correct the distortion of the adjustment process created by the private discount rate exceeding the social discount rate, the appropriate optimal intervention is to subsidize capital at a rate equal to the difference between the social and private rates. To correct the distortion created by capital owners undervaluing the net benefits of capital movement, the appropriate optimal intervention is a subsidy on capital movements.

The Assignment Rule must be applied cautiously. The examples discussed so far assume, unrealistically, that the intervening government is omniscient and altruistic. Apart from the design of optimal policies for each problem, economists must be careful in the design of the problems themselves. Quite a large body of literature on the theory of the second best has, in my opinion, been based on assumptions as to the nature of the second-best situation that are inappropriate. I have commented above on the unacceptability of the constraints in the literature on 'non-economic objectives'. Similarly, the literature on price distortions and piecemeal policy-making is based on an unquestioning assumption that there are pre-existing taxes–subsidies on certain commodities which are unalterable, and the policy problem is to find the optimal (second-best) policies subject to these distortions acting as a constraint on the economy. All taxes and subsidies are alterable; if some are deemed unalterable it is because of the inability or unwillingness of legislators to offend income groups dependent upon these prior interventions.

Economists have sometimes played into the hands of such groups by accepting too readily that these difficulties should be treated as permanent restrictions on the instrument set. As a third example, many economists have constructed models of policy-making in economies with rigid or sticky prices. In some instances such inflexibility is due to convention or institutional restraints when wages are fixed by wage-fixing bodies. Such restraints should be subject to analysis and policy recommendations rather than treated as taboos.

If an instrument that is not optimal is assigned to a problem, the theory of optimal interventions indicates that this choice imposes avoidable costs on some households in the economy. In this sense it is an ineffective assignment. It may also be an inefficacious assignment in the sense that it fails to achieve the stated objective (see Baldwin, 1982). Protection policy may be inefficacious because imports as the base of the explicit or implicit taxes are not closely related to the stated source of the problem. Thus, for example, in the context of the infant industry argument, Baldwin (1969) pointed out that border protection provides no incentive for a firm to acquire more knowledge than it otherwise would, even though the social gains from its doing so exceed the private gains. Similarly, a number of economists have recently emphasized that industry protection which was intended to protect jobs in declining industries such as textiles, clothing, footwear and steel has not prevented large declines in the aggregate employment levels of these industries (see for example Lawrence, 1985). Output protection does not ensure the protection of individual inputs.

Ultimately, the objection to distortionary trade policies is not that they impose costs on consumers and other income groups. Virtually any economic policy will adversely affect some group or groups in the economy. The objection is that they harm these groups unnecessarily because there are other policy options which achieve the objectives to a greater degree and reduce these costs. We need to emphasize that, aside from the terms-of-trade argument which is unimportant and/or infeasible for most countries, border protection is never the optimal instrument of government intervention.[5]

APPENDIX

Proof of Proposition 1

In the JBH model there are n zero-profit conditions for the n produced commodities:

$$A(u)u = p. \tag{A1}$$

These equations are not sufficient to determine the $(n+1)$ factor prices. However, substitution among the remaining equations of equations (5) gives the additional equation

$$\frac{a_L}{a_{Ki}}(u)K = L \qquad K = (K_1, \ldots, K_n)'. \tag{A2}$$

Differentiating (A1) and (A2) and transferring the terms involving inputs of commodities to the right-hand side, we have

$$\gamma \hat{u}^* = \hat{p}^* \tag{A3}$$

or, in full,

$$\begin{bmatrix} \theta_{L1} & \theta_{K1} & 0 \\ \vdots & \vdots & \vdots \\ \theta_{Ln} & 0 & \theta_{kn} \\ -\sum_j \lambda_{Lj}\theta_{Lj}\,(\sigma^j_{LL}-\sigma^j_{LK}) & \lambda_{L1}\theta_{K1}(\sigma^1_{KK}-\sigma^1_{KL}) & \lambda_{Ln}\theta_{Kn}(\sigma^n_{KK}-\sigma^n_{KL}) \end{bmatrix} \begin{bmatrix} \hat{u}_1 \\ \vdots \\ \hat{u}_n \\ \hat{u}_{n+1} \end{bmatrix} = \begin{bmatrix} \hat{p}^*_1 \\ \vdots \\ \hat{p}^*_n \\ S \end{bmatrix}$$

where

$$\hat{p}^*_i = (\hat{p}_i - \sum_{j\neq 1}\theta_{ji}\hat{p}_j)$$

and

$$S = -\sum_i \lambda_{Li}\sum_{j\neq 1}\theta_{ji}(\sigma^i_{jL}-\sigma^i_{jK})\hat{p}_j$$

where γ is an $(n+1)\times(n+1)$ matrix; u^* is the vector of specific and non-specific primary input prices; $(\theta_{Li}, \theta_{ki})$ are the shares of capital and labour costs and θ_{ji} is the share of input commodity j in the total cost of producing commodity i; λ_{Li} is the proportion of the labour stock employed in industry i; and σ^i_{rs} is the partial Allen–Uzawa elasticity of substitution between two inputs, r and s, in industry i.

The output prices can be varied singly; that is, $\hat{p}_i \neq 0$ and $\hat{p}_j = 0$ for $j \neq i$. Equation (A3) can be solved for $U = (\hat{u}_k/\hat{p}_i)$. By summation and substitution, it can be shown that the sum of the elements of each row is unity.

However, this summation property follows directly from the observation that the kth equation in the solution to equations (A1) and (A2),

$$u_k = u_k(p, L, K), \tag{A4}$$

is homogeneous of degree $+1$ in p. That is,

$$\sum_i \partial u_k/\partial p_i \, p_i = u_k$$

or

$$\sum_i (\hat{u}_k/\hat{p}_i) = 1. \tag{A5}$$

Similarly, in the Long Run version the solution of the n profit conditions yields n factor price equations, $u_k(p)$, which are homogeneous of degree $+1$ in p.

ϕ is also row-stochastic. Hence, for any household h earning its income from factor k,

$$\sum_j \hat{w}_k/\hat{p}_j - \sum_j \phi_{kj} = 1 - 1 = 0; \tag{A6}$$

that is, the rows of W sum to zero. Every row must have at least one negative and at least one positive element. Thus, the household earning its income from one factor must have at least one true friend. If any row of ϕ is replaced by the expenditure vector of any other household which also earns its income solely from this factor k but has different preferences and/or income, the same qualitative result applies.[6]

Proof of Proposition 2

For the ith commodity in equation (A3), we have

$$\sum_k \theta_{ki} \hat{w}_k = \hat{p}_i - \sum_{j \neq 1} \theta_{ji} \hat{p}_j \qquad j \neq i.$$

Setting $\hat{p}_i > 0$ and $p_j = 0$ for all $j \neq i$, this becomes

$$\sum_k \theta_{ki} \hat{w}_k = \hat{p}_i > 0. \tag{A7}$$

Since θ_{ki} are non-negative and less than unity, this implies that there exists at least one primary input g, for which $\hat{w}_g > \hat{p}_i$. The real income of this factor must increase in these circumstances. That is, for this factor commodity i is a true friend. Assume that the factor whose real income has increased is employed elsewhere in the economy, say, in the production of some commodity $h \neq i$. Then, from equation (A3), we have

$$\theta_{gh} \hat{w}_g + \sum_{k \neq g} \theta_{kh} \hat{w}_k = \hat{p}_h = 0. \tag{A8}$$

This implies that there is at least one other factor, f, for which $\hat{w}_f < 0$. The real income of this factor must decrease in these circumstances.

In the Jones (1975) model, all factors but one are specific to only one industry. However, in this model it turns out that all of the specific factors which are specific to industries other than industry i experience a decrease in nominal and real income. Inspection of equations (A7) and (A8) shows that the proof requires only that there be some factor in industry i whose nominal income increases ($\hat{w}_g > 0$) and which is employed elsewhere in the economy. In the Jones model this factor is labour, whose real income in the sense of the wage good commodity i need not increase ($0 < \hat{w}_L < \hat{p}_i$).

Q.E.D.

NOTES

1 Jones (1975, section III) actually considered a special case of the JBH model in which the intermediate inputs were pure intermediates that were traded but not produced locally.

2 These expressions ignore the redistribution of tariff proceeds to households. While some households in the economy must receive these revenues, it seems unreasonable to suppose that any group which coincides with a group of owners of one factor can claim them.

3 Bhagwati and Srinivasan (1969) endogenize the constraint by incorporating it into the objective function. This merely provides a maximization problem which validates the original solution: it does nothing to explain the underlying problem.

4 Ruffin and Jones (1977) use the terms W_{Li} to sign the change in utility for the mobile factor, labour, in the Jones model. Without the consumption effect, the change in real income of this factor in terms of a single wage good is ambiguous. They called this the 'Neoclassical ambiguity'. It is curious that Jones and Scheinkman (1977) did not use these terms to resolve the ambiguities of real income changes which remain when the analysis is conducted in terms of natural friends and enemies.

5 Johnson (1960) demonstrated that, if a maximum level of imports is added as a 'non-economic' constraint, the optimal policy is a tariff. Vandendorpe (1974) extended this to a uniform *ad valorem* tariff when the constraint is a maximum level of the value of imports for a set of commodities. In the JBH model this can be extended further to a uniform *ad valorem* tariff on all imports of final and intermediate goods when the constraint is a maximum for the net value of imports. However, this problem is subject to the objection of section 2 that this arbitrary constraint is not acceptable.

6 Two cases are of special interest. One is the $n \times n$ Heckscher–Ohlin model with no intermediate inputs. In this case equation (A3) reduces to $\theta\hat{u} = \hat{p}$ where θ is non-negative and row-stochastic (since the rows are the shares of the factors in the costs of producing commodities) but not column-stochastic. Hence, we have $\hat{u} = \theta^{-1}\hat{p}$. The elements of U can be identified as the corresponding elements of θ^{-1}. Since θ is row-stochastic, so its inverse, θ^{-1}. Consequently, $W = \theta^{-1} - \phi$ has rows with zero sums, as Cassing (1981) observed.

The second case is the Jones (1975) model, which is $n \times (n+1)$ but has no intermediate inputs. Again, the elements of U can be identified as elements of γ^{-1}.

However, if there are intermediate input flows, the elements of γ^{-1} are not elements of U, and γ is no longer a stochastic matrix. Since the proposition depends crucially on the homogeneity of the factor demand function, it applies more generally than the JBH model.

REFERENCES

Baldwin, R. E. (1969). 'The case against infant industry protection'. *Journal of Political Economy*, 77, 295–305.

Baldwin, R. E. (1982). *The Inefficacy of Trade Policy*. International Finance Section, 'Essays in International Finance', no. 150. Princeton: Princeton University Press.

Bhagwati, J. N. (1971). 'The generalized theory of distortions and welfare'. In J. N. Bhagwati et al. (eds), *Trade, Balance of Payments and Growth: Papers in Honor of Charles P. Kindleberger*. Amsterdam: North-Holland.

Bhagwati, J. N. and Srinivasan, T. N. (1969). 'Optimal intervention to achieve non-economic objectives'. *Review of Economic Studies*, 36, 27–38.

Bhagwati, J. N. and Srinivasan, T. N. (1976). 'Optimal trade policy and compensation under endogenous uncertainty: the phenomenon of market disruption'. *Journal of International Economics*, 6, 317–36.

Burgess, D. F. (1980). 'Protection, real wages, and the neoclassical ambiguity with interindustry flows'. *Journal of Political Economy*, 88, 783–802.

Cassing, J. (1981). 'On the relationship between commodity price changes and factor owners' real positions'. *Journal of Political Economy*, 89, 593–5.

Corden, W. M. (1957). 'Tariffs, Subsidies and the Terms of Trade'. *Economica*, n.s., 24, 235–42.

Ethier, W. J. (1984). 'Higher dimensional issues in trade theory'. In R. W. Jones and P. B. Kenen (eds), *Handbook of International Economics*, vol. 1. Amsterdam: North-Holland.

Hosios, A. J. (1982). 'Short-run and long-run equilibrium for a small open economy with intermediate goods'. *Journal of International Economics*, 13, 143–61.

Johnson, H. G. (1960). 'The costs of protection and the scientific tariff'. *Journal of Political Economy*, 68, 327–45.

Jones, R. W. (1971). 'A three-factor model in theory, trade and history'. In J. N. Bhagwati et al. (eds), *Trade, Balance of Payments and Growth: Papers in Honor of Charles P. Kindleberger*. Amsterdam: North-Holland.

Jones, R. W. (1975). 'Income distribution and effective protection in a multicommodity trade model'. *Journal of Economic Theory*, 11, 1–15.

Jones, R. W. and Scheinkman, J. A. (1977). 'The relevance of the two-sector production model in trade theory'. *Journal of Political Economy*, 85, 909–1035.

Khang, C. (1971). 'An isovalue locus involving intermediate goods and its application to the pure theory of international trade. *Journal of International Economics*, 1, 315–26.

Lawrence, R. Z. (1985). 'Industrial policy in the United States and Europe: economic principles and political practices'. Paper presented to the Fifteenth Pacific Trade and Development Conference, Tokyo, August 1985.

Mussa, M. (1982). 'Government policy and the adjustment process'. In J. N. Bhagwati (ed.), *Import Competition and Response*. Chicago: University of Chicago Press.

Neary, J. P. (1982). 'Intersectoral capital mobility, wage stickiness, and the case for adjustment assistance'. In J. N. Bhagwati (ed.), *Import Competition and Response*. Chicago: University of Chicago Press.

Ruffin, R. and Jones, R. W. (1977). 'Protection and real wages: the neoclassical ambiguity'. *Journal of Economic Theory*, 14, 337–48.

Stolper, W. and Samuelson, P. A. (1941). 'Protection and real wages'. *Review of Economic Studies*, 9, 58–73.

Tan, A. H. H. (1971). 'Optimal trade policies and non-economic objectives in models involving imported materials, inter-industry flows and non-traded goods'. *Review of Economic Studies*, 36, 105–11.

Vandendorpe, A. L. (1974). 'On the theory of non-economic objectives in open economies'. *Journal of International Economics*, 4, 15–24.

Young, L. (1980). 'Optimal revenue-rising trade restrictions under uncertainty'. *Journal of International Economics*, 10, 425–40.

3
Safeguards Policy and the Conservative Social Welfare Function

Alan V. Deardorff

1 INTRODUCTION

Max Corden has made many contributions to the theory of international trade policy, a number of which are celebrated in this volume.[1] One that has particularly intrigued me, especially as I have become more exposed in recent years to the intricacies of trade policy and the thinking of those who make it, is his notion of a Conservative Social Welfare Function (CSWF). This is a simple idea that Corden introduced some years ago in his *Trade Policy and Economic Welfare* (1974) as a convenient way of explaining what might otherwise be inexplicable uses of trade policy. In this essay I will use a simple model to show how the CSWF can be used to explain why countries might prefer the use of quotas instead of tariffs for dealing with injury due to surges in imports. I will conclude with a policy recommendation, based in part on this analysis, regarding the remedy to be included in the Safeguards Code that may emerge from the upcoming multilateral trade negotiations.

The CSWF embodies Corden's notion (1974, p. 107) that 'any significant absolute reductions in real incomes of any significant section of the community should be avoided.' Taken literally, this statement of the CSWF is probably too strong. It suggests that governments will resist major changes completely and for ever, and that they will certainly never engage in deliberate policies to redistribute income. Yet to varying degrees among the countries of the world, it is clear that many types of changes that help some at the expense of others are allowed to proceed unabated, that others are subjected to only temporary resistance, and that deliberate policies are undertaken that – intentionally or otherwise – redistribute income quite substantially. Thus it is hard to see how a CSWF can be the basis for all forms of public policy.

On the other hand, there are various areas of economic life, differing somewhat from country to country, in which governments do seem to have adopted the role of protector, and trade policy is certainly one of them. The reason for this may be better understood by comparing changes in trade with technological progress, which is another source of economic disruption, the policy response to which is typically much more passive.

A new source of cheap imports and a technological innovation are similar in that they both yield benefits that are spread over most of the population, yet cause substantial costs to groups of individual producers whom they displace. Trade policy is routinely used to protect individuals from the effects of the first of these disturbances, and its use is sanctioned in Article XIX of the GATT.[2] Victims of technological change, on the other hand, at least in the United States, are seldom given more than sympathy, and if they complain too loudly they may find even sympathy hard to come by.[3]

One difference between the two cases is presumably the ready existence of policies that are capable of dealing with trade, whereas, except where technology is already subject to licensing, there just is not much that a government can do to prevent workers being displaced by changes in technology. Another related difference is that trade itself is regarded as being potentially in the control of government, whereas technology is not. Thus governments are easily blamed when their actions or their failures to act concerning trade policy cause harm to their constituents.

But another difference is important and sheds light on how we should interpret the CSWF. A technological change is irreversible: a new product or technique can never be undiscovered. Thus, to protect those who would be displaced by technology either would require a long-term commitment on the part of government, or would serve merely to postpone the inevitable adjustment.

Trade, in contrast, is inherently volatile, even though we may think of it as based on rock-hard fundamentals of comparative advantage. A surge in imports may be the result of a permanent shift in comparative advantage, and thus be as permanent as a technological change, but this can never be known with certainty. There is always the chance that it is a temporary phenomenon and that temporary protection, if given, will enable the protected industry to avoid adjustment altogether.

Thus, one qualification that is reasonable to impose on the idea of the CSWF is that it be used as the basis for only temporary protection against injury.

How, then, does one model a CSWF that is subject to qualifications that it should apply to some situations but not others, and that its applicability should be explicitly temporary? I have no answers to this question. I cannot say whether the CSWF can provide the basis for a truly general theory of public policy, but it can provide a simple organizing principle for particular policy problems, as long as these qualifications are understood. That is how I will use the CSWF in this paper.

Thus I will look at the specific issue of safeguards: what policies a country might use to deal with injury from an upsurge in imports.[4] Injury is taken to mean a loss of utility by individuals within the economy, taking into account both the incomes they earn as producers and the prices they face as consumers. I will *assume* that the object of the policy is to prevent or redress that injury, without if possible causing injury to others, and thus will assume the essence of a CSWF. I do not suggest that the analysis should be extended to other areas of policy, even in international trade, without first evaluating whether these assumptions and the CSWF itself are appropriate in other contexts. And it should be understood, even though I will be using a static and hence timeless model, that the policies I am prescribing should be used only on a temporary basis.

The safeguards policies that I will consider and that are implied by the CSWF, then, are intended only for the temporary maintenance of the status quo. They are not intended, as economists more often recommend, to facilitate 'adjustment' in the sense of an orderly transition to a new equilibrium. This may seem to be a drawback of the analysis, especially considering the current emphasis in Washington on the need for industries to provide 'adjustment plans' in order to obtain escape clause relief.

In fact, however, the notion of adjustment in policy circles seldom corresponds to the economists' conception of adjustment from one equilibrium to another. Adjustment assistance programs have primarily involved extended unemployment benefits that have tended to discourage such movement.[5] And the adjustment programs that industries propose are typically designed to show how the industry will survive if only it is given temporary protection, rather than to ease the industry out of business. Thus I see the emphasis of the CSWF on the status quo as reasonably representative of the concerns of policy-makers, despite their occasional protestations to the contrary.

The structure of the paper is as follows. In section 2 I describe the simple model to be used, and examine the small-country, certainty case of that model in which the usual ranking of policies can be readily seen. Then in section 3 I add uncertainty about world prices to the model, and show that conventional first- and second-best policies now fail to satisfy the constraint imposed by the CSWF. Instead, an import quota serves the purpose better. The result is related to that of Eaton and Grossman (1985), who showed that tariffs may be beneficial in an uncertain world where absence of insurance markets prevents individuals from protecting themselves from changes in the terms of trade. It is also similar to the conclusions of Young and Anderson (1982) and of Falvey and Lloyd (1985), who show, with uncertainty and risk aversion, that quotas may be preferred to tariffs under certain conditions.

In sections 4 and 5 I bring the rest of the world into the model, first with a single exporting country and then with two countries. This allows me to extend the notion of the CSWF beyond domestic residents to foreigners, and to evaluate the effects of various policies on them as well. This extension of the CSWF to foreigners may go beyond what was envisioned by Corden, but it provides a simple way to build in the need for compensation in safeguards actions, and it may be motivated by the desire to avoid retaliation or other international political repercussions. It turns out that, among the safeguards policies I consider, the only one that performs well under a CSWF both at home and abroad is an externally allocated quota – one for which foreigners are allowed to garner the quota rents.

This leads me in my concluding section to elaborate on a recommendation that a safeguards code should incorporate such a quota as the approved remedy. To make this work as efficiently as possible, I suggest some details regarding how such a remedy might be implemented.[6]

2 A SMALL COUNTRY WITH CERTAINTY

In dealing with the safeguards remedy for import disruption, the central economic linkage is between the welfare of individuals and the prices of the goods that they help to produce in the short run. Therefore I will base my analysis throughout on an extreme specific factors model in which all factors are specific to the industries in which they initially produce. In such a model, so long as individuals own factors that are employed in only one industry – which I assume – the identities of separate factors within an industry are unimportant, and one can identify individuals with the goods they help to produce. Indeed, with constant returns to scale and perfect markets – which I also assume – production itself plays no essential role, since the specific factors will always produce the maximum of which they are capable and be remunerated in proportion to that output. Thus, the model is equivalent to one in which individuals are simply endowed with goods and then trade and consume them directly.

The reason for using this extreme specific factors model, as opposed to more conventional models in which one or both factors are mobile between industries, is primarily one of simplicity:[7] I wish to focus on the distributional effects of trade and trade policy with a minimum of complications. However, there is some precedent for using such a model, to be found as early as Cairnes's (1874) theory of non-competing groups, where factors of production are industry-specific even in the long run. Magee (1980) has found support for this assumption, at least in the short run, in the lobbying behavior of representatives of factors of production. These lobbyists tend to align along industry lines (import-competing vs. export) rather than along factor lines (capital vs. labor), suggesting that they perceive their fortunes to be tied to their industry of employment, just as they would be in an extreme specific factors model.

Such a model is illustrated in figure 3.1(a). The economy produces a fixed bundle of goods, X^0 and Y^0, at the endowment point E, and trades part of it at a given world price of X, namely p^0, in order to consume at I. I assume that individuals employed in the X industry and the Y industry, whom I will henceforth call X-factors and Y-factors, have identical and homothetic preferences, leading to a community indifference curve, u^0, tangent to the world price line at I.

The distribution of utility between the two factors can be read out of a variation of the familiar Edgeworth Box, the dimensions of which are the

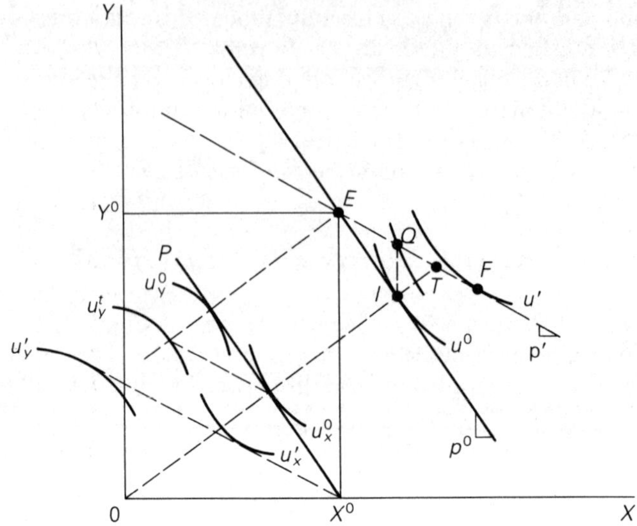

Figure 3.1(a)

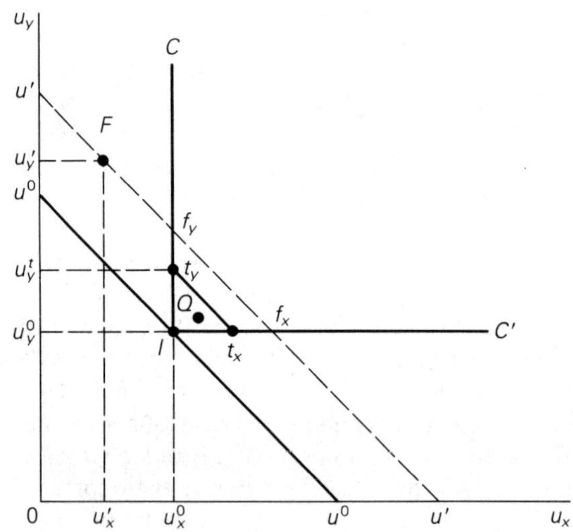

Figure 3.1(b)

economy's endowments of the goods. By drawing a price line, PX^0, from the lower right-hand corner of the box and parallel to the world price, p^0, one can find tangencies with indifference curves, u_x^0 and u_y^0, for the owners of the two factors. The former is drawn relative to the origin, O, while the latter is drawn relative to the endowment point, E. Under the stated assumptions, both tangencies occur at ratios of X to Y equal to that at I, and may be identified by the dotted rays from O and E of that slope.

These indifference curves allow us to infer utility levels of the factor owners if there is only one individual in each group or, more usefully, if the numbers in each group are constant and the utility functions are linearly homogeneous. Assuming the latter, these utility levels are plotted in utility space in figure 3.1(b) at point I.[8]

Given the price p^0, the only way to reach other utility combinations would be by a policy of income redistribution. By taxing one group and transferring the proceeds to the other, it is possible to shift the budget line of the two groups to the right or left within the box in figure 3.1(a). This in turn generates utilities for the two groups in figure 3.1(b) along a downward-sloping 45° line through I, with intercepts u^0. However, under a CSWF this redistribution would not take place, since any movement from point I hurts one of the groups. Instead, what the CSWF does is to impose a constraint, shown as the right angle CIC', on the utilities that are permissible. I will use this constraint to illustrate the need for some kind of policy response to a change in conditions of trade.

Suppose then that the world price of the imported good, X, falls to p'. As shown in figure 3.1(a), the budget line of the country as a whole becomes flatter, rotating through E, while the budget line of the two groups rotates in similar fashion but through X^0. A result is that a higher community indifference curve, u', is reached at F. Within the country, however, the two groups of consumer–producers are affected differentially, the utility of the Y-factor rising to u_y' and that of the X-factor falling to u_x'. Thus, with free trade this improvement in the terms of trade moves utilities in figure 3.1(b) to point F, which lies outside the constraint set imposed by the CSWF and requires some sort of policy response.

The optimal policy response, as usual in trade theory, is a policy of income redistribution, which now allows us to reach points on the utility possibility frontier $u'u'$ in figure 3.1(b). In particular, taxing the Y-factor and subsidizing the X-factor can move utilities down and to the right along this locus, to attain any of the points on the segment $f_y f_x$ above the constraint CIC$'$.[9]

If income redistribution is not a feasible policy for some reason, then some form of trade restriction can achieve a result consistent with the CSWF, though as usual such a policy is only second best. A tariff, for example, sufficient to move aggregate consumption to point T in figure 3.1(a), will restore a domestic price of p^0 and thus return factor incomes to their initial levels. In addition, by redistributing the tariff revenues to one or both of the groups of consumers, their utilities can be raised above initial levels. Thus, such a tariff distributed to the Y-factor will attain point t_y in figure 3.1(b), while if it is distributed to the X-factor it will attain point t_x.

An internally allocated quota, if set equal to the level of imports at point T in figure 3.1(a), will also restore the initial domestic price and will be exactly equivalent to the tariff just described. Depending on whether the rights to import under the quota are allocated to owners of Y, owners of X or both, the economy will again attain the utility possibilities at point t_y, point t_x or the line segment connecting them.

Finally, an externally allocated quota, set equal to the initial level of imports at *I*, will leave the economy at point *I* in both panels of the figure. Such an externally allocated quota is essentially the same as a voluntary export restraint, since the quota rents accrue to someone other than domestic residents. It is clearly an inferior policy in this version of the model, being dominated both by the first-best policy of income redistribution and by the equivalent second-best policies of a tariff and an internally allocated quota. The reason is that the latter policies make possible a limited amount of income redistribution themselves, accomplished by varying the allocation of the tariff revenues or quota rents. An externally allocated quota, on the other hand, merely locks in the initial situation and allows all of the rents from the policy to accrue to foreigners.

The policy is none the less worth looking at, because it will prove to be a more attractive policy in later sections of the paper. An externally allocated quota is, in a sense, the minimum policy capable of satisfying the constraint of the CSWF.

Before leaving this section, it will be useful to examine an internally allocated quota equal to initial imports. Such a quota does not put the equilibrium at point *I*, because of expenditure out of the extra income from the quota rents. Instead, consumption would be at point *Q*, which is on the p' price line directly above point *I*. The domestic price of X would then be given by the slope of the community indifference curve through *Q*, and thus, by homotheticity, would be above p^0. It follows that, even with the quota allocated to owners of good Y, owners of X must gain from this rise in domestic price. The effect on owners of Y, however, is ambiguous, since they gain quota rents but lose from the drop in the domestic price of Y. Assuming that the former effect dominates, the quota is shown as yielding the utilities at point *Q* in figure 3.1(b).[10]

3 A SMALL COUNTRY WITH UNCERTAINTY

Now suppose that the price of imports is uncertain; that, while it is known that the price will drop, it is not known by how much. Suppose in addition that policy must be put into place prior to the resolution of this uncertainty. These assumptions are similar to those that have been made in the literature on trade policy with uncertainty, such as Eaton and Grossman (1985), where the world price is a random variable and – in one scenario – tariffs are state-independent. My assumption differs from this only by allowing policy-makers to wait until the direction of the price change is known, but not its size. The difference reflects my perception that, as argued in Deardorff (1986), safeguards actions typically do wait until at least the threat of injury can be established. On the other hand, it is also crucial that some uncertainty persists at the time the policy is decided upon, since one can never know what further changes will occur subsequently.

With this uncertainty about the world price, the analysis of section 1 needs to modified. Now, as the reader can verify by working through diagrams like figure 3.1, any given policy may lead to a variety of outcomes in utility space, depending on the world price that obtains.

Figure 3.2 shows the various loci of utilities that may arise, each locus drawn for a given policy but for all of the variety of prices that may occur. These loci are similar to the utility possibility curves that have been the staple of welfare analysis in trade theory since Samuelson (1962), but they differ in an important respect. Samuelson's utility possibility curves show the various combinations of utilities attainable in a given state of the world, depending on various policies of income redistribution that are presumed to be in the control of the policy-maker. Thus the policy-maker can choose among the points on such a curve. Each curve in figure 3.2, on the other hand, shows the outcomes that may arise for a given policy depending on the state of the world – in this case, the world price – which is not under the control of policy. Thus the policy-maker by choosing a policy chooses one of these curves, but leaves to chance where along the curve the economy will end up.

Figure 3.2 shows as the curve *FI* the utility possibilities corresponding to free trade. Its extension, *IF'*, shows the utilities that would obtain if price were to rise rather than fall. *FIF'* is therefore the locus of all points like *F* in figure 3.1(b), traced out as the price in figure 3.1(a) is varied below p^0 (segment *FI*) and above p^0 (segment *IF'*). Note that, for some price line steeper than p^0, there will be a tangency with the community indifference

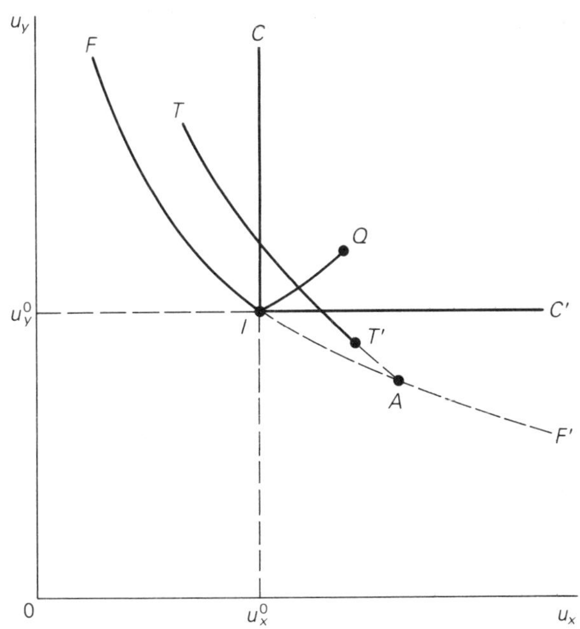

Figure 3.2

curve through E in figure 3.1(a) (not shown), and the country will not trade. This gives rise to the autarky utility possibilities at point A in figure 3.2, which is a benchmark that will be useful in a moment.

The curve TT' shows the possibilities that correspond to a tariff of a given size, the revenue from which is distributed in a given way. For example, it might be a 10 per cent *ad valorem* tariff with proceeds given to producers of good Y.[11] If so, then TT' would be the locus of points like t_y in figure 3.1(b), traced out as the price of X varies below p^0. Note that the point t_y lay on the vertical line IC only because the size of the tariff that was selected to restore the initial domestic price, p^0. With other world prices a given tariff will be either too large or too small to accomplish this, and the point t_y will lie to the right or the left of IC, respectively.

If the tariff were large enough to eliminate trade entirely at the initial price, then the locus TT' would include autarky at point A, but as drawn it stops short of A at T'. It is drawn as downward-sloping since, once the level of the tariff is given, a change in the world price redistributes welfare between the groups, just as with free trade. It is shown as extending both north-west and south-east of point I on the assumption that the range of possible prices is sufficiently large.[12]

Finally, TT' lies wholly above the free-trade locus, FAF', for the same reason that $t_y\,t_x$ in figure 3.1(b) lay north-east of I: any world price with free trade can be improved upon with a tariff of size t by a world price that is lower by that amount, since the latter will yield the same earned incomes for both groups plus some redistributed tariff revenue. Incidentally, the tariff locus $TT'A$ is one of a family of infinitely many such curves, each for a different size of tariff, that fan north-west from point A.

Considering next a quota, the curve IQ shows the utility possibilities for a quota that is set equal to the initial level of imports and is allocated internally to the Y-factor owners. It is the locus of points like Q in figure 3.1(b), again traced out as the world price in figure 3.1(a) varies. It includes the initial point I since, unlike a tariff, this quota would have no effect at all if price were not to drop. If price does drop, however, then the quota becomes equivalent to a positive tariff, sufficient to keep imports at their initial level. As already seen in figure 3.1, the domestic price of X rises as the world price of X falls, and this benefits owners of X and has an ambiguous effect on owners of Y. Assuming as before that the adverse price effect is dominated for the owners of Y by their receipt of the quota rents, I have drawn IQ as upward-sloping, with both factor groups benefiting as the world price of X falls.

Finally, an externally allocated quota equal to initial imports again holds utilities at point I, since there are then no rents to be spent internally.

The message is clear: with certain prices, a tariff may turn out to be too small to prevent harm to the import-competing group, or so large that it causes harm to the rest of the population. A quota, on the other hand, may be able to prevent harm to both groups, and can certainly do so if it is externally allocated. Thus, under a CSWF there would likely be a preference for a quota.

Though not shown in figure 3.2, a policy of redistributing income internally, if it were available, would not be chosen if it had to be implemented before prices were fully known. Such a policy would lead to a downward-sloping utility possibility curve, similar to the one for free trade, and would be likely to pass both north-west and south-east of *I*. The problem again is that one does not know how much income to redistribute until the price change is known, and there is a strong risk of leaving somebody worse off.

It should be noted that strict application of the CSWF to this uncertain situation could imply much more 'conservative' behavior than appeared in the model with certainty.[13] Depending on the constraints facing the economy, the CSWF would reject even a very large possible gain for some individuals in return for avoiding what may be a very small probability of loss, perhaps for the same individuals. Again, whether the CSWF is a plausible basis for policy analysis depends on the situation being examined, and I would not wish to apply it to all problems. My own view is that the alternatives depicted in figure 3.2 are not this extreme.[14]

4 TWO COUNTRIES WITH CERTAINTY

The next step in the analysis is to consider explicitly the foreign country from which the increased imports are coming. This is done using the offer curves of figure 3.3. As an importer of X, the domestic country A's free-trade offer curve is *OA*. Since the world market is now explicit, I can no longer make

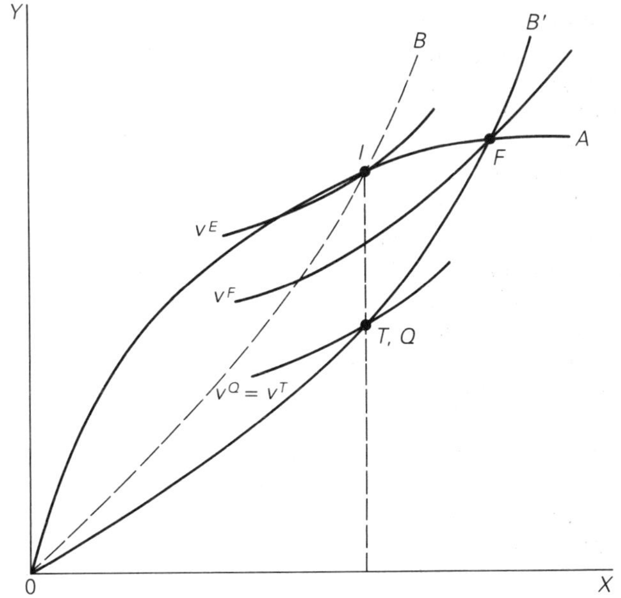

Figure 3.3

world prices exogenous as I did in sections 2 and 3. Instead, I will introduce a potential upsurge in country A's imports by having the other country's offer curve shift exogenously, owing to an increased capacity to produce good X. The source of this increased capacity is not important for its effect on country A. Thus, the foreign country B's initial offer curve is *OB*, but its increased capacity shifts this outward to *OB'*.

Country B's offer curves are taken to be exogenous, and therefore independent of the policy choice in country A. Thus I ignore both the possibility of *ex post* retaliation, as in Johnson (1954), and the *ex ante* efforts to reduce market disruption, as in Bhagwati and Srinivasan (1976). In fact, both countries have market power in this version of the model, and might be tempted to use an optimal tariff. I rule out such behavior on the grounds that it would violate the global application of the CSWF which I am about to pursue, since an optimal tariff necessarily hurts the rest of the world. However, one may prefer to view this global extension of the CSWF as reflecting not humanitarian concerns, but rather the desire to avoid retaliation that might be provoked by inflicting harm abroad.

Having already studied the welfare of country A, I will focus here on the welfare of country B as it depends upon the policy used by country A. I will consider only the aggregate welfare of the foreign country, not the welfare of individual groups within it. The latter is a distributional issue that should be handled by the government of country B, and not by the policy implemented by country A. Thus, the welfare of country B will be represented by trade indifference curves such as that shown as being reached by B's expanded offer curve in free trade, v^F.[15]

Without uncertainty, the effects on B's welfare of alternative policies are quite simple. By using either a tariff or an internally allocated quota, A can shift the equilibrium to *T*, lowering B's welfare to $v^Q = v^T$. By instead using an externally allocated quota, A can return the equilibrium to its initial position at *I*, and raise B's welfare to v^E.

Which of these policies should be chosen, based on the idea of the CSWF, is far from clear. First, country A may simply not care about the welfare of country B, and thus would chose the tariff or internally allocated quota. Second, even if there is in A a desire to avoid harming country B, it is not obvious what the base should be for representing the status quo. If that base is the new free trade equilibrium, then an externally allocated quota is the only one of the policies being considered that will avoid losses of welfare both at home and abroad.

But if the base for comparison is the old equilibrium at *I*, then further analysis is needed to determine what B's level of welfare was initially. The trade indifference curves shown in figure 3.3 are valid only in the new situation, and will presumably have shifted with whatever change it was that shifted the *OB* offer curve itself.

To be specific, let the structure of the economy in country B be analogous to that in country A, with fixed supplies of both goods, and suppose that the increased supply of X on the world market arises from an increased availability of X in B. As is well known, that increase could possibly be immiserizing for B even with free trade, and if so would surely be immiserizing if country A were to prevent imports from expanding via a tariff or quota. On the other hand, such growth need not necessarily be immiserizing even with such a response. Thus we cannot be sure *a priori* whether a tariff or conventional quota will deprive the foreign country of any gains from the expanded supply.

On the other hand, the externally allocated quota is guaranteed to leave country B better off than is was originally. The reason is that with this policy country A both imports and exports the same quantities as before, leaving country B free to consume its increased supply and to benefit from doing so. Thus, the externally allocated quota must satisfy the requirement of the CSWF, even if it may not be the only policy to do so. Therefore, if an importing country wishes to be sure of protecting its domestic residents from injury arising from an increased supply of imports from abroad, without preventing the foreign supplying nation from benefiting from its increased supply, an externally allocated quota is the only policy considered here that will be sure to work.

5 THREE COUNTRIES WITH UNCERTAINTY

In many cases when countries face increased imports, the source of the increase is limited to only a subset of the foreign countries that export the product – often to only one. While it may be questionable whether governments concern themselves with the welfare of countries whose exports to them have increased, it is quite common for them to wish to avoid policies which will damage other trading partners whom they view as innocent bystanders.

Thus, as a final case for analysis, suppose that there are now two foreign countries, B and C, both of them exporters of good X, but only one of them increasing its supply. And suppose too that the increase in supply from country B is known in direction but not in size, just as was assumed about prices in section 3. Then what are the implications of the various policy options available?

The increase in supply of X, regardless of its size, will lower its world price. But since the size of the increase in supply is uncertain, so will be the extent of the decline in price. Therefore the welfare of domestic residents in this situation has already been mapped out in section 3. What is interesting is to look at the welfare of residents of the two foreign countries.

Figure 3.4 shows utility possibilities for residents of countries B and C. Once again, point *I* is the initial position and the right angle *CIC′* shows the constraint on outcomes imposed by a CSWF, should we wish to acknowledge such a function defined on foreign welfare as constraining policy.

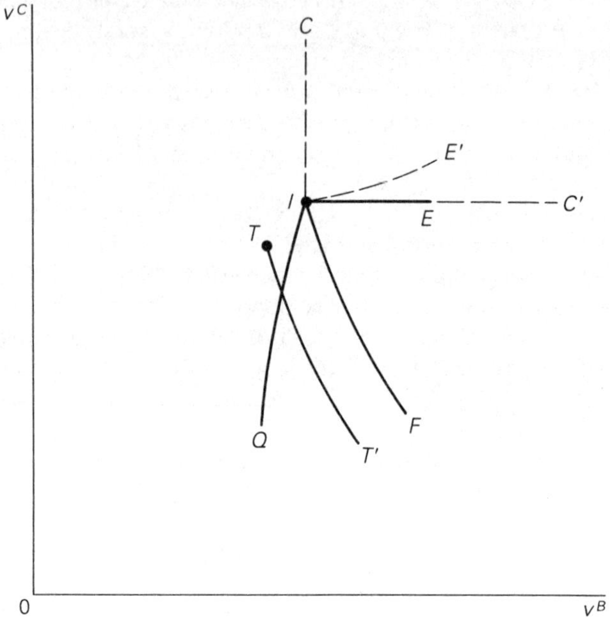

Figure 3.4

With free trade, the uncertain increase in supply of exports from country B is shown as implying a utility possibility locus of *IF*. The increase in exports certainly lowers their world price and hurts the other exporter, country C, which has no increase in supply to sell at the lower price. The effect on country B is in principle ambiguous, as discussed in section 4, since its growth could be immiserizing. However, in figure 3.4 this is assumed not to be the case, and the *IF* locus is drawn as downward-sloping.

Now if country A were to put a tariff on imports of X prior to knowing the size of the import surge, there is a possibility that import supply would not change at all and the tariff would simply lower welfare in both of the foreign countries. Thus the utility possibility curve for a given tariff starts at a point like *T* south-west of *I*. Then, given the tariff, growth of supply in B lowers welfare in C still further, but may raise welfare in B itself, so that the rest of the locus, *TT′* is downward-sloping in the same manner as *IF*.

Unlike a tariff, a quota will not bind at all if there is no shift in supply of X, so that the utility possibility locus for a quota begins at *I*. But as the supply of X grows, the quota becomes more and more binding, equivalent, if it is internally allocated, to a larger and larger tariff. Immiserizing growth in B, though still not inevitable, becomes more likely, and I have drawn the *IQ* locus as sloping down and to the left of *I*. In any case, the particular slopes of these three loci, *IF*, *TT′* and *IQ*, are not crucial to the argument below, which requires only that they extend below the constraint *CIC′*.

Now consider an externally allocated quota. One possibility for such a policy would be a quota on imports from country B only, leaving imports from C unrestricted. In this world of homogeneous products, however, such a partial quota would accomplish little, since the increased supply of X from B would merely be diverted to C, which would export a larger portion of its own product to A. Thus I will assume that the quota is levied against all exporters, whether or not they appear to be the source of the disturbance.

Suppose then that both countries B and C are allocated quotas allowing them to export to A the quantities that they exported in the initial equilibrium. How their welfare will be affected depends in part on how the governments of these two countries themselves respond to the restriction. But one thing is certain: neither country needs to lose from the policy.

Country C has, in the form of this quota, a licence to trade with A exactly the same quantity of X as it did before. Since A will be consuming the same bundle of goods entirely, C should be able to import the same amount of Y from A as well. Thus, by merely holding on to the status quo, country C can hold its level of welfare constant. If this happens, then country B, as argued in section 4, is left to consume the same amount of Y and a larger amount of X than it did initially, and so it must be better off. Thus one set of utility possibilities corresponding to this externally allocated quota is that shown as the horizontal line, *IE*, in figure 3.4.

In fact, country C can do better than this if it is able to take advantage of increased availability of X from B. Assuming it can solve its own problems of income distribution, then country C can raise its welfare by importing X from B and either re-exporting it to A under the quota, or consuming it and continuing to export its own product to A. Thus with optimal policy in C, its residents can enjoy a benefit from the increased supply of X and thus attain points along an alternative upward-sloping utility possibility locus, *IE'*.

Either way, it is clear that application of the principle of a CSWF to foreigners as well as to domestic residents leads to a preference for an externally allocated quota over the other policy options considered here. The externally allocated quota was seen in figure 3.2 to leave all domestic residents at unchanged levels of utility, and it is the only policy in figure 3.4 that does no harm abroad. Now an externally allocated quota is functionally equivalent to a voluntary export restriction (VER), and this conclusion may be surprising since VERs are normally viewed as inflicting considerable costs on domestic consumers. That is in fact the case, but only in an opportunity-cost sense. Without any policy at all, those who do not compete with imports would gain considerably from their lower price, as do the owners of Y at point *F* in figure 3.1(b). An externally allocated quota, or VER, deprives them of that gain and so could be said to impose a loss. But since it restores prices to what they would have been without the increased imports, it does not harm them absolutely.[16]

Now it may sound incongruous for a country's policy-makers to treat foreign residents as though they were constituents. In fact, though, there is a good deal of evidence that countries often do behave in this way, especially in the realm of trade policy. Governments routinely go out of their way to design trade policies that avoid harming innocent bystanders. Indeed, the preference of the European Community for selectivity in safeguards mechanisms may, perhaps too charitably, be viewed in this way. Or more realistically, one may view attempts to protect other countries from harm as a more indirect result of a desire to avoid retaliation or maintain political goodwill.

6 CONCLUSION AND POLICY RECOMMENDATION

This analysis suggests a conclusion that may have broader appeal than is evident from the simple model considered here. Based on the analysis, I would recommend that any new Safeguards Code to be negotiated under the GATT should incorporate what I have called here an externally allocated quota as the preferred remedy.[17] On the basis of my formal analysis, this recommendation is only as valid as the particular assumptions of my model, including the use of the CSWF as the basis for policy. However, the use of externally allocated quotas for safeguard purposes does have other attractive features, as well as certain qualifications, which are outside the model but should be considered.

My specific recommendation is that, once it has been decided that a domestic industry deserves some form of trade protection owing to its being injured by imports, the GATT should prescribe that the importing country institute an import quota, set at a level no less than some base-year level of imports prior to the injury. This quota should be implemented by issuing import licences in the amount of the quota and then allocating them to all exporting countries in the amounts of their base-year exports. The advantage of this policy within the context of this paper is that it is capable of preserving the levels of welfare of both consumers and producers in the importing country, and also of foreigners – even those in countries whose exports have not increased but who would be hurt by certain other policies such as a tariff.

An additional advantage of this policy beyond the context of the model here is that it automatically provides compensation to the country whose exports are restricted by the safeguards action. Compensation has always been a requirement of the GATT safeguard clause, but has been difficult to achieve in practice since it was attempted through offsetting trade concessions. The value of these were always questionable, and they did not, in any case, serve to compensate the private individuals who stood to lose from the action in the first place.

Having recommended that these quotas be allocated to the exporting countries, one could go further and say that they should be allocated to the foreign exporting firms themselves. This has some appeal, since it would assure that the compensation just mentioned would reach those in the private sector who would otherwise be harmed by the policy. But I do not recommend that it be a formal requirement of the proposal, since issues of income distribution within a country should best be left to the discretion of that country's own government. Furthermore, a viable safeguards code should be able to deal with cases involving non-market economies, where a requirement to allocate to firms might make no sense. I would therefore only suggest that the code contain a presumption in favor of governments who receive these allocations allocating them in turn to their own exporting firms.

Another feature of this proposal that I would insist on would be that, while these rights to import under a safeguards quota would be allocated to specific countries, they would be globally marketable and would not require that the imports actually come from the countries to which they were allocated. So it would be only the allocation of the quotas, and thus the quota rents, that would be country-specific: the quotas themselves would be global and globally marketable.

This feature would have the economic advantage of assuring that imports from all sources would be subject to a single quota premium, and thus would encourage imports from the least-cost source. In a changing world economy it would not freeze production patterns across exporting countries, and would permit entry by new low-cost suppliers. It would also mean that the quota, in terms of its effect on prices, would be equivalent to a most-favored-nation (MFN) tariff. This might make it acceptable to those countries, like the United States and many LDCs, who have insisted on an MFN provision in any negotiated safeguards code. At the same time, the ability to allocate quotas to specific foreign countries may satisfy at least part of the desire for selectivity on the part of the European Community.

Finally, the requirement that these quotas be global would eliminate the need for customs officers to monitor countries of origin. This would reduce the inefficiency, waste and sometimes corruption that country-of-origin requirements lead to, both in their enforcement and in their evasion.

This proposal is not without its dangers, and any code would have to anticipate and address them.

One such danger, argued forcefully by Michael Mussa (1974), is that this system creates property rights within the exporting nations that will make the quotas almost impossible to remove.[18] These property rights are in addition to the forces for continuing protection that will arise within the importing country regardless of what protective policy is used. This objection is certainly valid if the quotas are created on a year-to-year basis and without any orderly provision in advance for their removal. But I see no reason why such a provision could not be made. In the safeguards area temporary protection has always been the rule, and while that may be easier to assure with a tariff, the size of which can be reduced over time, it is not impossible with a quota. For example, the quotas when initially allocated could be defined as growing by some percentage each year thereafter. Thus the recipients would know in advance what their shares would be in the future, and would know also that the value of these rights would decline to zero over time. It would be necessary only to set the growth rate above the growth rate of demand for the product in order to assure that the level of protection provided by the quota would decline. By pre-specifying the rate at which total imports will grow under the quota, domestic import-competing interests should be deterred from further lobbying as well.

A second danger implicit in this proposal, as it is in all uses of quantitative restriction on trade, is that it will foster imperfect competition.[19] I view this as less of a danger here than in most other *ad hoc* systems of quantitative restrictions that we have today. By allocating the quotas to a large number of countries, they are initially spread out over the globe, and seem less likely to become concentrated in the hands of a few than if they were allocated domestically. Also, by allowing the quotas to be globally marketable, entry restrictions should be kept to a minimum.

Finally, I would note that it is no accident that this proposal comes very close to formalizing what is already the practice of many industrialized countries. It is my view that their negotiation of VERs and similar arrangements are often intended, in part, to secure much the same benefits that I have ascribed to this policy here. That they have done so without the sanction of the GATT has undermined the credibility of that institution. Yet the analysis in this paper has shown that some of the reasons for the use of such policies are legitimate. To ignore these reasons in reformulating the GATT would be foolhardy, since whatever new agreement would be reached would then almost certainly be ignored. A policy such as I have proposed here might well be not only agreed to, but also used, by the countries that have flaunted the GATT so readily in the past.

NOTES

1 After this paper was completed, I became aware of an essay by Corden (1984) that deals with a number of the same issues that I touch on here. Time has not permitted me to relate my analysis of his, the two of which are very complementary. The policy recommendation that concludes this paper grew out of discussions with John H. Jackson, and our experience together teaching an international law and economics seminar on safeguards. I have benefited greatly from discussions with Jackson, as well as from comments on an earlier draft from Bob Stern, Aquiles Almansi, Bernard Hoekman and Michael Leidy. The research underlying this paper was supported by the Ford Foundation.

2 Use of trade policy is also sanctioned in other articles of the GATT, of course, for dealing with 'unfair' trade practices.

3 They are, however, eligible for unemployment compensation.

4 According to Article XIX of the GATT, safeguards actions are permitted only when, in addition, the increased imports are in turn the result of 'the obligations incurred by a contracting party under' the GATT. In practice this qualification has not been meaningful, since any increase in imports can be viewed as resulting from the GATT obligation not to prevent such an increase by raising tariffs. I will therefore ignore it.

5 See Aho and Bayard (1984).

6 See Wolff (1983) for a good discussion of safeguards in the GATT.
7 See Jones (1971), Mayer (1974) and Mussa (1974) on the conventional specific factors model with one mobile factor, and Stolper and Samuelson (1941) and Jones (1956–7) on the all-factors-mobile Heckscher–Ohlin model.
8 Utilities in figure 3.1(b) are the aggregate utilities of all individuals in the respective groups. Per capita utilities would be obtained by dividing by the numbers of members in the groups.
9 Under the special assumptions of this model, these taxes and transfers could be paid in proportion to output, which is fixed. In general, of course, only lump-sum taxes and transfers can accomplish this redistribution without distorting behavior.
10 Point Q could be either to the right or the left of point t_x depending on the curvature of the indifference curves.
11 The locus for a specific tariff would be qualitatively similar to the locus for an *ad valorem* tariff, but somewhat steeper, since the *ad valorem* tariff to which it corresponds rises as price drops.
12 For example, as long as the price of X may drop below p^0 by more than the tariff, TT' will include points to the left of IC. And as long as the tariff itself is close enough to that which would eliminate trade at p^0, a sufficiently small drop in price will generate points below IC'.
13 I am indebted to Michael Leidy for pointing this out.
14 An alternative interpretation of the CSWF that would avoid this difficulty would rule out only losses in *expected* utility. The policy implications of this assumption are quite different, and do not conform well with what I perceive to be the motivation behind safeguards policies.
15 It is here that the source of the increased capacity to produce in B, and B's policy for dealing with it, may be important, since these could influence the interpretation of, and perhaps even the existence of, such trade indifference curves. I assume that whatever policies are employed in B are such as to leave it with trade indifference curves with the usual properties, and that these do represent social welfare.
16 This conclusion holds, of course, only if the VER is a response to an increase in the availability of imports from abroad, and thus a proper safeguards action. If a VER were used instead to protect producers from a shock that originates domestically, then it could certainly harm others in the country absolutely.
17 For other proposals to improve the safeguards and escape clause mechanisms, see Bhagwati (1977), Wolff (1983), and Hufbauer and Rosen (1986).
18 Mussa raised this objection during discussion of a version of this recommendation in Deardorff (1986) at the Spring 1986 Carnegie-Rochester Conference on Public Policy.
19 See Bhagwati (1965).

REFERENCES

Aho, C. Michael and Bayard, Thomas O. (1984). 'Costs and benefits of trade adjustment assistance.' In Robert Baldwin and Anne Krueger (eds), *The Structure and Evolution of Recent US Trade Policy*. Cambridge, Mass.: National Bureau of Economic Research.

Bhagwati, Jagdish N. (1965). 'On the equivalence of tariffs and quotas.' In R. E. Baldwin et al. (eds), *Trade, Growth, and the Balance of Payments: Essays in Honor of Gottfried Haberler*. Amsterdam: North-Holland.

Bhagwati, Jagdish N. (1977). 'Market disruption, export market disruption, compensation, and GATT reform.' In J. N. Bhagwati (ed.), *The New International Economic Order: The North–South Debate*. Cambridge, Mass.: MIT Press.

Bhagwati, Jagdish N. and Srinivasan, T. N. (1976). 'Optimal trade policy and compensation under endogenous uncertainty: the phenomenon of market disruption.' *Journal of International Economics*, 6, 317–36.

Cairnes, J. E. (1874). *Some Leading Principles of Political Economy*. London: Macmillan.

Corden, W. M. (1974). *Trade Policy and Economic Welfare*. Oxford: Clarendon Press.

Corden, W. M. (1984). 'Market disturbances and protection: efficiency versus the conservative social welfare function.' Discussion Paper no. 92, Centre for Economic Policy Research, Australian National University (March).

Deardorff, Alan V. (1986). 'Why do governments prefer nontariff barriers?' To be published.

Eaton, Jonathan and Grossman, Gene M. (1985). 'Tariffs as insurance: optimal commercial policy when domestic markets are incomplete.' *Canadian Journal of Economics*, 18, 258–72.

Falvey, R. E. and Lloyd, P. J. (1985). 'Uncertainty and the choice of protective instrument.' Working paper no. 125, Australian National University (June).

Hufbauer, Gary Clyde and Rosen, Howard F. (1986). *Trade Policy for Troubled Industries*. Washington: Institute for International Economics.

Johnson, Harry G. (1954). 'Optimum tariffs and retaliation.' *Review of Economic Studies*, 21, 142–53.

Jones, Ronald W. (1956–7). 'Factor proportions and the Heckscher–Ohlin model.' *Review of Economic Studies*, 24, 1–10.

Jones, Ronald W. (1971). 'A three-factor model in theory, trade, and history.' In J. N. Bhagwati, R. W. Jones, R. A. Mundell and J. Vanek (eds), *Trade, Balance of Payments, and Growth: Essays in Honor of Charles P. Kindleberger*. Amsterdam: North-Holland.

Magee, Stephen P. (1980). 'Three simple tests of the Stolper–Samuelson Theorem.' in Peter Oppenheimer (ed.), *Issues in International Economics*. Boston: Oriel Press.

Mayer, Wolfgang (1974). 'Short-run and long-run equilibrium for a small open economy.' *Journal of Political Economy*, 82, 955–67.

Mussa, Michael (1974). 'Tariffs and the distribution of income: the importance of factor specificity, substitutability, and intensity in the short and long run.' *Journal of Political Economy*, 82, 1191–1204.

Samuelson, Paul A. (1962). 'The gains from international trade once again.' *Economic Journal*, 72, 820–9.

Stolper, Wolfgang and Samuelson, Paul A. (1941). 'Protection and real wages.' *Review of Economic Studies*, 9, 58–73.

Wolff, Alan W. (1983). 'Need for new GATT rules to govern safeguard actions.' In William R. Cline (ed.) *Trade Policy in the 1980s*. Cambridge, Mass.: MIT Press.

Young, Leslie and Anderson James E. (1982). 'Risk aversion and optimal trade restrictions.' *Review of economic Studies*, 49, 291–305.

4

Voluntary Export Restrictions versus Import Restrictions: A Welfare-theoretic Comparison

Richard A. Brecher and Jagdish N. Bhagwati

The theoretical analysis of voluntary export restrictions (VERs) is notable for its paucity. In partial equilibrium, Takacs (1978) has compared with them alternative trade restrictions from the viewpoint of 'equivalence' as defined and considered by Bhagwati (1965; 1968; 1969, ch. 9) and later writers. Subsequent to theoretical work of Falvey (1979) and Rodriguez (1979), Feenstra (1984) has demonstrated elegantly that Japanese VERs on auto exports to the United States have induced a shift toward higher-quality exports, and has calculated the magnitude as well as analyzed the implications of this shift.

As a long-standing part of the conventional wisdom, moreover, there is also the following principal proposition on VERs: VERs, relative to import restrictions, would be beneficial for the exporting country and detrimental to the importing country in a two-country framework, since they would appropriate[1] to the former the restriction-induced rents that would otherwise accrue to the latter. In fact, in the policy-oriented discussions, as in the analysis of market disruption and proposed changes to GATT Article XIX, it is generally assumed that VERs build into themselves automatic compensation to the exporting countries whose markets are being restricted, and that therefore no explicit compensation needs to be paid when VERs are imposed.[2]

It is the purpose of this paper to subject this conventional wisdom to analytical examination. Our results, in general equilibrium analysis, are startling: they demonstrate that the question is more complex than has been assumed to date.

For helpful comments and suggestions, thanks are due to Robert Feenstra, Gene Grossman, Rachel McCulloch, Makoto Yano and the participants at the Third Annual Conference on International Trade Theory at the University of Western Ontario. Bhagwati's research has been partially supported by the National Science Foundation.

Section 1 briefly outlines the conventional wisdom and its customary theoretical foundation in partial equilibrium analysis. Section 2 then introduces general equilibrium analysis of the problem, demonstrating the need for, and analyzing the differential consequences of, the following two alternative assumptions: (1) the policy objective of the two alternative restrictions being compared is to fix the volume of home imports; (2) the objective is instead to fix the home price ratio. For analytic convenience only, we assume that the VERs and the import restrictions are 'price' (rather than 'command') instruments: that is, we compare export duties abroad with import duties at home.[3] Since either policy therefore generates revenue, the former abroad and the latter at home, we extend our analysis in section 3 to the case where the policies lead to 'revenue-seeking,' as in Bhagwati and Srinivasan (1980); the revenue in this analysis is not assumed to be redistributed in a lump-sum fashion to consumers but instead is assumed to be dissipated to the clients of revenue-seeking lobbyists. Thus, our analysis in section 3 is yet another application of what Bhagwati (1982) has termed the theory of 'directly unproductive profit-seeking' (DUP) activities, and indeed is a further demonstration of how the introduction of DUP activities has a critical impact on theoretical analysis.

1 THE CONVENTIONAL ARGUMENT

The proposition that VERs, relative to import restrictions, benefit the foreign country while hurting the home country is demonstrated readily with well-known partial equilibrium reasoning.

In figure 4.1, DD' and SS' are the home import demand and foreign export supply curves. With an import tariff at *ad valorem* rate FG/GQ, the demand curve shifts to D_tD_t', the international price falls to HO, the domestic price in the home country becomes $HO+EH=EO$, imports are reduced to OQ, and the area of rectangle $EFGH$ represents the revenue accruing to the home government. Now shift the policy to a VER, i.e., an export duty at rate FG/FQ by the foreign government. In this event, the supply curve shifts to S_tS_t' (whereas the demand curve returns to DD'); the domestic price in the foreign country remains HO; the international price rises to EO, which now becomes also the domestic price in the home country; and the revenue represented by rectangle $EFGH$ now is clearly earned by the foreign government. Since the real equilibrium at home and abroad is otherwise undisturbed, the conventional proposition readily follows: VERs, relative to import restrictions, benefit the foreign country and harm the domestic country.

Figure 4.1 clearly assumes perfect competition. To ensure consistency of comparison, the rest of this paper will therefore continue to focus on the perfectly competitive case.

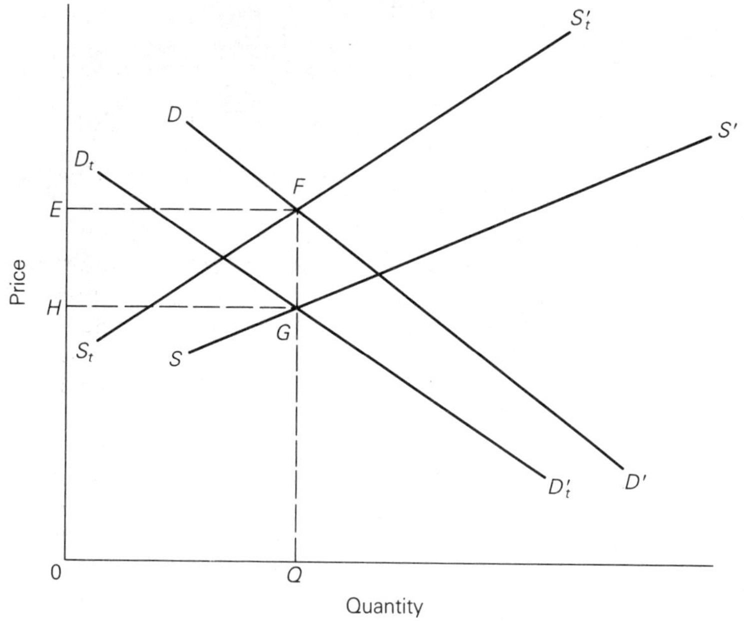

Figure 4.1

The area of rectangle *EFGH*, accruing originally as revenue to the home country, subsequently accrues instead as revenue to the foreign country when the policy is shifted from a home import duty at *ad valorem* rate *FG/GQ*, to a foreign VER at rate *FG/FQ*.

2 GENERAL EQUILIBRIUM ANALYSIS

Once we shift to general equilibrium analysis, however, the implicit partial equilibrium assumption – that the underlying supply and demand curves are independent of the policies being compared – is no longer valid. In analyzing the switch from one policy to the other, we must now take into account the general equilibrium effects of the international purchasing-power transfer represented by rectangle EFGH in figure 4.1. Once these effects are considered, VERs and import restrictions are no longer 'equivalent' policies in Bhagwati's (1965) well-known sense; in other words, the replacement of one policy instrument by the other does not yield an identical real equilibrium. It equally follows that we must now distinguish between alternative objectives (or constraints) subject to which foreign VERs are compared with home import tariffs, as we do immediately below.[4]

It would appear that there are two important reasons for restricting trade. There may be either a quantity objective, in the sense of a maximum acceptable level of home imports, or a price objective, in the sense of a minimum acceptable level for the relative price of the importable within the home country. We consider these objectives now, in turn, comparing a home-country import tariff with an alternative foreign-country VER export tariff

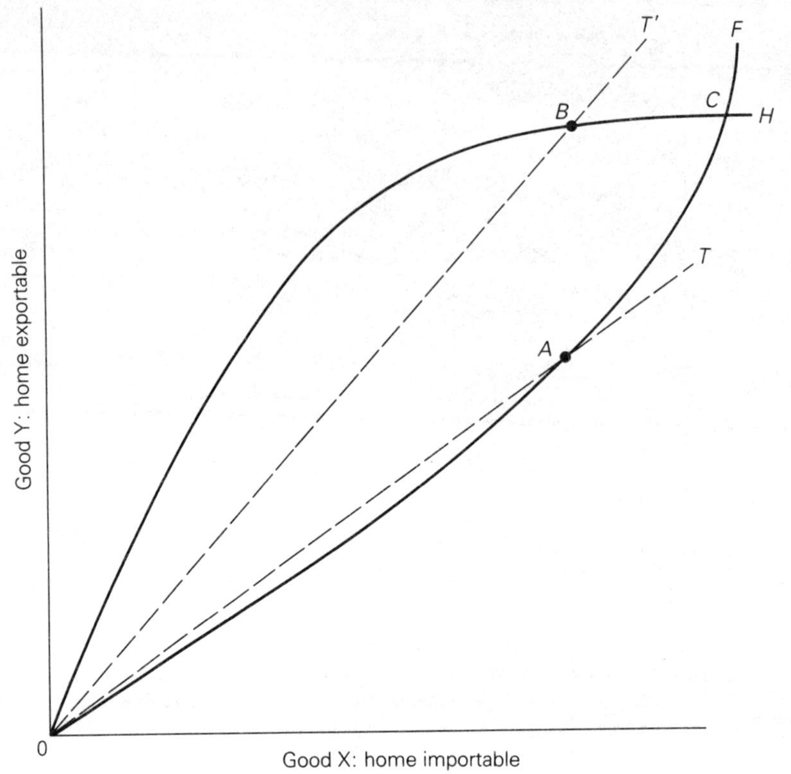

Figure 4.2

in each instance.[5] The revenue generated in either case is assumed in this section to be redistributed to consumers in a Meade-like lump-sum fashion as in conventional general equilibrium tariff theory.

Case 1: Fixed Volume of Home Imports

In figure 4.2, OH and OF are the free trade offer curves of the home and foreign countries, which export goods Y and X, respectively. As usual, we assume that all offer curves are well behaved, in the sense of never bending back towards the origin. Also, for simplicity of exposition only, all offer curves are assumed to be elastic.

To restrict its imports below the free trade level at point *C*, the home country can use an import tax to shift curve *OH* inwards to pass through (say) point *A*. Alternatively, to achieve the same reduction in trade of good X, the foreign country can impose an export tax which shifts curve *OF* inwards to pass through point *B* (vertically above *A*). By drawing in the usual trade indifference curves, we could readily see that the move from *A* to *B* unambiguously raises foreign and lowers home welfare, since the foreign

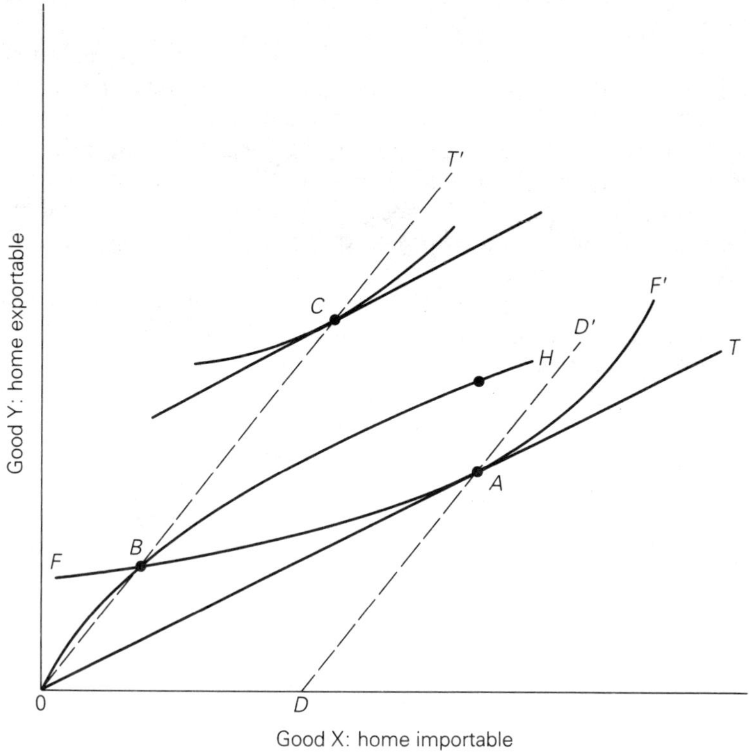

Figure 4.3

(home) country gets increased (constant) imports for constant (increased) exports. Thus, in this particular case, the welfare effects of switching from home to foreign taxation accord with the conventional wisdom.

It is easy to see intuitively why the conventional wisdom holds here. Home welfare must necessarily decline on shifting from *A* to *B* by changing from the import to the export tax, since the terms of trade worsen (from *OT* to *OT'*) without any mitigating improvement as the volume of imports does not increase. Foreign welfare, on the other hand, must necessarily improve since the terms of trade improve with no offsetting deterioration as the volume of exports does not diminish.

Case 2: Fixed Home Price Ratio

In figure 4.3, where *OH* is the free-trade offer curve of the home country, an import tax of this country leads to (say) point *A*, at which the ratio of international (and foreign) prices is given by the slope of ray *OT*, while the home price ratio is given by the necessarily greater slope of line *DD'*. Foreign welfare is represented by the trade indifference curve *FF'*, tangent to ray

OT at point *A*, whereas home welfare is given by the trade indifference curve (not shown) tangent to line *DD'* at *A*.

When the home country's import tax is replaced by a foreign tax on exports, the equilibrium shifts to point *B*, where the ray *OT'* (parallel to *DD'*) intersects *OH*, so that the home price ratio remains unchanged. By requiring a foreign export *tax* (rather than subsidy) to keep the home price ratio constant, we are implicitly assuming no Metzler Paradox for the home country. Also, without this assumption the home country would have paradoxically used an import *subsidy* (rather than tax) to achieve the price objective in the first place.

The move from *A* to *B* clearly lowers home welfare because home expenditure declines, at constant prices, by *OD* units of good X. In the case illustrated, however, foreign welfare remains unchanged at the level defined by curve *FF'*. For this constant-welfare result to occur, we must have point *B* lying south-west of *A*, thereby implying that good Y is inferior in home consumption.[6] (Note that, as at point *A*, the home country has an undrawn trade indifference curve tangent to the home-price line through point *B*.) If the home country had a smaller (larger) marginal propensity to consume good Y, *ceteris paribus*, foreign welfare would fall (rise). Thus, in the event of shifting to the export from the import tax, a rise in foreign welfare would be ensured by normality in home consumption.[7]

Again, the intuition behind this result is readily spelled out. The home country is necessarily hurt by the shift to VERs because, with the domestic price ratio fixed, this shift must imply worsened international terms of trade with no offsetting production and consumption gain. On the other hand, for the foreign country the corresponding improvement in the international terms of trade and hence welfare can be offset by diminished gains from a reduced volume of exports (which may be a sufficiently large reduction if the home country's exportable good Y is inferior in consumption and therefore the home country's demand for imports falls sharply as its real income falls).

The move from *A* to *B* can be decomposed, as follows, into two conceptual stages that provide further insight into our analysis. In the first stage, the home import tax is replaced by a foreign export tax that leaves the domestic price ratios of both countries constant, with the following consequences: the home country goes to *B*; the foreign country moves to point *C*, where its (unlabelled) trade indifference curve cutting the new international terms-of-trade ray *OT'* has a tangent parallel to *OT*; and (in the example illustrated) the world develops an excess supply of good X (and demand for Y), which is represented by line segment *BC*. This market imbalance is eliminated in the second stage, by raising the export tax of the foreign country until this country reaches *B*. The first-stage impact on welfare is negative for the home but positive for the foreign country (as in the partial equilibrium analysis), since we essentially have the primary (constant-price) effect of a purchasing power transfer of *OD* units (evaluated at the new international terms of trade) from the former to the latter country. The second-stage impact on welfare, however, is zero for the home country, but (in the present illustration) sufficiently negative for the foreign country to offset exactly the first-stage gain of this country. Thus, this case can be interpreted as another example of a transfer payment that paradoxically fails to enrich a recipient whose tax-affected importable is inferior in the donor's consumption, in consonance with results reported by Brecher and Bhagwati (1982) and Bhagwati, Brecher and Hatta (1985).[8]

As demonstrated by the foregoing treatments of cases 1 and 2, our general equilibrium analysis depends importantly on the importing country's underlying objective, namely, quantity or price. Which of these two objectives is the more realistic? At first glance it may appear that the quantity objective is the appropriate one, since exporting countries and industries are often forced to agree to specific export levels. However, this view is probably naîve, since the quantities fixed thus, as with the well-known VERs on autos from Japan, are only an instrumentality through which the government of the importing country seeks to maintain the import-competing industry's price (and hence output): quantities are, in fact, continually renegotiated to ensure such an outcome. If anything, therefore, we would argue that the price objective, distinguished in our formal analysis, is quite possibly the more appropriate one.

3 INTRODUCING REVENUE-SEEKING

We now extend our analysis to incorporate revenue-seeking activity, which draws scarce primary inputs away from the production of goods X and Y, assumed (as usual) to be the only arguments in the national utility functions. Since the burden of DUP activity is shifted from the home to the foreign country when the former's import tax is replaced by the latter's export tax, we would intuitively expect that home welfare may increase at the expense of foreign welfare. This outcome is indeed possible under certain specific conditions, as shown by the following analysis.

Case 3: Revenue Seeking with Home Imports Fixed[9]

Consider now figure 4.4, where the production possibility frontier for the home country is QQ', drawn for the fixed endowments of capital and labor under constant returns to scale. Initially, with the home country taxing imports, the home price ratio is given by the slope of line AC, which touches curve QQ' at point A. Now, as Bhagwati and Srinivasan (1980) have shown, consumption must then take place on a community indifference curve at point C, where national welfare is maximized subject to expenditure equalling income at factor cost, if (as we assume) revenue-seeking occurs and results in a wastage of resources worth the fully dissipated proceeds of the import tax. Moreover, as they establish, production takes place at B, which is the point of intersection for the following two lines: the international price line

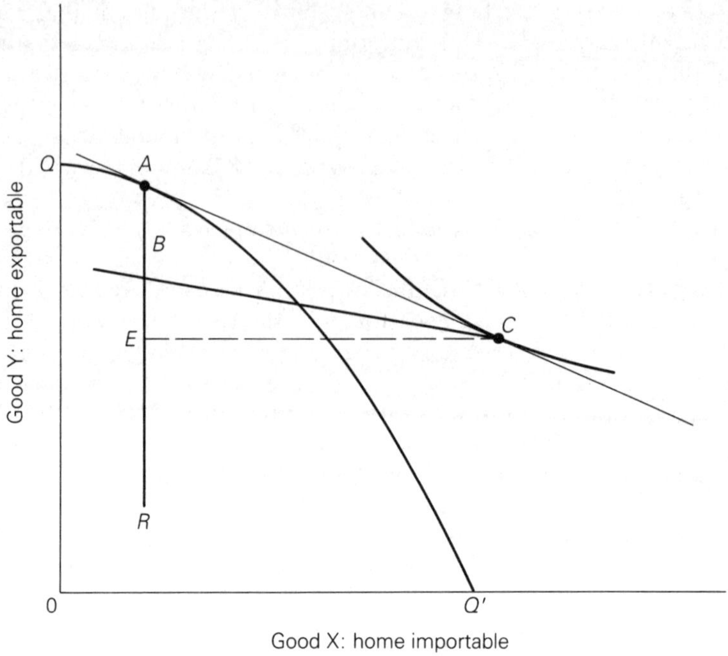

Figure 4.4

BC, drawn through *C*; and the (generalized) Rybczynski line *AR*, drawn through *A*, for the withdrawal of productive factors into revenue-seeking activity.[10]

The Rybczynski line is drawn vertical in figure 4.4, to illustrate the break-even case where a shift from the import to the export tax will have no impact on home welfare. (As we shall subsequently show, moreover, this case readily suggests the alternative conditions under which such a policy shift will instead improve or worsen welfare.) To see the logic of the break-even case, replace the import tax by an export tax such that the international price line facing the home country worsens to *AC*, which therefore continues to be the domestic price line at home (now that the import tax has been eliminated). Under these circumstances, production remains at point *A*, consumption stays at point *C*, and home country's imports of good X remain fixed at *CE*, as required under the quantity objective. In this case, since consumption is at point *C* under both the import tax and the export tax, we clearly have the same level of home welfare under either policy.

By similar reasoning, if the Rybczynski line through point *A* passed instead to the left or right of vertical line *AR*, replacement of the import tax by the export tax would cause home welfare to rise or fall, respectively. In the former case, for example, the Rybczynski line would intersect the international price line *BC* to the left of point *B*, and hence the initial level of home imports would exceed *CE*. To keep imports fixed at the initial level as required, the

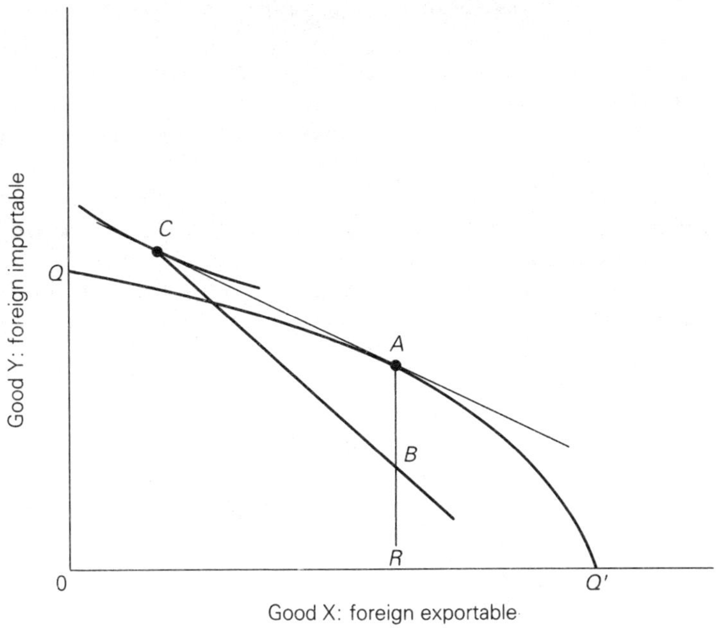

Figure 4.5

home price line would have to flatten (from AC) when the import tax was replaced by the export tax. Thus, the home country would clearly reach a higher indifference curve under this tax replacement scheme. The change in foreign welfare can be evaluated symmetrically to show a gain or loss, respectively, as the foreign Rybczynski line passes to the left or right of a vertical line through the initial production point.

Case 4: Revenue-seeking with Home Price Ratio Fixed

Since the home price ratio is fixed by assumption, national income at factor cost remains unchanged when the home tax is replaced by the foreign one. Thus welfare of the home country is correspondingly constant, unambiguously. The situation could be described again by figure 4.4 without modification.

To analyze the change in foreign welfare, however, introduce figure 4.5, where QQ' is the production possibility frontier for the foreign factor endowments under constant returns to scale. Initially, given the home country's tax on imports, production is at point A and consumption is at point C, with the slope of line AC giving the ratio of international prices. After the shift to the foreign country's tax on exports, the ratio of international prices is given by the slope of the necessarily steeper line BC (parallel to AC of figure 4.4). If the Rybczynski line AR has the same slope as its home-country counterpart, foreign consumption would remain at point *C* while production shifted to point *B*, since the trade triangle constructible from line segment *BC* of figure 4.5 is then equal to the analogous triangle corresponding to line segment *AC* of figure 4.4. (This result does *not* require that the Rybczynski lines be vertical, but only that they be equally sloped.) Thus, in this case foreign welfare too is unchanged when the import tax is replaced by the export tax.

Suppose instead that the foreign Rybczynski line passed to the right of the vertical line *AR*, while the home Rybczynski line was still vertical. Then, the foreign tax needed to keep consumption at point *C* in figure 4.5 would raise foreign exports (and hence home imports) above the level consistent with the fixed home price ratio in figure 4.4. Thus, the foreign country would have to raise its tax somewhat more, thereby increasing its domestic relative price of good Y, to keep the international price ratio (now equal to the fixed home price ratio) constant. Therefore foreign welfare would be diminished in figure 4.5, as the foreign price line flattens relative to *AC*. (Again, what matters is the *comparative* slopes of the Rybczynski lines, not the absolute slope of either one.) By similar reasoning, a Rybczynski line passing to the left of *AR* in figure 4.5 (given figure 4.4 as drawn) would imply a rise in foreign welfare.[11]

4 CONCLUDING REMARKS

Our analysis casts doubts on the conventional wisdom, according to which the home country loses while the foreign country gains if responsibility for trade restriction passes from the former to the latter. In fact, the actual welfare outcomes depend importantly on the objective of trade restriction and on the method of disbursing the resulting (tariff) revenues or (quota) rents.

We have been asked, how important are these analytical complexities *in practice*? Should we not continue believing that, for all practical purposes, VERs replacing import restrictions harm the importing country and enrich the exporting country?

The honest answer has to be that it depends on the case at hand. Evidently, the received doctrine relies on restrictive assumptions, although this reliance has not been appreciated to date. Are these assumptions, such as the absence of lobbying generated by the restrictions, sensible to make most of the time? Apparently not. Reverting to the revenue-seeking analysis, for example, we find that few analysts today would reject out of hand the argument that *some* fractional revenue-seeking activity must be allowed for. In fact, let us take its more intuitive quantity counterpart, premium-seeking: can there be any doubt that firms will tend to compete for a share of the trade-restricting, premium-fetching licenses? We would argue that this competition is generally an important consideration in the case of quantity-constraining VERs[12] such as those set through the Multifibre Arrangement (MFA) on textiles. Lobbying for licenses occurs not only among firms within each MFA country, but also among the MFA countries themselves, and indeed between these countries and new entrants (as was doubtless the case when China was recently negotiating its textiles share with the United States and therefore impacting on the older exporters' market shares).

NOTES

1 Diagrammatic partial equilibrium discussions of this appropriation may be found in a variety of places; see, for example, Bergsten (1975) and Caves and Jones (1973, p. 289). Concern over the international distribution of rents from trade restriction appears also in Meade (1951, ch. XXI), who paid careful attention to whether the importing or exporting country enjoys 'the margin between the buying and selling price.'

2 See Bhagwati (1977) for an analysis of the question of market disruption in the context of GATT Article XIX, and Bhagwati and Srinivasan (1976) for a theoretical analysis of the issue. The former accepts the conventional wisdom on VERs which is re-examined in the present paper.

3 Given the assumptions specified below, our results would hold equivalently for a comparison between export quotas abroad and import quotas at home. Thus, our analysis should be viewed generally as comparing trade-restricting actions by exporters versus importers, regardless of whether the restrictions are imposed by taxes or quotas. Also see n. 12 below.

4 This has been done also in the 'equivalence' literature on tariffs versus quotas, as in the important papers by McCulloch and Johnson (1973), Pelcovits (1976) and others. See Bhagwati (1978) for a detailed review and synthesis.

5 As shown by Lizondo (1984), a home import restriction and foreign VER that give rise to the same volume of trade may lead to different domestic price ratios for the home country in a general equilibrium context.

6 This implication is evident from a comparison of points *A* and *B*. At *A*, where home welfare is higher, exports of good Y are greater. Thus, with home production unchanged because of a constant domestic price ratio at *A* and *B*, home consumption of good Y at *A* must be less than at *B*, implying that Y is an inferior good in the home country.

7 If foreign welfare remains constant, as in figure 4.3, the domestic relative price of good X within the foreign country falls, since curve FF' is flatter at point *B* than at *A*. A fall in this price would still occur if the foreign country instead suffered a deterioration in welfare, given that FF' belongs to a family of non-intersecting trade indifference curves. Thus, foreign welfare would rise if the domestic relative price of good X in the foreign country remained unchanged (as in the partial equilibrium case of figure 4.1) or became larger, although a rise in foreign welfare might occur even with a fall in the domestic relative price of good X within the foreign country.

8 An alternative two-stage decomposition, along the following lines, is also worth considering. In the first stage, the home import tax is replaced by a foreign export tax that leaves constant the volume of international trade in good X, thereby leading both countries to move (as in case 1) vertically from point *A* to curve *OH* in figure 4.3, and (in the situation illustrated) causing the home price line to flatten. Therefore, to restore the home price ratio to its original level, the second stage

requires raising the foreign export tax until the world reaches final equilibrium at point *B*. (*Ceteris paribus*, the magnitude of this tax rise depends positively on the home offer curve's elasticity, which in turn depends negatively on the marginal propensity to consume good Y.) Whereas the first-stage impact on welfare is (as in case 1) unambiguously beneficial to the foreign but detrimental to the home country, the second-stage impact happens (in the present illustration) to be harmful for both countries. Home welfare must thus undergo an overall decrease, while foreign welfare remains (in the example depicted here) unchanged on balance.

9 The following analysis can be readily translated into offer-curve diagrammatics, but is more intuitively understood as developed below.

10 To obtain the equivalence mentioned in n. 3 above, we would clearly have to assume the same technology for rent-seeking with quotas as for revenue-seeking with taxes.

11 If the Rybczynski line in figure 4.4 is not vertical, home output of good X will change. Thus, we must now distinguish between the possible aims of fixing the domestic output of this good and fixing the internal product price ratio, exactly as Bhagwati and Srinivasan (1980) were forced to distinguish between the Metzler output paradox and the Metzler price paradox. Our analysis can be extended readily to handle an output constraint, subject to which the foreign country might still fail to gain at the home country's expense.

12 Note also that the use of VERs, which evidently are an *instrument* constraining quantities, is not to be regarded as automatically implying import restraint as the *objective*. As emphasized by our discussion in section 2, a quantity instrument such as a VER may be deployed to achieve a price objective. Failure to make this important distinction could seriously flaw the analysis and interpretation of VERs.

REFERENCES

Bergsten, C. Fred (1975). 'On the non-equivalence of import quotas and "voluntary" export restrictions.' In C. Fred Bergsten (ed.), *Towards a New World Trade Policy: The Maidenhead Papers*. Lexington, Mass.: Lexington Books.

Bhagwati, Jagdish N. (1965). 'On the equivalence of tariffs and quotas.' In Robert E. Baldwin et al. (eds), *Trade, Growth and the Balance of Payments: Essays in Honor of Gottfried Haberler*. Chicago: Rand McNally.

Bhagwati, Jagdish N. (1968). 'More on the equivalence of tariffs and quotas.' *American Economic Review*, 58, 142–7.

Bhagwati, Jagdish, N. (1969). *Trade, Tariffs and Growth: Essays in International Economics*. Cambridge, Mass.: MIT Press.

Bhagwati, Jagdish N. (1977). 'Market disruption, export market disruption, compensation, and GATT reform.' In Jagdish N. Bhagwati (ed.), *The New International Economic Order: The North–South Debate*, Cambridge, Mass.: MIT Press.

Bhagwati, Jagdish N. (1978). *Anatomy and Consequences of Exchange Control Regimes*. Cambridge, Mass.: Ballinger Press.

Bhagwati, Jagdish N. (1982). 'Directly unproductive, profit-seeking (DUP) activities.' *Journal of Political Economy*, 90, 988–1002.

Bhagwati, Jagdish N., Brecher, Richard A. and Hatta, Tatsuo (1985). 'The generalized theory of transfers and welfare: exogenous (policy-imposed) and endogenous (transfer-induced) distortions.' *Quarterly Journal of Economics*, 100, 697–714.

Bhagwati, Jagdish N. and Srinivasan, T. N. (1976). 'Optimal trade policy and compensation under endogenous uncertainty: the phenomenon of market disruption.' *Journal of International Economics*, 6, 317–36.

Bhagwati, Jagdish N. and Srinivasan, T. N. (1980). 'Revenue seeking: a generalization of the theory of tariffs.' *Journal of Political Economy*, 88, 1069–87.

Brecher, Richard A. and Bhagwati, Jagdish, N. (1982). 'Immiserizing transfers from abroad.' *Journal of International Economics*, 13, 353–64.

Caves, Richard E. and Jones, Ronald W. (1973). *World Trade and Payments: An Introduction*. Boston, Mass.: Little, Brown.

Falvey, Rodney E. (1979). 'The composition of trade within import-restricted product categories.' *Journal of Political Economy*, 87, 1105–14.

Feenstra, Robert C. (1984). 'Voluntary export restraints in US autos, 1980–81:, quality, employment and welfare effects.' In Robert E. Baldwin and Anne O. Krueger (eds), *The Structure and Evolution of Recent US Trade Policy*. Chicago: University of Chicago Press (for National Bureau of Economic Research).

Lizondo, Jose Saul (1984). 'A note on the nonequivalence of import barriers and voluntary export restraints.' *Journal of International Economics*, 16, 183–7.

McCulloch, Rachel and Johnson, Harry G. (1973). 'A note on proportionally distributed quotas.' *American Economic Review*, 63, 726–32.

Meade, J. E. (1951). *The Balance of Payments*. Oxford: Oxford University Press.

Pelcovits, Michael D. (1976). 'Quotas versus tariffs.' *Journal of International Economics*, 6, 363–70.

Rodriguez, Carlos Alfredo (1979). 'The quality of imports and the differential welfare effects of tariffs, quotas, and quality controls as protective devices.' *Canadian Journal of Economics*, 12, 439–49.

Takacs, Wendy E. (1978). 'The nonequivalence of tariffs, import quotas, and voluntary export restraints. *Journal of International Economics*, 8, 565–73.

5
Factor Shadow Prices in Distorted Open Economies

Alasdair Smith

1 INTRODUCTION

Much attention in the theory of cost–benefit analysis has been given to the proposition advanced by Little and Mirrlees (1969) that in an open economy, even in the presence of distortions, world prices measure the social opportunity costs of goods and so are the appropriate shadow prices for project appraisal. The proposition is valid in a wide range of circumstances, the key requirements being that world prices be exogenous and that the distortions do not include quantitative restrictions on foreign trade. The derivation and properties of shadow prices for non-traded factors of production when traded goods are valued at world prices is discussed by Diamond and Mirrlees (1976), Findlay and Wellisz (1976), Srinivasan and Bhagwati (1978), Bhagwati and Wan (1979) and Bertrand (1979). Bhagwati, Srinivasan and Wan (1978) observed that such factor prices could be negative, giving a nice treatment in the 'dual' of the phenomenon of immiserizing growth, while Smith (1980) and Neary and Ruane (1985) use factor shadow prices to derive the Brecher and Diaz Alejandro (1977) result on the immiserizing effects of foreign-owned capital in the presence of a tariff protecting a capital-intensive importable.

The aim of this paper is to present a derivation of factor shadow prices in the rather general model of constant-returns competitive production developed by Diewert and Woodland (1977); to show that careful treatment of the role of the government deals with the difficulties identified by Bertrand (1979) in the case where more goods are produced than there are factors of production; and finally to present some further examples of the usefulness of factor shadow prices in the analysis of distorted open economies.

The issue being considered is the evaluation of the social cost of factors of production withdrawn from competitive private-sector production for use in the public sector. In the two-factor, two-good, constant-returns economy analysed by Findlay and Wellisz and further discussed by Srinivasan and

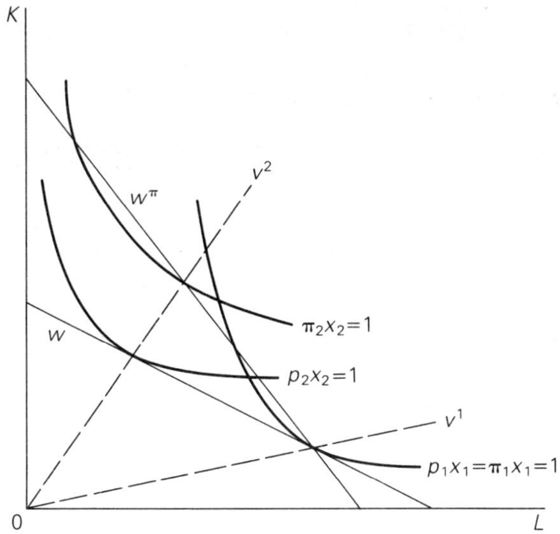

Figure 5.1

Bhagwati, 'foreign-exchange-equivalent' factor shadow prices (w_2^π, w_2^π) are defined by

$$\begin{aligned}\pi_1 &= w_1^\pi a_{11} + w_2^\pi a_{21} \\ \pi_2 &= w_1^\pi a_{12} + w_2^\pi a_{22}\end{aligned} \tag{1}$$

where (π_1, π_2) is the vector of world prices which gives the social value of goods, and a_{ij} is the quantity of factor i used in the production of a unit of good j, these input coefficients being chosen by private producers who face domestic prices for goods which are different from world prices. Findlay and Wellisz's justification for the prices w^π defined by (1) being shadow prices is based on the standard derivation of linear programming shadow prices.

Figure 5.1 illustrates the case where there is a tariff (or subsidy) on the more capital-intensive good. The domestic producer prices of the goods are p_j, and the tangent w to the domestic unit-value isoquants $p_jx_j=1$ determines the input coefficients and the market prices of the factors of production. However, the factor shadow prices are shown as the line w^π which passes through the corresponding points on the world unit-value isoquants $\pi_jx_j=1$. The market prices overstate the true value of the capital-intensive good, and this is reflected in the market price of capital being higher than its shadow price.

So long as the factor supplies available to the competitive production sector lie inside the cone v^1Ov^2, the shadow prices will not change as public sector production draws factors out of the competitive sector. The factor shadow prices are, in the terminology of Bhagwati and Wan, stationary.

Figure 5.2 illustrates a simple case in which there are more factors of production than there are goods produced: the trivial case where two factors

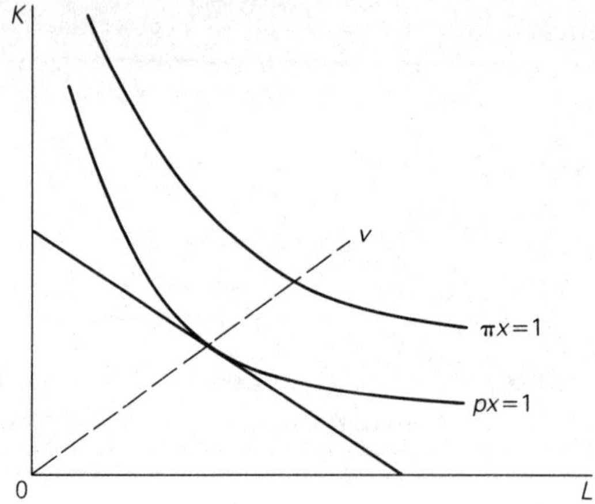

Figure 5.2

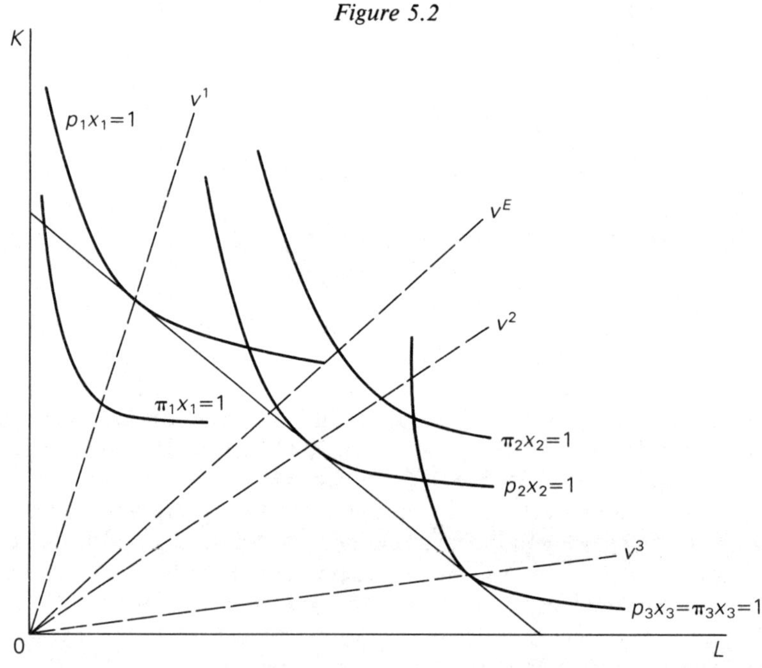

Figure 5.3

are used to produce one good. There is clearly no difficulty about defining factor shadow prices, given the world unit-value isoquant $\pi x = 1$, but equally clearly, the factor shadow prices are not stationary, as their value will almost certainly change as the public sector draws factors out of the competitive sector.

Finally, figure 5.3 shows a case in which there are more goods produced than there are factors: in fact, it is the case of three goods and two factors

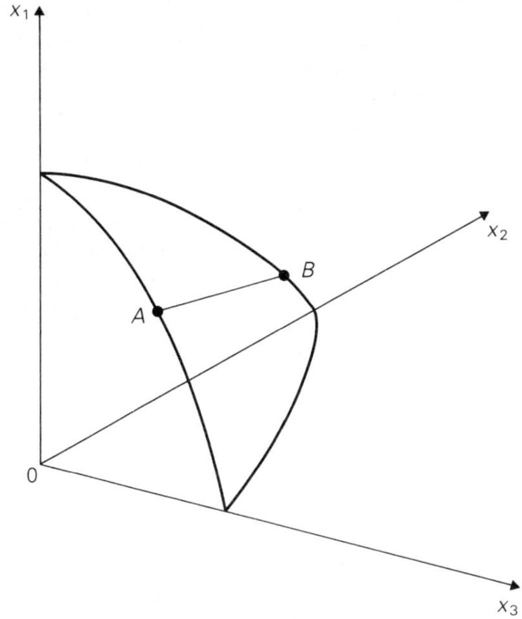

Figure 5.4

that is analysed by Bertrand (1979). Production of good 1 is taxed at the rate t_1 so that $p_1 = \pi_1(1 - t_1)$. Production of good 2 is subsidized at the rate s_2, and $p_2 = \pi_2(1 + s_2)$. Production of good 3 takes place at the world price.

In the absence of intervention, good 2 would not be produced, while the tax and subsidy rates have been chosen so that production of all three goods is competitive. The rays v^k show the proportions in which factors will be used in the respective sectors, and if the economy's endowment ratio of factors is inside the cone $v^1 Ov^3$, production of all three goods will be compatible with full employment, but the amounts of each good produced will be indeterminate. The effect of intervention on factor prices is to raise the relative price of labor.

It is immediately evident that a unique set of factor shadow prices cannot be derived from figure 5.3. In the particular case illustrated, in which v^E represents the factor endowment ratio, it would be compatible with full employment and competitive pricing to produce only goods 1 and 2, or only goods 1 and 3, though not to produce only goods 2 and 3. If a public sector project drew factors out of competitive production, the social cost in terms of foreign exchange would depend on which competitive outputs were reduced.

Another way to see this problem is to observe that, with more goods than factors, there is not a well-defined relationship between the factor supplies and the commodity outputs in the competitive sector. In the three-dimensional commodity space, the transformation surface has the property of being a ruled surface: to every set of domestic prices compatible with the production of all three goods (such as the set of domestic prices shown in figure 5.3) there corresponds a straight line lying along the transformation surface; and the *domestic* value of output is constant along this line, but the value of output *at world prices* varies along the line. The social value of inputs cannot be calculated without knowing how the inputs are used, and the use of inputs seems to be indeterminate.

Figure 5.4 illustrates the full three-dimensional transformation curve, and the straight line *AB* is the locus of points corresponding to the domestic prices of figure 5.3: at *A* there is specialization in goods 1 and 3, at *B*, specialization in goods 1 and 2, and any linear combination of the two points is compatible with full employment at the same prices.

However, one cannot sensibly analyse a case such as this one without giving an explanation of how it comes about that goods prices happen to satisfy the precise relationship that enables more goods to be produced than there are factors of production. In the case illustrated in figures 5.3 and 5.4 welfare is not constant with respect to changes in production plan, as is most easily seen by supposing that there are no consumption distortions, so that consumer prices are world prices, and that there is a single representative consumer in the economy, with any surplus or deficit arising from the production taxes and subsidies being distributed in lump-sum fashion to the consumer. Then, if the plane through *A* representing world relative prices (not shown in the figure) lies strictly above the rest of *AB*, it follows that consumer welfare is higher with production at *A* than with production anywhere else on *AB*. Optimal production of good 2 is zero, and this equilibrium is attainable by a suitable self-financing lump-sum payment by the government to the consumer.

Point *A* is not the point at which the value of output is *maximized* at world prices, for there is still a tax on good 1: the value of output at world prices would be higher with more of good 1 and less of good 3 than are produced at *A*. There is a possible rationale for the intervention: the tax and subsidy shift the distribution of income in favour of the owners of factor 2. However, factor prices are independent of how much of each good is actually produced, and it is desirable to drive production of the subsidized good to zero. To put the same point another way, there is no rationale for the subsidization of good 2, for the same apparent policy objectives are better met by taxing only good 1.

Once production has been driven to the point *A* in figure 5.3, the same number of goods is being produced as there are factors of production, and there will be no difficulty about deriving foreign-exchange-equivalent shadow prices.

Alternatively, one might suppose that production of good 2 is being held at a positive level in order to satisfy some non-economic objective. If, however, this were the case, then the evaluation of the social cost of withdrawing factors out of the competitive production sector must take explicit account of the constraint on the output level of good 2, so only outputs of goods 1 and 3 will change, and again the shadow prices of factors will be well defined.

These examples suggest that the apparent indeterminancy of factor shadow prices when there are more goods than factors may be resolved by the introduction into the analysis of an explanation for the diversification of production. In the next section, after a formal treatment of the simpler cases, I offer a rigorous argument to this effect.

2 THE FORMAL MODEL

Consider a competitive economy in which n goods are produced using m factors of production. Suppose that consumer preferences can be aggregated, and let $c(q, u)$ be the compensated demand function of the representative consumer, where c is an n-dimensional vector of goods consumed, q is the corresponding n-dimensional vector of domestic consumer prices for goods, and u is a measure of real income. Domestic private net outputs of goods are given by the n-dimensional vector x. The public sector may also engage in production, and the net outputs of goods by the public sector are given by the n-dimensional vector g. World prices are fixed at π, and domestic consumer and producer prices are therefore fixed also if trade taxes and consumer taxes are given. Denote by p the n-dimensional vector of prices faced by domestic producers. In equilibrium, the value of consumption at world prices must be equal to the value of total production:

$$\pi c(q, u) = \pi x + \pi g. \tag{2}$$

The factor endowments of the economy are given by the m-dimensional vector v, and competitive factor prices are given by the m-dimensional vector w. Competitive producers faced by a constant-returns technology choose cost-minimizing input coefficients; and the typical entry a_{ij} of the $m \times n$ matrix A is the cost-minimizing quantity of input i used in the production of a unit of good j. A will, in general, depend on w, and the competitive producer prices p will satisfy

$$A'w = p. \tag{3}$$

In competitive equilibrium, it is also required that all factors be fully employed. Let v^x be the factors used in the private sector:

$$Ax = v^x \tag{4}$$

so that, if v^g are the factors used in the public sector, full employment requires that

$$v = v^x + v^g. \tag{5}$$

It is important to understand the connection between (2), which is a balance of payments equation, and the government's budget equation. Total consumer income m satisfies

$$\begin{aligned} m &= qc \\ &= (q-\pi)c + \pi(x+g) \\ &= (q-\pi)c + (\pi - p)x + (\pi g - wv^g) + wv \end{aligned} \tag{6}$$

using (2)–(5). (Note how (3) and (4) give the standard result that, in a constant-returns economy, the value of output to producers will be the same as the value of factor earnings.) The first three terms on the right of (6) are net government revenues from taxation of consumption, taxation of private production, and public production. Thus, consumer income is the sum of government revenue and factor incomes; so any government surplus or deficit from taxes and subsidies is distributed as a lump sum to the consumer.

The differentials of the $m+n$ equations (3) and (4) are

$$A'dw = dp \tag{7}$$

$$Adx + Sdw = dv^x \tag{8}$$

where $S = x\partial A/\partial w = (\Sigma_j x_j \partial a_{ij}/\partial w_k)$ and where the envelope property $dA'w = 0$ is used in deriving (7).

Cost–benefit analysis is modelled here by considering a 'project' (dg, dv^g) which is a perturbation in the public sector production plan and deriving its effect on real income u.

Consider first the case where $m = n$. (3) and (4) define x and w as functions of p and v^x. If A is non-singular, (7) and (8) may be inverted to give

$$dw = A'^{-1}dp \tag{9}$$

$$dx = -A^{-1}SA'^{-1}dp + A^{-1}dv^x. \tag{10}$$

With consumer and producer taxes and subsidies fixed, q and p are fixed by world prices, and the effects of changes in g, v^g and v are given by (2), (10) and (5) as

$$\begin{aligned} (\pi c_u)du &= \pi dx + \pi dg \\ &= (\pi dg - w^\pi dv^g) + w^\pi dv \end{aligned} \tag{11}$$

where

$$w^\pi = \pi \partial x(p, v^x)/\partial v = \pi A^{-1}. \tag{12}$$

It is easy to see that πc_u is positive. If it were nonpositive, (2) shows that welfare could be increased by disposal of production; or, from (6), a welfare-improving positive transfer to the consumer would increase the right-hand side of (6) by at least as much as the left-hand side, and thus would not reduce government revenue. (See Hatta, 1977, for further details.) Thus (11) shows that the effect of a public project on welfare is found by valuing goods at world prices and factors at the Findlay–Wellisz/Srinivasan–Bhagwati shadow prices defined by (12). In fact, (12) shows explicitly how the factor shadow prices value at world prices the marginal contributions of factors to national product at the distorted equilibrium.

When the number m of factors exceeds the number n of goods, the derivation of factor shadow prices is a little more complex. Diewert and Woodland (1977) show that, if $AA' - S$ is nonsingular with inverse Z, then (7) and (8) can be inverted to give

$$\partial x/\partial v = (A'ZA)^{-1}A'Z. \tag{13}$$

So again (11) follows from (2) and (5), but now with

$$w^{\pi} = \pi\partial x(p, v^x)/\partial v = \pi(A'ZA)^{-1}A'Z. \tag{14}$$

Because this case does not have the property of local factor price equalization, unlike the case where $m = n$, the factor shadow prices are not 'stationary': the shadow prices w^{π} depend on v^x, through Z. As Bhagwati and Wan (1979) have discussed, factor shadow prices will in general vary as the public sector draws factors away from the private sector, even with goods prices constant.

Now consider the case where $m < n$. Consumer and producer taxes, and therefore prices, are fixed, and factor prices also are determined by the fixed producer prices through (3). Let public production and factor use also be constant. With more factors than goods, there will typically be multiple equilibria, since the output vector is not uniquely determined. Consider how the equilibrium changes with x. The only other variable that may change is u. (2) and (4) require that such changes satisfy

$$(\pi c_u)du = \pi dx \tag{15}$$

$$Adx = 0 \tag{16}$$

and the change will be welfare-improving if

$$du > 0. \tag{17}$$

Motzkin's theorem (see Diewert, 1983, n. 8) states that *either* there exists a solution x to the matrix inequalities $Ex \gg 0$, $Fx \geq 0$, $Gx = 0$ (where the matrix E is non-vacuous) *or* there exist solutions $y^1 > 0$, $y^2 \geq 0$, y^3 to $y^1E + y^2F + y^3G = 0$; but not both. Thus there exist no du, dx satisfying (15)–(17) if and only if there exist scalars $\lambda > 0$ and μ, and an m-dimensional vector w^{π} such that

$$\lambda = \mu(\pi c_u) \tag{18}$$

$$\mu\pi = w^{\pi}A. \tag{19}$$

Equations (18) and (19) are conditions for optimal choice of u and x, and they have natural interpretations in terms of shadow prices. λ is the social value of utility, μ is the shadow price of foreign exchange, and (18) requires that the marginal benefit and cost by utility should be equated, and will be positive. (19) requires the equality of the social marginal benefit and cost of production of each good. (Note that, if we replaced the equalities in (15) and (16) with inequalities permitting excess supply of foreign exchange and of factors, it would follow that $\mu \geq 0$, and $w^{\pi} \geq 0$.) (18) implies that μ is in fact positive also, and without loss of generality μ can be set to 1 in (18) and (19).

Now as (6) has shown, government budget balance through lump-sum redistribution is implied in this model. Therefore, as we vary x and u in (15)–(17) we are varying lump-sum distribution. In fact, the government can choose the highest value of u compatible with existing taxes, factor supplies and public production simply by choosing the appropriate levels of lump-sum distribution and letting the economy choose the corresponding equilibrium. Referring back to figure 5.4, we see that the government can ensure that the economy chooses point A by giving the consumer the appropriate level of expenditure.

Now (19) asserts the existence of Findlay–Wellisz/Srinivasan–Bhagwati factor shadow prices *if* no solutions to (15)–(17) exist, that is, *if* the government has used its power of lump-sum distribution to ensure that the welfare-maximizing equilibrium is chosen given the fixed prices, taxes and public production. Now from (8), with w constant, and from (19), with $\mu = 1$, (11) again follows, and the w^{π} are confirmed to be the appropriate shadow prices.

The central point of the argument above in the case where $n > m$ is that the derivation of shadow prices for public production in the presence of a set of fixed distortions requires one to assume that the government is making appropriate use of those policy instruments which it *does* control. The importance to the theory of shadow prices of the assumptions made about the rationality of and constraints upon other public sector policies is a central theme of Drèze and Stern (1986).

The argument is not that we will not observe an economy in which there are more goods produced than there are factors: it is that such an economy cannot be modelled simply by inserting a suitable set of taxes and subsidies into a model like the one set out above, for there is, in such a model, an unexplained implicit irrationality in government policy: if the objective of the government when it imposes distorting taxes is to influence factor prices and the distribution of income, then selection of the best among the continuum of equilibria which satisfy this objective will imply that shadow prices are well defined and will usually, though not necessarily, imply that production of all but m goods will be driven to zero.

However, another interpretation is that there are further constraints on government actions which have not yet been made explicit. Suppose, specifically, that (for strategic or political or other reasons) the subset x^f of the private production vector is seen by the government as subject to a constraint that outputs must not fall below certain levels. The government might not be able to satisfy such a constraint simply through lump-sum distribution, and it might need direct control over output levels, although, with production of all goods equally profitable, there would be no cost to producers in complying with such a request. We have to add to (15)–(17) the inequality of

$$dx^f \geq 0 \tag{20}$$

and Motzkin's theorem now implies that the assumption that the government is optimizing with respect to its existing policy options is equivalent to the existence of a positive scalar λ, a non-negative n-dimensional vector η, a scalar μ and an m-dimensional vector w^π such that

$$\lambda = \mu(\pi c_u) \tag{21}$$

$$\eta + \mu\pi = w^\pi A \tag{22}$$

where η has the property that it has zero entries corresponding to the goods not in the constrained vector x^f, and non-negative entries corresponding to goods in x^f.

It is certainly true that factor shadow prices do not now satisfy the Findlay–Wellisz rule; but this is for the simple reason that world prices are not goods shadow prices. The shadow prices of goods whose production levels are constrained have a component reflecting the social cost of that constraint. It remains the case, however, that factor shadow prices are well-defined if optimal use is made of the policies which *are* available to the government. In the example of figure 5.3, if production of good 2 were constrained to be positive, the shadow prices of goods 1 and 3 would be their world prices; the factor shadow prices would be the prices at which production of goods 1 and 3 would be just profitable at world prices, given the distorting effect of the tax on good 1 on the choice of technique of production; and the shadow price of good 2 would actually exceed both the domestic price and the world price.

One other type of explanation can be offered for diversification with $n > m$: goods prices may be endogenous, and may adjust so that the world as a whole produces all goods demanded by consumers. Discussion of this case is beyond the scope of the present paper, but it is sufficient to observe that, when world prices are endogenous, world prices are not the correct shadow prices for goods (see Smith, 1980). There is then not any basis for supposing that factor shadow prices should satisfy a relationship such as (1) or, more generally, (22).

Note finally that, in the three cases respectively, (12), (14) and (19) satisfy the property

$$\pi = w^\pi \mathrm{A} \tag{23}$$

which reflects a more general proposition established by Diamond and Mirrlees (1976) that, at the optimal level of public production in a distorted economy with constant returns to scale in the private sector, public sector shadow prices should have the property that private production activities make zero profits when evaluated at shadow prices. Although the present class of models is less general than that of Diamond and Mirrlees, the derivation above does not require that public production be at an optimal level.

3 SOME APPLICATIONS OF FACTOR SHADOW PRICES

In the model of the previous section, aggregate factor supplies were allowed to vary as well as public sector production, and this allows us to see at once that the shadow prices w^π also evaluate the effects of exogenous factor growth. It is a simple matter to generate examples in which elements of the shadow price vector are negative, and this provides, as Bhagwati, Srinivasan and Wan (1978) observed, a compact derivation of the phenomenon of immiserizing growth.

To allow for the existence of foreign-owned factors of production, let

$$v = v^h + v^f \tag{24}$$

where v^h are domestically owned and v^f are foreign-owned factors. The balance of payments equation (2) is now replaced by

$$\pi c(q, u) = \pi x + \pi g - w v^f \tag{25}$$

and (10) becomes

$$(\pi c_u)du = (\pi dg - w^\pi dv^g) + w^\pi dv^h + (w^\pi - w)dv^f. \tag{26}$$

Now growth in a factor supplied by foreigners will be immiserizing if $w_i^\pi < w_i$, so the foreigners are paid more than the social value of the factor. In a two-good two-factor model, a tariff on a capital-intensive importable will imply that capital imports are immiserizing: we have $p_1 = \pi_1$, and $p_2 > \pi_2$, while the Rybczynski theorem implies that $\partial x_2/\partial v_2 > 0$ if good 2 is the capital-intensive importable and factor 2 is capital. Since $w = p\partial x/\partial v$ and $w^\pi = \pi\partial x/\partial v$, it follows that $w_2^\pi - w_2 = (\pi_2 - p_2)(\partial x_2/\partial v_2) < 0$, the Brecher and Diaz Alejandro (1977) result.

Now I turn to a rather different application, to the small open economy models with Harris–Todaro unemployment discussed elegantly by Corden and Findlay (1975). The derivation of shadow factor prices in these models is different in detail from the models discussed in the previous sections, since now we are looking at models in which the distortion is in a factor market rather than the goods markets. (There is a discussion of the general principles of cost–benefit analysis in models of rent-seeking, the Harris–Todaro model being one such, in Foster (1981), but Foster's approach is rather different from the one adopted here.)

Consider first the two-by-two Heckscher–Ohlin model. The equilibrium is described by

$$K = a_{KA}A + a_{KX}X + K_G \tag{27}$$
$$L = a_{LA}A + (1+u)(a_{LX}X + L_G) \tag{28}$$
$$p_A = ra_{KA} + wa_{LA} \tag{29}$$
$$p_X = ra_{KX} + w_u a_{LX} \tag{30}$$
$$w_u = (1+u)\,w \tag{31}$$

where A is the output of the agricultural sector, X the output of the private urban sector, K_G and L_G the public sector's employment of the factors, and u the urban unemployment rate; w is the endogenous wage in the agricultural sector and w_u the fixed urban wage, and equation (31) is the Harris–Todaro equilibrium condition. Public sector production is assumed to be located in the urban economy. In order to focus only on the implications of the unemployment, suppose that there are no output distortions, so that the prices p are both domestic and world prices.

With w_u and p_X fixed, (30) implies that r is fixed, so (29) implies that w is fixed, and therefore, from (31), that the unemployment rate is fixed. Consider the effect of a change (dG, dK_G, dL_G) in public sector production, where dG is the output of the public sector project. Let p_G be the shadow price of public sector output, which will be a world price if the good is traded. The value of the consequent change in outputs is

$$\begin{aligned} p_G dG + p_A dA + p_X dX &= p_G dG + r(a_{KA}dA + a_{KX}dX) + wa_{LA}dA + w_u a_{LX}dX \\ &= p_G dG + r(dK - dK_G) + w\{dL - (1+u)\,dL_G\} \\ &= (p_G dG - w_u dL_G - rdK_G) + rdK + wdL \end{aligned} \tag{32}$$

which shows that the shadow price of capital is the market price r, and the shadow price of new labour endowment is the agricultural wage w (for the labour either contributes w in the agricultural sector or, with probability $1/(1+u)$, contributes w_u in the urban sector); but the shadow price of labour to the public sector is the urban wage w_u, reflecting the fact that each job created in the urban public sector attracts $1+u$ migrants out of the agricultural sector.

The story is a little more complicated in the other model considered by Corden and Findlay, in which capital is sector-specific. Now the equilibrium equations are

$$K_A = a_{KA}A \tag{33}$$
$$K_X = a_{KX}X + K_G \tag{34}$$
$$L = a_{LA}A + (1+u)(a_{LX}X + L_G) \tag{35}$$
$$p_A = r_A a_{KA} + wa_{LA} \tag{36}$$
$$p_X = r_X a_{KX} + w_u a_{LX} \tag{37}$$

and, of course, (31) continues to hold.

Since the urban wage and the output prices are fixed, equation (37) shows that r_X is fixed. Factor prices in the agricultural sector are not fixed, but changes in the input coefficients satisfy the envelope result:

$$r_A da_{KA} + w da_{LA} = 0. \tag{38}$$

Now the equation analogous to (32) is

$$\begin{aligned} \mathrm{p_G dG + p_A dA + p_X dX} &= p_G dG + r_A a_{KA} dA + r_X a_{KX} dX + w a_{LA} dA + w_u a_{LX} dX \\ &= p_G dG + r_A dK_A + r_X(dK_X - dK_G) \\ &\quad + wdL - duw(a_{LX}X + L_G) - w_u dL_G \\ &= (p_G dG - w_u dL_G - r_X dK_G) \\ &\quad + r_A dK_A + r_X dK_X + wdL - duw(a_{LX}X + L_G). \end{aligned} \tag{39}$$

Apart from the final term, this is essentially the same as (32): if there were no change in unemployment, the shadow prices of the factors are their market prices, with the urban wage being the shadow price of public sector employment. Derivation of the full effects of factor changes requires solving the model for the effects of such changes on u. However, the analysis of Corden and Findlay (1975), based on their figure 1 (p. 61), shows how growth in factor supplies will be associated with changes in the unemployment rate, and it is easily seen that changes in public sector activity will have corresponding effects. An increase in capital stock (or a reduction in the public sector's use of capital) raises the agricultural wage, and so reduces the unemployment rate. An increase in the labour stock (or a reduction in public sector employment) reduces the agricultural wage. Hence the shadow prices of the capital inputs are above r_A and r_A, the shadow price of labour is below w, and the shadow price of public sector labour is below w_u.

In short, derivation of factor shadow prices in the version of the Harris–Todaro model presented by Corden and Findlay gives a very compact treatment of some important aspects of the welfare economics of that model and confirms the effect on the properties of the model of different assumptions about intersectoral factor mobility.

REFERENCES

Bertrand, Trent J. (1979). Shadow pricing in distorted economies. *American Economic Review*, 69, 902–14.

Bhagwati, Jagdish and Wan, Henry Jr (1979). The 'stationarity' of shadow prices of factors in project evaluation, with and without distortions. *American Economic Review*, 69, 261–73.

Bhagwati, Jagdish, Srinivasan, T. N. and Wan, Henry Jr (1978). Value subtracted, negative shadow prices of factors in project evaluation, and immiserizing growth: three paradoxes in the presence of trade distortions. *Economic Journal*, 88, 121–5.

Brecher, Richard A and Diaz Alejandro, Carlos F. (1977). Tariffs, foreign capital and immiserising growth. *Journal of International Economics*, 14, 317–22.

Corden, W. Max and Findlay, Ronald (1975). Urban employment, intersectoral capital mobility and development policy. *Economica*, 42, 59–78.

Diamond, Peter and Mirrlees, James (1976). Private constant returns and public shadow prices. *Review of Economic Studies*, 43, 41–7.

Diewert, W. Erwin (1983). Cost–benefit analysis and project evaluation: a comparison of alternative approaches. *Journal of Public Economics*, 22, 265–302.

Diewert, W. Erwin and Woodland Alan D. (1977). Frank Knight's theorem in linear programming revisited. *Econometrica*, 45, 375–98.

Drèze, Jean and Stern, Nicholas (1986). The theory of cost–benefit analysis. In Alan Auerbach and Martin Feldstein (eds), *Handbook of Public Economics*, vol. 2. Amsterdam: North-Holland.

Findlay, Ronald and Wellisz, Stanislaw (1976). Project evaluation, shadow prices and trade policy. *Journal of Political Economy*, 84, 543–52.

Foster, Edward (1981). The treatment of rents in cost–benefit analysis. *American Economic Review*, 71, 171–8.

Hatta, Tatsuo (1977). A theory of piecemeal policy recommendations. *Review of Economic Studies*, 44, 1–21.

Little, Ian M. D. and Mirrlees, James A. (1969). *Manual of Industrial Project Analysis in Developing Countries*, vol. 2. Paris: OECD.

Neary, J. Peter and Ruane, Frances P. (1985). International capital mobility, shadow prices and the cost of protection. Centre for Economic Policy Research, Discussion Paper no. 58.

Smith, Alasdair (1980). Optimal public policy in open economies. Economics Research Paper no. 176, University of Warwick.

Srinivasan, T. N. and Bhagwati, Jagdish (1978). Shadow prices for project selection in the presence of distortions: effective rates of protection and domestic resource costs. *Journal of Political Economy*, 86, 97–116.

6

Industrial Policy and Trade Policy: The Connections

Richard E. Caves

Industrial policy has emerged as a recognized category of economic policy dealing with the allocation of the nation's resources among various sectors and activities. That definition of industrial policy is formidably broad, and as a result the public agenda of issues and policy prescriptions docketed under this heading has varied widely among nations and over time.

Economists' interests in industrial policy, similarly selective, have recently focused on those aspects with affinities for current fashions in theoretical microeconomics – notably, those of behavior and policy raised by conjunctions of externalities (e.g., innovation or learning) and international strategic behavior. While many interesting results have been obtained, this literature suffers from a certain lack of perspective that may be due to its detachment from the traditional theory of trade controls and welfare:

1 We have neglected some propositions that establish the link between the locus of a resource misallocation and the type of policy that is first-best to repair it.
2 While we accept the proposition that nations' trade policies represent public choices of their political systems, we have not similarly investigated what bases in public choice may explain the selection of industrial policies.
3 We have embraced the viewpoint of national welfare in the setting of policy without giving 'equal time' to global welfare or the types of bargains that would be needed to reconcile maximum global and national welfare.[1]

The present paper is an extended version of chapter 3 of *Industrial Policies for Pacific Economic Growth*, edited by H. Mutoh et al. and published by Allen & Unwin Australia, in association with the Pacific Trade and Development Conference Secretariat, the Australian National University, in Sydney 1986, and is reproduced here with permission.

Accordingly, this paper is an essay in consolidation. It delineates the analytical territory that we can call industrial policy and probes these points of contract with the traditional theory of trade control.

1 THE DOMAINS OF INDUSTRIAL POLICY AND TRADE POLICY

The breadth of our definition of industrial policy flags the problem of treating it cogently: so little is left out.[2] We can achieve reasonable coherence only by restricting ourselves to those policies adopted *primarily* to affect the activity level of some sector and omitting those (such as the corporation income tax) that have this incidental result. Even with that restriction, the category includes everything from agricultural subsidies through competition policy to restrictions on industrial pollution.

It is useful to state the relevant neoclassical core of analysis, as it comes from the theory of trade control, before proceeding to novel issues. Market forces are expected to deliver the wrong scale of output in an industry if some externality or distortion renders the marginal private and social values of the resources committed to the industry unequal. With monopoly (and competition policy) put aside for the moment, the relevant distortions turn on external economies or diseconomies and industry-specific distortions in input prices. External economies or diseconomies make the marginal social value of a sector's output diverge from its marginal private value to the output setter. As we shall see, it is important whether the difference obtains only within the nation or in the world as a whole. Price distortions giving rise to excess supply or demand in input markets for a particular sector are especially relevant to the optimality of the speed of adjustment in the short run. Tax/subsidy correctives of the relevant marginal inequivalences and the 'standard fix' for both externalities and price distortions.

Political decision-makers commonly seize upon trade policy as an instrument readily available to enlarge the output of an import-competing industry that has been forced to contract. If we assume for the moment that the industry's output is indeed sub-optimal, a familiar result (for example, Johnson, 1965) shows that the use of, say, a tariff to enlarge domestic production is a second-best remedy, because it effects an undesirable contraction in domestic consumption at the same time as it accomplishes its stated goal of expanding domestic production.[3] A domestic production subsidy in this case is the first-best solution. The same theorem of course applies to trade controls as correctives for non-optimal levels of domestic consumption: a tariff to discourage goods with external diseconomies undesirably expands their domestic production. In this context a tariff should be used only to remedy an inequivalence between the marginal cost and benefit of trade flows themselves. The obvious example (from the viewpoint of the single nation) is a tariff to maximize the nation's benefits from the exploitation of its monopoly/monopsony power in world markets. The terms-of-trade argument for a tariff usually stands as the only one passing the test of a trade restriction that is first-best for the country imposing it. Thus, most problems imputed to trade policy really call for industrial policy corrections – a conclusion of many years' discussions that plays to the new-found interest in policies focused directly upon distortions in the domestic market of open economies.

Just as the analysis of tariffs regularly includes a horrified glance at fallacious but evergreen arguments for protection on the basis of misconstrued market failures, so has the public discussion of industrial policy issued many dubious calls for action. These include preferences for high-wage or high-skill industries, for 'thick' value-added slices or for fast-growing sectors. In the third section of this paper I shall consider the possibility that these preferences (or 'sectoral fetishisms') may reflect not economic confusion but political equilibrium.

2 PROBLEMS OF RESOURCE MISALLOCATION AND INDUSTRIAL POLICY

Discussions of industrial policy have emphasized three sources of unsatisfying performance that involve genuine problems of market failure and may indeed call for policy correctives. One of these lies in externalities associated with research and proprietary knowledge, the second in international competition in oligopolistic markets, and the third in processes of adjustment.

Production and Appropriation of Proprietary Knowledge

A long history of discussions of property rights in industrial knowledge has clarified the problem that reposes here. In general, we expect that optimal provision requires the producer of knowledge to be able to appropriate fully the rents that are generated, if socially optimal investments are to be made in innovative activities. However, full appropriation normally (that is, unless the owner can practice perfect price discrimination) is second-best in that it results in the knowledge (or the output embodying it) being sold to users only at a price exceeding its marginal cost. It is widely accepted that a patent grant of some limited duration is the optimal compromise, trading off the underprovision of innovative effort against the loss of welfare arising from the monopoly pricing of proprietary innovations. The optimum pertains to global welfare, in the sense that it encompasses gains to all the producers and consumers of knowledge and assumes that in general changes in their welfare are weighted equally. The degree to which the international patent system actually attains this global second-best is considered below.

This analysis carries a number of qualifications that are important for industrial policy. Investments in proprietary knowledge may have positive externalities in the form of revealing further knowledge-creation opportunities to other firms and thus increasing the productivity of their investments in knowledge (Spence, 1984). In that case firms tend to underinvest in knowledge even if they can perfectly appropriate its direct benefits. However, appropriation itself becomes inefficient to the extent that society's grant of the patent privilege falls short of its goal of obtaining full disclosure of new knowledge in exchange for conferring a property right in it.

Other qualifications concern the social optimality of the aggregate investments that firms make to obtain knowledge. The amounts of knowledge that firms privately commit in races to obtain discoveries may exceed the socially optimal amount; even if each additional would-be inventor increases the chances that a discovery will be obtained by a given time, it also generates a negative externality by lowering the expected profitability of other firms in the race. Thus, if firms may join the race freely (paying a fixed cost plus an outlay per period of time) and have rational expectations, then too many enter, and excess resources are committed (Tandon, 1983; Dixit, 1985).[4] This externality problem pertains more obviously to resources that firms invest in order to obtain knowledge already possessed by other firms (to invent around established patents, or to appropriate knowledge that owners keep secret). First-best correctives for these externalities (to the extent that they are feasible) generally involve taxes or subsidies on R&D inputs or on revenues from discoveries.

These principles can be applied straightforwardly in the international economy to any policies designed to correct the provision of industrial knowledge from a purely national viewpoint. Take the simple problem of appropriability. If each domestic innovator can protect its proprietary knowledge, either through patents or by keeping its discoveries secret, then no problems arises for national policy. Similarly, industrial policy can make no contribution if knowledge escapes or diffuses freely into the world at large. Then domestic firms have an incentive to underprovide it, but so does each single country as a whole. Any one country will rationally choose to ride free on the research investments of others, and the resulting under-allocation of resources to research can be solved only at a global level. The opportunity for national public policy comes in the intermediate case, where the research outlays of domestic firms have externalities for other domestic firms, but lesser externalities (or none at all) for firms located abroad. Then domestic innovative effort should be promoted up to the point where the marginal gain to the nation from external benefits of innovation offsets the difference between the private benefits and costs of innovative activities.

How to accomplish that promotion, however, brings us back to the relation between trade and industrial policy. Tariffs have been repeatedly advanced as the appropriate policy for import-competing 'high technology' industries. Yet they are of dubious national value, quite apart from their clear inconsistency with global welfare. As Baldwin (1969) pointed out, protecting an industry that would otherwise under-invest in research raises its product price, but it also induces a larger number of firms to enter the market. Furthermore, it raises their incentives to invest in imitating or matching innovations. Both the increased number of would-be imitators and their enlarged incentives to invest in imitation reduce the expected profits of innovators, making it unclear that the individual firm's incentive to seek original inventions actually increases. The optimal remedies to research externalities affect the revenues from or outlays on research directly and not the price of research-embodying goods or imports that compete with them.

While restrictions on trade have no direct role in promoting the optimal provision of innovative effort, they are effective (if not necessarily optimal) for promoting another sort of proprietary knowledge – that associated with learning by doing, in which a producer's costs decrease with cumulative output or with the elapsed time during which production has taken place. As Krugman (1984a) pointed out, the existence of an activity that enjoys learning-curve gains may provide a case for tariff protection (or production subsidies) to maximize national welfare. Indeed, this may be the most cogent formulation that can be given to the classic 'infant industry' case for the restriction of imports. A market failure occurs, however, only if learning benefits are not internalized. If benefits from learning by doing accrue only within the enterprise, then it presumably internalizes the benefit and prices its output in the short run in recognition of the gains yielded by each unit of output on day *t* in lower costs of producing all subsequent units of output.[5] As Corden (1974, ch. 9) pointed out, a firm might fail to obtain internalized learning advantages because of a lack of information on the prospective gain (in which case the appropriate policy is to disseminate the information); or it might fail owing to capital market imperfections associated with the fact that the lender covering losses during the period when learning occurs has no tangible security.

If learning does have spillover benefits to other firms producing the same good or using the same technology in other product markets, then both national and global problems of market failure may arise. Suppose that learning flows freely among firms in the national industry, making the unit costs of all national producers depend on cumulative industry output and not on its distribution among these firms. Then individual producers set their short-run outputs without taking account of all national benefits, and policy intervention is again warranted to maximize national welfare. A tariff is not first-best, because the specific market failure is associated with insufficient domestic output rather than excessive imports. However, a tariff comes closer to the mark in the case of learning benefits than it does in the case of R&D externalities, because the spillover problem is (by hypothesis) proportional to quantity produced in the case of learning, whereas R&D expenditures are linked to output levels only through a complex chain of behavioral relations.

The discrepancy between national and global welfare again depends on whether external benefits from learning stop at the national boundary or are diffused internationally. If learning diffuses internationally, of course, the activity will be underprovided globally, but the single small nation does best by riding free on other producers' investments in knowledge. Our factual knowledge on these points is unfortunately quite limited. One excellent study (Lieberman, 1984) shows that cost reduction in US processing industries is related to cumulative industry rather than cumulative firm output. But there is little systematic evidence on the relative extents of diffusion to domestic and to foreign products.[6]

The uncertain appropriabilities of both innovations and learning by doing complicate reconciliation of the interests of national and global welfare. Governmental effusions over promoting national 'high tech' industries convey a belief in vast domestic externalities flowing from both research and production coupled with a disregard certainly of international spillovers and arguably of resource wastage through races to obtain innovations or production learning. Also evident are governmental inclinations to support 'national champions' in international races, with the policy-makers falling into the role of Bertrand competitors. These circumstances suggest a strong possibility of globally excessive resources dedicated to some forms of research and innovative production – whether tariffs or direct subsidies serve as the operative policy instrument.

International Oligopoly

The second valid problem of market failure that has been stressed in discussions of industrial policy is that of international oligopoly. Recent contributions on this subject were preceded by an extensive literature that recognized the conflict between national and global interests in competitive international markets. The focus of recent writings has shifted to the problem of oligopoly and international market rivalry from that of national monopoly. That older literature remains useful background to the new developments. If a country enjoys monopoly power over an export (monopsony over an import) that is not fully exploited by its domestic suppliers (buyers), then the government has an incentive to impose a tariff as a first-best remedy. In the case of the export, a second-best solution is monopolizing the domestic industry (second-best because of the distortion that results in domestic consumption). A tariff may be beneficial against a monopolistic supplier of imports even if the monopolist has constant long-run marginal costs if, by shriveling the domestic demand for monopolized imports, a tariff can cause the monopolist to reduce his price (Katrak, 1977).[7] The optimal policy response to a foreign monopoly could, however, be a subsidy on the monopolized imports rather than a tariff: the subsidy becomes appropriate either if the monopolist enjoys decreasing marginal cost or if the curvature of the domestic demand curve is such that the monopolist's price for imports falls by more than the unit subsidy (Brander and Spencer, 1984).

Policies toward external monopolists also take account of how tariff protection affects the prevalence and efficiency of domestic competitors. For example, an import duty might suffice to bring a domestic rival into existence, which under certain conditions could increase national welfare even if the domestic seller behaves oligopolistically and/or has a cost disadvantage (Corden, 1974, p. 217). On the other hand, tariff protection also has effects on the structures of protected markets that amplify the welfare loss associated with an inefficient tariff protecting a competitive industry. Consider the theoretical case of a small country's tariff which protects an industry whose firms are subject to scale economies but otherwise enjoy free entry. A possible outcome is that in equilibrium the domestic price equals the world price plus the tariff, with domestic producers entering to the point where their profits are eliminated. A good deal of empirical evidence supports the explanatory power of this model for the import-competing manufacturing sectors of countries such as Canada and Australia.[8]

New theoretical developments associated with industrial policy address international oligopoly and strategic behavior, chiefly situations in which a domestic producer or oligopoly group faces similar competitors in the world market. The analytical results of all these cases flow from the fact that the income of the home nation includes any profits that domestic producers earn from foreign markets, so that national income can be increased by any policy that enlarges the national producers' share of world sales and profits, unless the benefit should be offset by losses in the distortion of domestic consumption of the commodity in question.

This literature comprises a number of specific models. Some of them focus on the possibility that the government can effect commitments for its national duopolist (say, through a subsidy to the firm's research and development activities) that maneuver the national champion into a position of Stackelberg leadership over its foreign rival (and away from a symmetrical Cournot equilibrium). If the two duopolists sell only in a third market and the government can effect a commitment that the firm itself cannot, then the national welfare is increased by the excess of Stackelberg-leader profits over Cournot profits. The relevance of this case for policy of course depends on whether governments in fact enjoy any advantages that firms do not when it comes to making commitments. The modern theory of entry deterrence in fact points to a rich assortment of investment-type outlays that can yield first-mover advantages (deterring a potential competitor, in this literature; but also reducing the set of opportunities of an incumbent rival). Governments, on the other hand, lack instruments that allow them to make credible binding policy commitments. As Harry Johnson once remarked in the context of host governments' dealings with multinational companies, a government can promise that it will not expropriate, but it cannot credibly promise that it will remain in power six months later.

Other models of policy for international oligopoly put aside the scope for commitment and simply raise the question whether the government can fruitfully intervene to improve the national firm's position in a Nash equilibrium. With output the policy variable that the duopolists utilize, a subsidy to the domestic firm's exports causes the foreign duopolist to contract output, which raises the national duopolistic profit and thus the national welfare. However, in a duopoly with price as the decision variable the case comes out the other way, with a tax on the domestic producer's exports required to cause the foreign producer to reduce output (Grossman and Richardson, 1985, pp. 10–15). This difference between the cases of quantity and price reactions is rather subversive for the policy relevance of these models of profit-shifting, because the mode of oligopolistic reaction is not among the readily observable attributes of a market.[9]

In conclusion, tariff and industrial policies have new theoretical roles for maneuvering the nation's domestic producer(s) into a more favorable position in an international oligopoly. The stringency of the information requirements for correct policies in these cases, however, makes one pessimistic about their direct empirical application. Still, the proposition stands out clearly enough that governments can raise national welfare by intervening to tilt the oligopoly bargain so as to shift rents toward the national income.[10]

Somewhat lost from sight in this discussion is the *global* interest in a coordinated competition policy that forces the 'international duopoly' to sell as a price equal to marginal cost. To put it another way, the national discrepancy between marginal social and private value (profit-maximizing price minus actual price) is not the same as the global discrepancy (price minus marginal cost). This problem is discussed below in section 4.

Failures in the Adjustment Process

Another market failure associated with industrial policy lies in the reallocation of resources among industries in response to international disturbances. Earlier research on this subject (such as Mussa, 1978) suggsted that, with positive costs of adjustment, rational expectations concerning future prices and only a single source of friction, private allocation decisions would correspond to socially optimal ones, and public intervention to affect the reallocation of capital from declining to expanding sectors could make no positive contribution to welfare.[11]

Neary (1982) showed, however, that this conclusion fails to hold if the economy suffers from several sources of stickiness in the reallocation process, such as inflexibility of wages in the short run and capital embodied in sector-specific plant and equipment or subject to costs of reallocation. The adjustment process then may involve phases of 'immiserizing reallocation' in which private decisions lower real national income, owing to the combination of two sources of allocative inefficiency. Neary showed that, in order to eliminate the difficulty, the government needs instruments sufficient to control the speeds of adjustment in both the capital and labor markets. The optimal general policy is likely to call for subsidizing the movement of capital, but, if the speed of adjustment of wages cannot be affected by policy, then the optimal second-best policy will in many cases imply a reduction in capital's speed of adjustment. This is more likely, the slower the speed of adjustment of wages and the smaller the potential for input substitution between capital and labor. Rational expectations do not avert the need for policy because wage rates, even if perfectly foreseen, do not reflect the social opportunity cost of labor.

Interferences with international trade once again provide only a second-best remedy. If the basic problem for policy is to provide differential incentives for the movement of capital and labor, one strategy is to employ trade restrictions as a control on the average or overall incentive affecting factor movements from a sector coupled with another instrument that operates only on the movement of capital or labor.[12]

The issue of failures in the adjustment process is related to the question of whether private information failures may impair the dynamic allocation of resources – the old question of 'indicative planning.' Economists have recently tended to treat this as one of the fallacious bases for industrial policy, pointing out that it amounts to asking the government to pick 'growth stocks' more effectively than the private sector can. Furthermore, the private sector of an advanced industrial society expends considerable resources gathering information in attempts to predict accurately the marginal productivity of resources committed to various sectors. None the less, one cannot be dogmatic about the general efficiency of private decisions on intersectoral allocation for at least two reasons. First, the public good character of information implies that it can be privately overprovided in pursuit of speculative returns (Hirshleifer, 1971) and that *in principle* pre-emptive public provision could be superior. Second, when the addition of resources to a sector involves races among entrepreneurs to make commitments and obtain first-mover advantages, the movement to equilibrium can involve inefficient sequences of excess or deficient capacity. But that possibility still leaves copious room for doubt that governments can forecast better and, if so, whether they can impose their forecasts on private investment decisions without finding themselves running cartel operations.

3 POLITICAL ECONOMY OF INDUSTRIAL POLICY

The framework for analyzing industrial policy should embrace the political economy surrounding it, taking a lesson from the positive political economy of tariffs. One reason for this need is the prevalence among the objectives advanced by the proponents of industrial policy of economic goals or criteria that offer no plausible claim to increase national economic welfare but that may serve non-economic preferences about the economy's sectoral composition. The other reason is that choices of public policy can sometimes be explained as the result of rational actors maximizing their welfare through allocations determined by the political process – allocations that in general will not serve to maximize national welfare. In the case of tariffs, economists have come to accept that differences in the rates of protection that industries obtain seem to reflect their differing structural accesses to the political process. The same proposition seems likely to hold for other instruments of industrial policy.

Models of Political Choice

A variety of approaches have been put forth to explain political decision-making economically on the basis of rational actions by individual political actors or cooperating groups. These include the familiar models of voting in national elections or by geographic representations; they also include lobbying activities of interest groups interacting with political or bureaucratic actors.

These models of public choice have proved successful for explaining tariffs and other policy choices. I suspect, however, that they may miss important bases for the industrial policies that have been chosen, especially in the mature industrial countries. I have in mind the notable proclivity of industrial policies in the United States and Europe to support the losers rather than aid the winners among industries facing international competition. The conventional vote-maximizing model of political behavior implies that a government will enact any measure that a majority of voters perceive to provide them with benefits in excess of the associated tax costs. Such a model is consistent with helping losers if we assume a taste for a collective good that is the sense that fellow citizens are being treated fairly in light of their reasonable expectations. Equivalently, the public sector may provide insurance of last resort against economic disasters that the public view as being visited unfairly upon the victims.[13]

If the political process balances perceived equities in this fashion, we can explain several aspects of aid to losers that are otherwise puzzling. Why should economic disturbances emanating from imports bring political assistance when an equivalent domestic disturbance would not?[14] Why should the public readily support assistance to import-competing industries whose unionized employees command above-median incomes? One can note a few examples of symmetrical penalties imposed on 'undeserving' winners, such as those who enjoyed capital gains from increasing energy prices. This political process of balancing equities is not the only concept of rational political action useful for explaining the orientation of US and European industrial policy oriented toward aiding losers, but a collective preference for perceived equitable treatment can explain features of public choice that are otherwise obscure.

In the nations of Western Europe, more than in the United States, assistance to losers seems to focus mainly on the preservation of jobs, and this fact points to another concept that seems useful for explaining the propensity of their industrial policies to aid the losers. As Houseman (1985, ch. 4) suggested, a great deal of public policy can be characterized as conferring on workers limited property rights in their jobs. These rights are never unlimited in time, nor do they necessarily guarantee preservation of real incomes at the full levels previously attained. But they do treat a person's job as an endowed asset that warrants limited compensation if it should be lost, or protection if it is threatened. Because neoclassical economics has generally been unsympathetic toward such a property right, we may note that it can be given a straight-forward analytical interpretation. Assume that a person obtains certain non-marketed satisfactions that are attached to the job, the workplace or a geographic place of residence that is viable only because he or she holds this job. Then loss of the job entails not just the conventionally recognized cost of retraining and relocation, but also an increase in the cost of obtaining the previous bundle of non-marketed satisfactions.[15]

Implications for Industrial Policy

If these elements of collective equitable treatment and job property rights do characterize the political process surrounding industrial policy, they hold a number of implications for both national and international policy-making. At the national level, a policy of supporting the losers is to be expected, and one's expectations about any systematic policy-making aimed at identifying and backing winners must be lowered. It is implied, however, that the support for losers will be limited in time and amount; the thrust of policy intervention is to delay adjustment processes rather than to forestall them permanently. This implication matches rather well such patterns as the use of voluntary export quotas to curb the expansion of imports' share of the domestic market but not to fix it permanently. The normal turnover of a sector's employees may set a limit on the rate at which adjustments in its level of activity and employment can proceed without triggering intervention to sustain workers' property rights in their jobs.[16]

That public policy preserves limited property rights in jobs and otherwise serves a collective interest in equitable treatment seems the most important implication of collective goods for explaining industrial policy, but it is not the only one. The economically specious arguments for industrial policy mentioned in section 1 may indeed make some claim for coherence along the line. Breton (1964) argued that middle-class voters may gain utility from the knowledge that the economy's sectoral mix is one that provides a rich array of middle-class jobs – skilled labor, research, middle management and other non-production activities. Such a collective preference is consistent with electoral support for measures to promote or preserve high-wage, high-skill industries and those supporting substantial research activities. Thus, industrial policy may be called upon to serve collective interests of the middle class in the sectoral composition of the economy. Collective-good preference may also explain public support for technically spectacular but low-return investments (e.g., the supersonic transport aircraft) that contribute to a collective sense of national achievement. Also, a collective disutility in seeing the nation lose a race for such an achievement can certainly explain Bertrand-type competition in providing public sector support for innovation races.

4 INDUSTRIAL AND TRADE POLICIES AND INTERNATIONAL RELATIONS

I have proposed that industrial policy can be regarded either as a conventional normative areas of economic policy-making at the national level or as a behavioral phenomenon that can be explained by the choices of national policies made by political actors. Either way, it affects policy-making at the national level toward both sectoral activity levels and international trade. Most bases for industrial policy, both normative and behavioral, imply as first-best policy governmental intervention with tax/subsidy measures to affect sectors' levels of activity in either the short or the long run. Affecting sectoral allocations through tariffs or subsidies on international trade is for most purposes second-best. Public choice can supply an explanation of why this second-best approach prevails. If political decision-makers perceive a substantial shadow price on sources of government revenue, then a tax incentive will be preferred to a subsidy even if it imposes some extra deadweight loss. If a sector is to be enlarged (or its shrinkage averted), a tariff on competing imports has an obvious fiscal attraction over a subsidy on domestic output, especially if the subsidy cannot be applied only at the margin. By extension, expanding a sector through subsidizing exports becomes preferable to subsidizing all of its output, including that sold on the domestic market, especially if (as is likely) export demand is more elastic.

Whether national governments select first-best or second-best policies, international ramifications must be expected. Except in special cases (such as Brander and Spencer, 1981), a production subsidy (tax) increases (decreases) net exports of the affected sector, just as a tax (subsidy) on imports or a subsidy (tax) on exports does. As US public policy keenly recognizes, production and trade measures when taken in a large country exert similar quantitative effects on sectoral production levels in other trading countries. Therefore, industrial policy raises essentially the same questions of the international coordination of policies that have stood before the General Agreement on Tariffs and Trade since World War II. It therefore provides another valuable comparison between the two lines of policy.

International Coordination: the General Issue

It is worth knowing where significant payoffs could be achieved in the international coordination of economic policy, however pessimistic one may be about attaining them. We assume that no problem arises with policies that favorably affect the perceived welfare of the country imposing them and inflict no harm on other countries: they will be put into effect. The substantial cases calling for international coordination are those in which one country's policy exerts a spillover effects, favorable or unfavorable, on the perceived welfare of another country or countries. A standard approach to this problem is to assume an initial Cournot equilibrium in which each country has set one or more policy instruments without taking account of their effect on the foreign country's welfare (we address the two-country case, for simplicity) or its optimal policy response.

The analysis of international policy coordination then follows as an application of bargaining over externalities in a market setting, but with the possibility noted that direct pecuniary compensation is awkward to arrange between sovereign nations, so that barter in policies is an important route to mutual gains. Policy spillovers may take either negative or positive forms. Suppose a policy that improves country 1's welfare has (at the margin) a negative effect on 2's welfare, and that country 2 has no property right in freedom from such effects.[17] The standard theory identifies 2's preferred option as a bribe to effect a reduction of the policy's intensity to the point that diminished losses to 2 from the spillover at the margin just offset diminished benefits to 1 from the policy. With a positive spillover, the optimal bribe expands the policy to the point where 2's spillover benefits at the margin match 1's opportunity loss from 'overkill.'

Another useful way to frame bargaining over policies is to set a barter between two symmetrically positioned countries, each plying a policy instrument that imposes spillovers on the other. Efficient trade in policies then is the counterpart of mutually beneficial exchange from a Cournot equilibrium to one that is Pareto-optimal, and it may involve a marginal increase or decrease in either country's instrument, depending on the sign of the spillover. Each country's gross benefits from policy trade take the form of increased welfare for 2 – say, a function of unit increases in 1's policy beyond the 'Cournot' level that 1 would select on its own, when the spillover is a positive one. For a negative spillover, the benefits repose in the increases in 2's welfare that stem from unit reductions in the intensity of 1's policy from its Cournot level. Country 1's benefits from changes in 2's policies are analyzed symmetrically. One can think of these benefit functions as giving rise to offer curves that describe the opportunities for mutually beneficial policy trade that is analytically identical to the neoclassical model of two-country barter in goods.

Applications to Industrial Policy

These approaches to policy spillovers are at once analytically familiar and too abstract to enrich the preceding analysis greatly. Yet they do have important practical lessons for the international coordination of policy. Consider, for example, the rounds of tariff reduction that have occurred under the aegis of the General Agreement of Tariffs and Trade. If we assume that countries' pre-negotiation tariffs represented equilibrated choices of output structures made by their national political systems, then the successive rounds of international negotiations (such as the most recent Tokyo Round) can be thought of as policy barter to cut back these tariffs and curb negative spillovers that has taken the form of worsened terms of trade for the tariff-setting country's trade partners. Economists obsessed with the belief that few tariffs make any contribution to the tariff-setting country's own welfare have resisted this behavioral interpretation of the tariff bargaining process, yet it elucidates many features of the GATT rounds.

Let us consider policy spillovers in light of the substantive issues of industrial policy identified in section 2. International oligopoly poses the simplest problem, is that the profit-shifting policies proposed for national industrial policy are entirely redistributive between countries and at best themselves have no effect on global real income. Although countries have not obviously responded to these new theoretical invitations to seek rents from their neighbors, there is a well established practice of exempting from a country's competition policy any national monopolies or cartels seeking to extract rents from foreign markets (Auquier and Caves, 1979). One might hope for a GATT-type agreement for each country to enforce its competition policy even-handedly as to benefits that it will yield to domestic and foreign buyers. This arrangement will not generate equiproportional benefits for every trading country, but neither do multilateral tariff reductions under the GATT, yet each procedure offers a rough likelihood that the gains to each country from global reductions in allocative inefficiency will more than offset any curtailment of the rents it obtains from foreigners.[18]

International interests in research and development and in proprietary learning pose more complex issues. In the case of R&D, the international patent system already provides a limited assignment of property rights to nationals who devise patentable inventions, with countries that accord patent rights to foreigners forswearing the spillover benefits that they could otherwise obtain by freely copying foreigners' innovations. Thus, to the extent that the universal patent is the best available compromise for rewarding inventive effort, the patent system has already sought out a global solution that keeps nations from fencing over rents and spillover benefits from individual inventions. However, this global solution really describes only the arrangement among the leading industrial countries, for nations outside this group typically choose to some extent to ride free by according property rights in patentable innovations only to their own citizens.[19]

Obviously not every industrial country benefits proportionally from the international patent system, and some on balance may not benefit at all. That is, they might gain from free-riding on other countries' innovations even if other industrial nations were to retaliate by denying patent privileges to their own citizens. None the less, the system works rather like GATT-negotiated tariff reductions to pursue a global optimum on the mutually accepted assumption that its benefits are proportionally distributed.

The issue newly raised under the banner of industrial policy is nations' efforts to maneuver their home producers into a priority of discovery of patentable innovations or of similar proprietary assets such as learning curve knowledge. These have spillover effects in the opportunity-cost sense that one nation's investment in supporting its national industry precludes foreign countries' access to the potential rent stream. The international interest here lies in averting the waste of resources in competitive rent-seeking.[20] There may also be gains in minimizing the world's real cost of output, in so far as industrial policy maneuvers some national producer other than potentially the most efficient into the 'lead' position (this case is particularly clear in regard to learning-curve benefits). However, making this global interest prevail against national policy is not easy for exactly the reason that the international patent system reveals. In any particular innovation race, an efficient solution requires that the 'best' (most skillful inventor; lowest-cost manufacturer when all learning gains have been obtained) producer bribe others who are effectively in the race to let it go ahead. Compensation could conceivably take the form of a binding commitment to limit the price–cost margin on the efficiently produced innovation or output, but credibility and enforcement problems make this unlikely. The only practical prospect seems to be the same type of compromise embedded in the patent system, which is to assume that commercial victories will be spread more or less proportionally among the major industrial countries so that governments mutually agree to maintain a hands-off policy.

Problems of efficient adjustment in the short run also have potentially important ramifications for international policy coordination, although their structure is not so readily predicted. A country that optimally delays the contraction of its i industry can generate either negative or positive spillovers abroad. Perceived negative spillovers arise if the i industry abroad is also subject to excess capacity. Positive spillovers obtain should the foreign country's expanding industry avert overshooting and excessive entry into industry i by investors with biased expectations. Because of the short-run and specific nature of such effects, international coordination requires a framework for continuing coordination rather than a definitive international resolution. One can imagine a framework that contemplates intertemporal policy-trading, with country 1 tolerating an adjustment-related trade restriction by 2 at one time on the understanding that 2 will reciprocate on a future occasion. The lower the correlation over time between countries' levels of unemployment, the better prospect is such balancing.

NOTES

1 This paper neglects a fourth candidate for this list: general equilibrium qualifications to the partial equilibrium analysis of tariffs have not always found their counterparts in partial equilibrium treatments of industrial policy.

2 One is reminded of Baldwin's (1970) effort to classify non-tariff barriers to trade, which wound up including all policies designed to affect consumption or production of the competing domestic sector's output.

3 Corden (1974, chs. 2, 3) synthesized this analysis and reviewed the qualifications to the first-best status of subsidies to remedy underproduction.

4 Various authors have noted that rivalry to innovate resulting in overcommitment of research resources in light of expected private returns might simply serve to offset the incomplete private appropriation of social gains from innovation (private returns fall short of social), leaving the net distortion of the allocation of resources to research uncertain but possibly small.

5 As Dasgupta and Stiglitz (1985) emphasized, the logic of the learning curve suggests that monopoly will indeed emerge, making internalization of learning benefits a likely outcome. Where actual or potential rivals are present at the outset, the rate at which learning occurs and the discount rate are both relevant to determining the equilibrium market structure.

6 A few studies such as Benvignati (1982) suggest that domestic diffusion of innovations is speedier than diffusion abroad.

7 Brander and Spencer (1981) showed that, if the foreign monopolist is limit-pricing to preclude the rise of domestic competition, such a tariff is (up to a point) a free ride for the nation imposing it, having no cost from the distortion of domestic consumption.

8 Product differentiation also plays a role in determining the viability of suboptimal-scale producers. See, among other sources, Corden (1974, pp. 213–14). Corden (p. 221) also pointed out that the administration of 'made to measure' production fosters such sub-optimal equilibria by truncating the returns expected by any domestic producer who expands in an effort to seize much greater economies of scale; if he succeeds and obtains rents, protection may be reduced.

9 The usual problem arises of the relative efficiency of taxes/subsidies on production and on exports. From the national viewpoint the distortion lies in trade, so that a production tax/subsidy is second-best if the good is also consumed domestically.

10 An example is Japan's apparent success in reducing the market price of international technology licenses by restricting the number of Japanese companies allowed to enter into negotiations with foreign licensors (M. J. Peck, in Patrick and Rosovsky, 1976, pp. 544–58).

11 Of course, the absence of perfect foresight also provides grounds for intervention. For example, if expectations are static so that capital owners expect intersectoral differences in rates of return to persist, capital will be reallocated between sectors at a faster rate than is socially optimal (given the assumed existence of adjustment costs of reallocating it). See Mussa (1978).

12 Houseman (1985, ch. 5) built upon Spencer and Brander (1983) to show a role for national public policy in an international declining industry. Public assistance to a national duopolist in such an industry may provide the commitment that leaves a foreign rival no option but to exit first, letting the domestic seller collect from foreign buyers some terminal monopoly rents that contribute to the national income.

13 This formulation was suggested to me by Donald McFetridge.

14 To appreciate the importance of perceived fairness as an influence on policy, at least in the United States, notice that assistance to domestic industries facing import competition is heavily although not exclusively conditioned on the subsidization of foreign exporters or their use of price discrimination. If the issue were simply one of preserving existing jobs or altering private markets' rates of adjustment, the basis for the intervention should not depend on the reasons for the advantage held by foreigners.

15 Devotees of rational expectations have argued that the expectation of losses would be built into the supply price of labor, so that the wage precompensates workers for such welfare losses. The logical force of this point is somewhat blunted by the long time-horizons of many workers' attachments to their jobs, which limit their ability to distinguish job-loss probabilities in the far-distant future. It is also blunted if the political process of balancing equities that was hypothesized above fails to perceive the premium for risk-bearing built into the wage.

16 Grossman and Eaton (1985) provided a normative model that draws upon risk aversion to demonstrate that free trade may not be optimal even for a small country when the terms of trade are uncertain and markets for contingent claims are incomplete.

17 Only limited property rights exist guaranteeing countries the right to compensation

for spillovers from foreign policy measures, such as selected articles of the General Agreement on Tariffs and Trade.

18 The more closely correlated among countries are consumers' losses of surplus to profits of (domestic or foreign) monopoly and domestic producers' monopoly profits exacted from consumers (at home or abroad), the more likely is it that each nation gains from a global policy of promoting competition. The fact that international oligopolies and differentiated-product industries (even without oligopoly elements) tend to undertake intra-industry trade – a central conclusion of modern theoretical research – favors just this correlation. A presumption is supported that parallel applications of pro-competitive policies in the leading producer countries will increase each country's welfare as well as bring the international economy closer to a global optimum.

19 We might also expect the generosity of the terms of a country's patent grant to increase with the importance of domestic relative to foreign applications for patents. Casual evidence seems consistent with this.

20 Suppose that we accept the model of excessive rival investments in innovation (Dixit, 1985). Then any one nation's tax on the costs of inventive activities has a positive externality abroad, averting the negative externality that otherwise curtails foreign inventors' expected profits.

REFERENCES

Auquier, Antoine A. and Caves, Richard E. (1979). Monopolistic export industries, trade taxes, and optimal competition policy. *Economic Journal*, 89, 559–81.

Baldwin, Robert E. (1969). The case against infant-industry tariff protection. *Journal of Political Economy*, 77, 295–305.

Baldwin, Robert E. (1970). *Nontariff Distortions of International Trade*. Washington: Brookings Institution.

Benvignati, Anita M. (1982). The relationship between the origin and diffusion of industrial innovation. *Economica*, 49, 313–23.

Brander, James A. and Spencer, Barbara J. (1981). Tariffs and the extraction of foreign monopoly rents under potential entry. *Canadian Journal of Economics*, 14, 371–89.

Brander, James A. and Spencer Barbara J. (1984). Trade warfare: tariffs and cartels. *Journal of International Economics*, 16, 117–31.

Breton, Albert (1964). The economics of nationalism. *Journal of Political Economy*, 72, 376–89.

Corden, W. M. (1974). *Trade Policy and Economic Welfare*. Oxford: Clarendon Press.

Dasgupta, Partha and Stiglitz, Joseph (1985). Learning-by-doing, market structure, and industrial and trade policies. Centre for Economic Policy Research, Discussion paper no. 80 (London).

Dixit, Avinash (1985). The cutting edge of international technological competition. Institute for International Economic Studies, Seminar Paper no. 342 (Stockholm).

Grossman, Gene M. and Eaton, Jonathan (1985). Tariffs as insurance: optimal commercial policy when domestic markets are incomplete. *Canadian Journal of Economics*, 18, 258–72.

Grossman, Gene M. and Richardson, J. David (1985). *Strategic Trade Policy: A Survey of Issues and Early Analysis*. Special Papers in International Economics, no. 15. Princeton: International Finance Section, Princeton University.

Hirshleifer, Jack (1971). The private and social value of information and the reward to inventive activity. *American Economic Review*, 61, 561–74.

Houseman, Susan N. (1985). Job security and industrial restructuring in the European Community steel industry. PhD dissertation, Harvard University.

Johnson, Harry G. (1965). Optimal trade intervention in the presence of domestic distortions. In Robert E. Baldwin et al. (eds.), *Trade, Growth and the Balance of Payments: Essays in Honor of Gottfried Haberler*. Chicago: Rand McNally.

Katrak, H. (1977). Multi-national monopolies and commercial policy. *Oxford Economic Papers*, 19, 283–91.

Krugman, Paul R. (1983). Targeted industrial policies: theory and evidence. Paper presented at a symposium on Industrial Change and Public Policy, sponsored by Federal Reserve Bank of Kansas City.

Krugman, Paul R. (1984a). Import protection as export promotion: international competition in the presence of oligopoly and economies of scale. In Henryk Kierzkowski (ed.), *Monopolistic Competition and International Trade*. Oxford: Clarendon Press.

Krugman, Paul R. (1984b). The US response to foreign industrial targeting. *Brookings Paper on Economic Activity*, 1, 77–121.

Lieberman, Marvin B. (1984). The learning curve and pricing in the chemical processing industries. *Rand Journal of Economics*, 15, 213–28.

Mussa, Michael (1978). Dynamic adjustment in the Heckscher–Ohlin–Samuelson model. *Journal of Political Economy*, 86, 775–91.

Neary, J. Peter (1982). Intersectoral capital mobility, wage stickiness, and the case for adjustment assistance. In J. Bhagwati (ed.), *Import Competition and Response*. Chicago: University of Chicago Press.

Patrick, Hugh and Rosovsky, Henry (eds.) (1976). *Asia's New Giant: How the Japanese Economy Works*. Washington: Brookings Institution.

Spence, Michael (1984). Cost reduction, competition, and industry performance. *Econometrica*, 52, 101–21.

Spencer, Barbara J. and Brander, James A. (1983). International R&D rivalry and industrial strategy. *Review of Economic Studies*, 50, 707–22.

Tandon, Pankaj (1983). Rivalry and the excessive allocation of resources to research. *Bell Journal of Economics*, 14, 152–65.

7
International Capital Mobility and the Dutch Disease

Ronald W. Jones, J. Peter Neary and Frances P. Ruane

1 INTRODUCTION

One of the striking features of the 1970s and early 1980s has been the importance of major resource shocks, in the form both of discoveries and exploitation of new reserves, and of dramatic changes in resource prices. As might be expected, such resource-based booms have, in general, been of more benefit to resource-rich countries than to others. However, it is just as true in practice, although less immediately evident, that resource booms have created major internal problems for resource-rich countries.[1] Such problems have arisen because of the structural adjustments which resource booms have induced, problems which have been given the title of the 'Dutch Disease'.[2]

Academic economists have not been slow to investigate these issues, and a sizeable literature has now emerged dealing with both theoretical and empirical aspects of the Dutch Disease.[3] However, a characteristic feature of most of this literature to date is that it assumes that all factors of production are trapped within national boundaries. The implications for the analysis of the Dutch Disease of potential international mobility of some factors have not yet been explored, despite the fact that, as we hope to show, a number of interesting possibilities are introduced when these two phenomena are examined together. Such an exploration is particularly appropriate in a volume of essays in honour of Max Corden, since has has made important contributions to the literature on both of these topics.[4]

The model used most frequently in discussing the implications of a resource boom for output changes is the Specific Factors model.[5] Two traded sectors make use in common of a mobile resource, which we shall refer to as labour,

---

Jones's research is supported, in part, by National Science Foundation Grant no. SES-8510697.

as well as of a resource or type of capital that is adapted for specific use in only one sector. A boom that takes the form of an expansion in one of these specific factors causes the transformation schedule to shift outwards, thus opening up the potential for both sectors in the economy to expand. However, if both sectors are trading outputs at given world prices, the sector making use of the booming resource must expand at the expense of the other sector. In this basic model the phenomenon of the Dutch Disease is not only possible, but cannot be avoided.

The model we wish to develop in this paper is richer in its productive base, and this opens up the possibility that the severe consequences of the Dutch Disease may be moderated, if not altogether averted. Furthermore, it is a model which allows us to consider international mobility of capital without implying an implausible degree of specialization in the output of tradable goods. Although it turns out that the Dutch Disease is still highly prevalent even in this expanded setting, the model reveals how certain types of internal or external links may ease the adjustments required in the rest of the economy following a boom specific to one sector.

In our discussion of the Dutch Disease we limit ourselves to the case of a resource boom. An alternative scenario, in which the world price of a country's export commodity rises, is explicitly ignored, even though its analysis is similar in many respects. However, there is one important difference. In a context of a model in which rates of return to capital may be set on world markets, it is inappropriate to analyse a small open economy's reaction to a change in world commodity prices without at the same time investigating the likely consequence of such price changes on world returns to capital. International capital mobility thus adds a further dimension to the Dutch Disease by drawing attention to this significant difference between price and quantity booms. In what follows we ignore the issues raised by price booms and concentrate on productive relationships within a small price-taking economy faced with a resource boom which is purely internal in its origins.

2 THE MODEL WITH NATIONALLY TRAPPED CAPITAL

The extended version of the Specific Factors model we wish to analyse considers two tradable commodities, which we refer to as the booming sector (B), and the traditional manufacturing sector (M). Both sectors are assumed to use three factors of production, but the extent and kind of mobility of each of these factors is different. As in the standard Specific Factors model, labour is assumed to be perfectly mobile between both sectors of the economy; but such mobility stops at the water's edge. By contrast, capital will, in the subsequent treatment, be considered to have a world market, but none the less will be restricted in its use by functional specificity. Thus capital used in traditional manufacturing is never appropriate as an input in the booming sector. Finally, there is a third type of factor, which we call resources. This

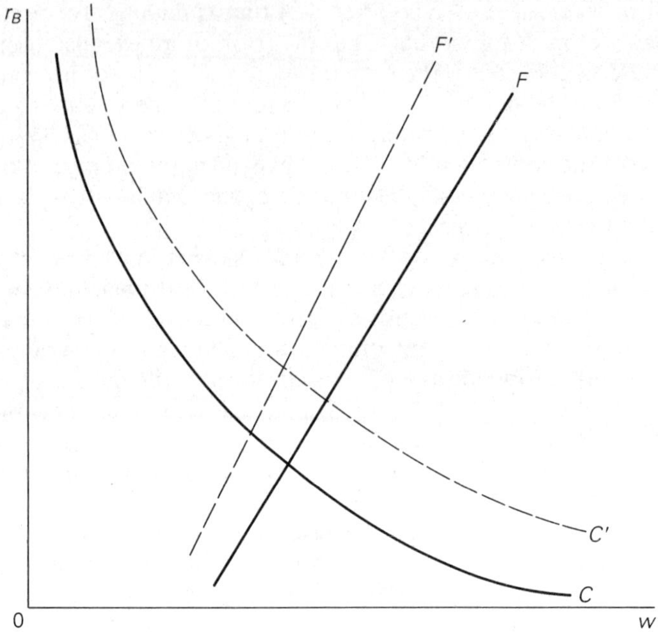

Figure 7.1 Response to a fall in resource price

is both functionally specific, like capital, and internationally immobile, like labour.

Although we are interested in the consequences of international capital mobility for the phenomenon of the Dutch Disease, it is useful to begin by considering a resource boom when capital is tied down both geographically and functionally. Such an exploration provides a point of comparison when we consider international factor mobility, and also serves to reveal how this extended model allows a moderation of the form of the Dutch Disease found in the traditional Specific Factors model. We begin with the competitive profit conditions of change in the booming sector. Let L_B, K_B and V_B denote, respectively, the quantities of labour, capital and resources used in the booming sector. If output prices remain unaltered, a boom in resources will affect factor prices, but unit costs in this sector must remain constant. This requires a weighted average of factor price changes, with the weights provided by the distributive factor shares, to vanish. Let θ_{iB} refer to factor i's distributive share in the booming sector, and let the returns to labour, capital and the resource be denoted by w, r_B and s_B, respectively:[6]

$$\theta_{LB}\hat{w} + \theta_{KB}\hat{r}_B + \theta_{VB}\hat{s}_B = 0. \tag{1}$$

Explicit solutions for this model are worked out in the Appendix. It is clear, however, that a resource boom must serve to lower the return to resources, s_B, allowing a potential improvement in the return to the other two factors used in the booming sector. Whether or not both these factors indeed share in the potential gain depends upon the relative degrees of substitutability among factors. As we now investigate, if labour does not gain, the resource boom will not require any output reduction for traditional manufactures.

For an initial value of the return to resources, the *C* curve in figure 7.1 illustrates the possible values for the wage rate and return to capital in the booming sector as of a given product price. This curve, convex to the origin to reflect the convexity of technology, illustrates the trade-offs represented by the competitive profit equation of change, (1). When a resource boom occurs, the return to resources must fall, and this causes an upward shift in the *C* curve to *C'*. A second curve, *F*, drawn with a positive slope, indicates that, for the initial value of the return to resources and given factor supplies to the booming sector, an increase in the return to capital, r_B, must be matched by an increase in the wage rate, w, to keep the proportions of labour and capital demanded in balance with the ratio of supplies.[7] The reasoning is straightforward. An increase in r_B must, on its own, reduce the use of capital. Moreover, if labour and capital are substitutes, the demand for labour will rise. Even if they are complements in production, we assume the degree of complementarity is limited so that an increase in r_B must lower the capital – labour ratio used. To restore this ratio to the full employment levels, the wage rate must rise. As drawn in figure 7.1, the *F* curve is 'inelastic', reflecting an assumption that a greater relative increase in r_B than in w is required to maintain full employment. As we now argue, such an asymmetry is indicative of a presumed greater degree of substitutability between resources and labour than between resources and capital in the booming sector.

From an initial equilibrium point where the *C* and the *F* curves intersect in figure 7.1, imagine an equiproportionate increase in w and r_B. This is equivalent, in its effect on factor usage, to a reduction in the return to resources, s_B, as of fixed w and r_B. If resources are just as good a substitute for labour as for capital, this factor price change leaves undisturbed the ratio of labour to capital demanded. (In such a case, the *F* curve would be a ray from the origin and would not be affected by changes in s_B.) If labour and resources are better substitutes for each other than are capital and resources, the equiproportionate rise in w and r_B must create an excess demand for capital (relative to labour), necessitating an equilibrating further rise in r_B to restore full employment. Such an asymmetry was assumed in drawing the *F* curve inelastic in figure 7.1, and for precisely the same reasons the fall in s_B which accompanies a resource boom shifts the *F* curve upwards to position *F'*.

Figure 7.1 illustrates the way in which a greater degree of substitutability between resources and labour than between resources and capital leads to an asymmetric share of potential gains to capital and labour. A sufficient degree of asymmetry in this respect could lead to an actual reduction in the wage rate. Figure 7.2 illustrates the different possible outcomes from an alternative perspective, depicting relationships explicitly derived in the Appendix. In this diagram the vertical axis measures the changes in w and r_B relative to the change in the resource endowment. The horizontal axis

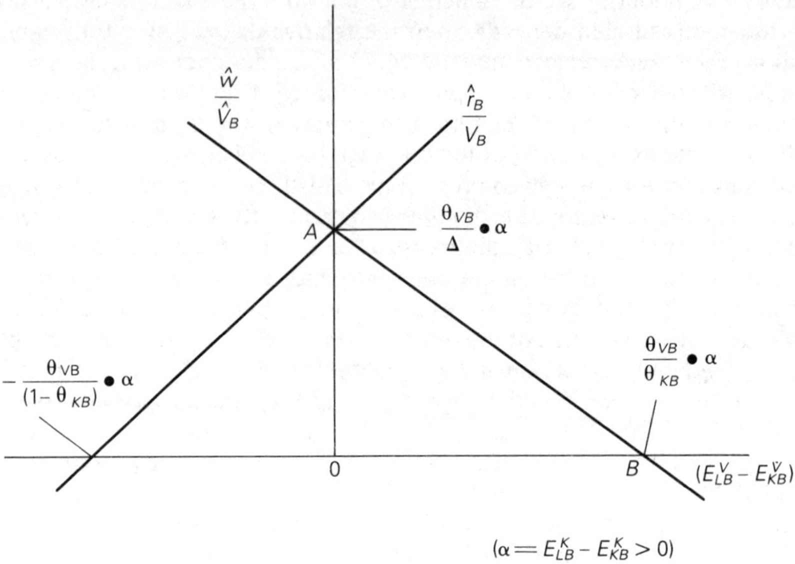

Figure 7.2 Factor prices and relative substitutabilities
$\alpha \equiv E^K_{LB} - E^K_{KB} > 0$

measures the relative extent to which resources are a better substitute for labour in the booming sector than they are for capital. The term E^i_{jB} is defined as the relative change in the quantity of factor *j* used per unit output in the booming sector brought about by a 1 per cent rise in the return to factor *i*. Thus, $E^V_{LB} - E^V_{KB}$ measures the effect of a rise in the return to resources on the labour-capital ratio in production. In the case of separability, this ratio is undisturbed and an increase in the supply of resources would raise wages and the return to capital by the same relative amount. (In figure 7.1 this would be shown by the intersection of an unshifting *F* ray through the origin with the *C′* curve; in figure 7.2 it corresponds to point *A*.) But the more substitutable are resources for labour as compared with capital, the more will the increase in V_B benefit capital at the expense of labour. Figure 7.2 illustrates how a sufficiently high degree of asymmetry (such that $E^V_{LB} - E^V_{KB}$ exceeds the distance *OB*) can actually cause the boom to lower the wage rate. In such a case, labour and resources are relatively such good substitutes that an increase in V_B not only lowers s_B, but drags *w* down as well. That is, the increase in V_B has lowered labour's marginal product in the booming sector.

The possibility that labour and resources are relatively such good substitutes provides a rationale for the traditional manufacturing sector to avoid the Dutch Disease in our model. The reasoning is clear: with capital and the type of resources required in manufacturing fixed in supply, any lowering of the wage rate (brought about by the effect of the resource boom on the marginal product of labour in the booming sector) must serve to raise the use of labour in manufacturing. Output must rise. In effect, the sector-specific shock to the economy represented by the resource boom has been transformed into an economy-wide shock by the high degree of substitutability between mobile labour and the booming resource. (By analogy, in the Specific Factors model a genuine increase in the economy's supply of labour would serve to raise outputs in both sectors.) Less pronounced asymmetry in the relative degree of substitutability will not suffice to reverse the phenomenon of the Dutch Disease. However, any asymmetry whereby labour and resources are better substitutes than are capital and resources must to some extent mitigate the required output reduction in manufacturing, since it serves to limit the extent of the wage increase.

3 THE MODEL WITH INTERNATIONAL CAPITAL MOBILITY

In the traditional scenario describing the Dutch Disease, the manufacturing sector loses resources to the booming sector. But the possibility that manufacturing could obtain resources from abroad introduces an alternative route whereby productive activity in the traditional manufacturing sector can avoid being hurt by the resource boom in the other sector. Although relief through world capital markets thus appears possible, note that the line of argument in the preceding section, whereby traditional manufactures could benefit if the wage rate falls, no longer applies. With capital internationally mobile, its rental rate in the booming sector is determined on world markets. As a consequence, the fall in resource rentals following the resource boom must serve to drive up the wage rate.[8] The traditional manufacturing sector is forced to release labour to the booming sector.

Although this route for avoiding Dutch Disease is thwarted, the international mobility of capital suggests an alternative mechanism. Since the volume of resources specifically suited for use in the manufacturing sector is unchanged, any alteration in the capital flow is reflected in a change in the capital–resource ratio adopted in traditional manufactures. That is, the resource boom in the other sector serves to attract capital from abroad into manufacturing if the expression shown in equation (2) is positive:[9]

$$\hat{a}_{KM} - \hat{a}_{VM} = (E^L_{KM} - E^L_{VM})\,\hat{w} + (E^V_{KM} - E^V_{VM})\,\hat{s}_M. \tag{2}$$

If resources and capital in manufacturing are substitutes, the second bracketed term, $(E^V_{KM} - E^V_{VM})$, is positive. Even if these two factors are complements in production, this term is positive as long as we continue to assume that a rise in any factor return always lowers the ratio of that factor's use compared with any other. Therefore, the drop in the return to resources used in manufacturing must by itself encourage a capital outflow. Since the wage rate must rise, attention centres on the sign of the first bracketed expression.

This term contrasts the relative degree of substitutability of labour and capital, on the one hand, and labour and resources, on the other.

The significance of this term can be revealed by considering two examples. The first assumes separability between labour and the other two factors in the sense that an increase in the wage rate does not alter the capital–resource ratio utilized in manufacturing (so that $E^L_{KM}=E^L_{VM}$). If this condition prevails, the reduction in s_M (forced by the increase in wages) would unambiguously lower the ratio of capital to resources; capital would flow out of the manufacturing sector to the rest of the world. International capital mobility will have accentuated the Dutch Disease difficulties faced by the traditional manufacturing sector. In the second example, suppose that the resource coefficient of manufacturing output is absolutely rigid, with the technology requiring a fixed value for a_{VM}. In this case the term $(\hat{a}_{KM}-\hat{a}_{VM})$ in equation (2) reduces to $E^L_{KM}\,\hat{w}$, so that the increase in the wage rate must encourage an *inflow* of capital into the manufacturing sector from abroad.

Although international capital mobility might provide a route whereby the traditional (non-booming) sector acquires resources from overseas, can such a capital inflow ever be sufficient to guarantee that manufacturing output does not contract? Since the quantity of local resources available for manufacturing is fixed, any increase in output must be matched by a fall in the resource content per unit of output:

$$\hat{x}_M = -\hat{a}_{VM}. \tag{3}$$

This change in the input–output ratio must be linked to factor price changes, so that

$$\hat{x}_M = -E^L_{VM}\,\hat{w} - E^V_{VM}\,\hat{s}_M. \tag{4}$$

It is immediately apparent that, if labour and resources are substitutes, output must fall since the wage increase and fall in return to resources would both encourage a rise in a_{VM}. What if labour and resources are complements in manufacturing (a negative value for E^L_{VM})? By well-known symmetry relationships,

$$\frac{\partial a_{VM}}{\partial w} = \frac{\partial a_{LM}}{\partial s_M}$$

Translating into elasticity terms yields equation (5):

$$\theta_{VM}\,E^L_{VM} = \theta_{LM}\,E^V_{LM}. \tag{5}$$

Furthermore, by the competitive profit equations of change in manufacturing (analogous to equation (1)), $\theta_{VM}\,\hat{s}_M = -\theta_{LM}\,\hat{w}$, since the return to capital is fixed by the world market. Substitution into equation (4) reveals that

$$\hat{x}_M = -\frac{\theta_{LM}}{\theta_{VM}}(E^V_{LM} - E^V_{VM})\,\hat{w}. \tag{6}$$

Our previously invoked limit on the extent of complementarity requires this entire expression to be negative, except for the limiting case which we already described, in which resources are rigidly linked to output. (In such a case x_M remains constant.) Even if capital is attracted from abroad, it can never make up for the loss of labour to the booming sector; manufacturing output must fall in the Dutch Disease fashion.

Two kinds of asymmetries in relative degrees of factor substitutability have emerged as crucial in reversing or alleviating the Dutch Disease phenomenon for traditional manufactures. If capital were immobile between countries and labour and resources were particularly good substitutes, the resource boom might actually cause the wage rate to fall. This is the only route by which traditional manufactures can expand, and it is a route that is blocked off in the case of international capital mobility. In this latter case the wage rate must rise and traditional manufactures must lose labour. The effect of this loss of labour to the booming sector on manufacturing output would be accentuated by a capital flow abroad unless labour and capital in manufacturing were particularly good substitutes (relative to labour and resources in manufacturing). With the wage rate rising and the return to resources in manufacturing falling, the manufacturing sector can attract inputs from abroad only if these inputs (capital) are particularly good substitutes for the local input that has gone up in price (labour). Even if it succeeds in attracting capital from abroad, the effect on output is never sufficient (unless the resource–output ratio is rigid) to outweigh the internal loss of labour to the booming sector.

4 A BOOM IN A TRADED RESOURCE

The boom which we have analysed above takes the form of a resource discovery, where that resource cannot be traded directly. Instead, it is used as an input into a commodity which is traded. An alternative possibility – that the resource itself can enter international trade, at a price given on world markets – has far-reaching implications for internal factor allocations and the possibility of Dutch Disease. In order to adhere to the distinctions we have already made, assume that the boom (discovery) takes place not in the form of an increase in V_B, but rather in the form of ownership claims to internationally traded, but functionally specific, capital used to produce output in the booming sector.

The existence of an international market for sector-specific capital serves to transform the sector-specific shock into an economy-wide *wealth* shock. If, further, we adhere strictly to the output assumptions made previously, whereby only two goods are produced and both are traded on world markets, the boom in owned type-B capital is absorbed with no changes in factor prices or, indeed, in output in either sector. Consumption levels rise, and this is financed by an outflow of capital from the booming sector.

To progress to a more interesting scenario, introduce a non-traded good sector in addition to the two traded goods. One of the principal directions which the original literature on the Dutch Disease took involved exploring the distinction between the fate of such a final, non-traded commodity and that of a traditional traded commodity not sharing in the boom (our 'manufacturing' sector). As was pointed out in these contributions, the price of this non-traded good is determined within the economy and, given the favourable income effects of the boom, would be expected to rise as demand shifts outwards. What is of interest in our present discussion is that, with such local activity taking place, the wealth effects of the increase in owned capital will spill over and raise the return to some non-traded productive factor, such as labour. If so, output in the 'booming' sector, i.e. the sector utilizing the kind of capital which has increased in local supply, will actually get squeezed.[10]

These remarks serve to highlight the crucial role played by international trade in the resource. The output activity which utilizes the booming resource benefits specifically from this boom only to the extent that input price falls, helping to attract other inputs as well into this activity. International trade in this resource cuts this direct link between resource availability and output. To take an example, secondary industry in a country such as Canada could not expect to have its external competitive position strengthened by new discoveries of oil and natural gas if these command world markets. Not only would income effects tend to drive up factor prices, but any direct requirement for labour and other inputs to develop these resources serves further to attract resources away from traditional secondary industries using energy inputs.[11] This is a kind of 'self' Dutch Disease.

5 CONCLUDING REMARKS

One of the most classic propositions in all of economics is Ricardo's doctrine of comparative advantage. It establishes that any country can find some commodities in the production of which it can successfully compete in world markets. It also suggests how, with the close link between a nation's consumption and production patterns dissolved by the possibility of international exchange, a nation's resources tend to get concentrated in a few lines of production. Any individual productive activity which faces a world market need no longer be supported by a reservoir of local demand. A sector-specific shock favouring one traded activity will generally draw resources out of other traded activities. When all goods are traded, the phenomenon of the Dutch Disease is simply a corollary of the doctrine of comparative advantage.

The extended version of the Specific Factors model explored in this paper reveals how the tendency for a traditional traded sector to lose resources to a booming sector may be moderated by asymmetries in substitution relationships among inputs. In each case these asymmetries had something in common: the traditional sector may be a net recipient of some factor which is obtainable elsewhere (labour from the booming sector in section 2, capital from the rest of the world in section 3), and which has fallen in price relative to some other factors used in production. Our model emphasizes the pricing relationships among factors in developing these possibilities, but less formally suggests that other ways of attracting resources to the traditional sector may help moderate the Dutch Disease. Thus a resource boom typically leads to increased government tax revenues, and some of these revenues might be channelled to subsidize inputs used in the traditional traded sector. Probably the development of public inputs such as roads or other forms of social overhead capital (or development of human capital in a form of productive relevance to traditional sectors) comes most readily to mind. The role of international trade in productive factors should not be ignored in considering this wider framework within which to view the Dutch Disease. The historical record is rich in instances of booming sectors attracting resources from abroad, and of these resources, in turn, helping to develop productive potential in other lines of activity. Notwithstanding these possibilities, the message of the Dutch Disease remains clear: resource gains specifically tied to one traded sector tend to attract non-traded factors, and these are to be found in other traded sectors not blessed by the resource gain.

APPENDIX

The basic characterization of substitution possibilities among factors utilized in figure 7.2 is found in the term E^i_{jB}. A 1 per cent rise in the return to factor i results, by definition, in an E^i_{jB} per cent increase in the use of factor j per unit output in the booming sector. All 'own' substitution terms, E^i_{iB}, are negative. Furthermore, by zero degree homogeneity of factor demands,

$$E^L_{jB} + E^K_{jB} + E^V_{jB} = 0 \text{ for } j = L, K, V.$$

Figure 7.2 shows the effect on wages and the return to capital of an increase in the quantity of resource, V_B, made available to that sector assuming the quantity of labour and capital available in the booming sector is (temporarily) kept constant. The change in any input–output coefficient is given by the factor price changes and the appropriate elasticities:

$$\hat{a}_{jB} = E^L_{jB}\,\hat{w} + E^K_{jB}\,\hat{r}_B + E^V_{jB}\,\hat{s}_B.$$

Full utilization of factors available to the booming sector requires:

$$\begin{aligned} a_{LB}\,x_B &= L_B \\ a_{KB}\,x_B &= K_B \\ a_{VB}\,x_B &= V_B. \end{aligned}$$

Output change is restricted by the availability of labour, so that, for given L_B,

$$\hat{x}_B = -\hat{a}_{LB}.$$

The following three relationships can then be used to determine the effect of an increase in V_B on factor returns:

$$\begin{aligned} \theta_{LB}\,\hat{w} + \theta_{KB}\,\hat{r}_B + \theta_{VB}\,\hat{s}_B &= 0 \\ (E^L_{KB} - E^L_{LB})\,\hat{w} + (E^K_{KB} - E^K_{LB})\,\hat{r}_B + (E^V_{KB} - E^V_{LB})\,\hat{s}_B &= 0 \\ (E^L_{VB} - E^L_{LB})\,\hat{w} + (E^K_{VB} - E^K_{LB})\,\hat{r}_B + (E^V_{VB} - E^V_{LB})\,\hat{s}_B &= \hat{V}_B. \end{aligned}$$

The first equation is the competitive profit equation of change for the booming sector, equation (1) in the text, with θ_{iB} representing factor i's distributive share. The second equation states that the capital–labour ratio is fixed, while the third allows the resource–labour ratio to rise only by the relative increase in the resource base, $\hat{V}_B$. Figure 7.1's C and C' curves illustrate the manner in which the first equation's relationship between w and r_B is altered when s_B falls (as a consequence of a rise in V_B). The F and F' curves in figure 7.1 picture the comparable links between w and r_B found in the second equation.

Formal solutions are shown by

$$\frac{\hat{s}_B}{\hat{V}_B} = -\left\{\frac{\theta_{LB}(E^K_{LB} - E^K_{KB}) + \theta_{KB}(E^L_{KB} - E^L_{LB})}{\Delta}\right\}$$

$$\frac{\hat{w}}{\hat{V}_B} = \frac{-\theta_{KB}(E^V_{LB} - E^V_{KB}) + \theta_{VB}(E^K_{LB} - E^K_{KB})}{\Delta}$$

$$\frac{\hat{r}_B}{\hat{V}_B} = \frac{\theta_{LB}(E^V_{LB} - E^V_{KB}) + \theta_{VB}(E^L_{KB} - E^L_{LB})}{\Delta}$$

By the assumed concavity property of the production function, the determinant, Δ, must be positive and an increase in V_B must lower own-return, s_B. Furthermore, although complementarity is allowed, we rule out 'super-complementarity', wherein a rise in a factor price would not only lower the intensity of that factor's use, but would also reduce the input of a complementary factor by even more. Thus terms like $(E^L_{KB} - E^L_{LB})$ are all positive. Finally, since by homogeneity

$$(E^L_{KB} - E^L_{LB}) = (E^K_{LB} - E^K_{KB}) + (E^V_{LB} - E^V_{KB}),$$

the expression for the changed return to capital can be written as

$$\frac{\hat{r}_B}{\hat{V}_B} = \frac{1}{\Delta}\{(1 - \theta_{KB})(E^V_{LB} - E^V_{KB}) + \theta_{VB}(E^K_{LB} - E^K_{KB})\}.$$

Figure 7.2 plots the relationship between $\hat{w}/\hat{V}_B$ and $\hat{r}_B/\hat{V}_B$ on the one hand, and the degree of asymmetry between resource substitutability with labour and with capital on the other. A relatively high degree of substitutability between resources and labour could lower the wage rate (labour's marginal product in the booming sector), thus releasing labour to the rest of the economy.

NOTES

1 For empirical evidence relating to a number of countries, see the contributions in Neary and van Wijnbergen (1986).
2 Resource booms also raise issues of depletion and stabilization policies, which we shall not consider here.
3 For overviews, see Corden (1984), Neary (1985), and Neary and van Wijnbergen (1986).
4 On international capital mobility, see especially Corden's important paper, Corden (1967). On the Dutch Disease, see his illuminating remarks in Corden (1981), subsequently developed in Corden and Neary (1982) and Corden (1984).
5 This model is developed in Jones (1971) and Samuelson (1971).
6 A circumflex denotes a proportional rate of change; e.g., $\hat{X} = dx/x$.
7 An analogous diagram for a three-factor, two-sector economy is described in Jones and Easton (1983).
8 This strong result depends upon there being only three factors in the booming sector. With capital's return pegged to world markets, a resource boom must raise the return to some factor other than capital or resources. If there were additional factors, labour's return could conceivably fall, for reasons similar to those developed in section 2.
9 a_{ij} denotes the amount of factor i per unit of output in sector j. Thus $\hat{a}_{KM} - \hat{a}_{VM}$ is the change in the capital–resource ratio in manufacturing.
10 An example of this outcome is given in Jones, Neary, and Ruane (1983, p. 360, n. 6).
11 These themes are explored as well in Jones (1980, 1986).

REFERENCES

Corden, W. M. (1967). Protection and foreign investment. *Economic Record*, 43, 109–32.

Corden, W. M. (1981). The exchange rate, monetary policy and North Sea oil: the economy theory of the squeeze on tradeables. *Oxford Economic Papers*, 33, 23–46.

Corden, W. M. (1984). Booming sector and Dutch Disease economics: survey and consolidating. *Oxford Economic Papers*, 35, 359–80.

Corden, W. M. and Neary, J. P. (1982). Booming sector and de-industrialization in a small open economy. *Economic Journal*, 92, 825–48.

Jones, R. W. (1971). A three factor model in theory, trade, and history. Chapter 1 in J. N. Bhagwati, R. W. Jones, R. A. Mundell and J. Vanek (eds), *Trade, Balance of Payments, and Growth: Essays in Honor of Charles P. Kindleberger*. North-Holland: Amsterdam.

Jones, R. W. (1980). Comparative and absolute advantage. *Swiss Journal of Economics*, 3, 235–60.

Jones, R. W. (1986). The Dutch Disease: a trade-theoretic perspective. In Neary and van Wijnbergen (1986).

Jones, R. W., Neary, J. P., and Ruane, F. P. (1983). Two-way capital flows: cross-hauling in a model of foreign investment. *Journal of International Economics*, 14, 357–66.

Jones, R. W. and Easton, S. T. (1983). Factor intensities and factor substitution in general equilibrium. *Journal of International Economics*, 15, 65–99.

Neary, J. P. (1985). Real and monetary aspects of the Dutch Disease. In K. Jugenfeld and D. Hague (eds), *Structural Adjustment in Developed Open Economies*. London: Macmillan.

Neary, J. P. and van Wijnbergen, S. (1986). *Natural Resources and the Macroeconomy*. Oxford, Basil Blackwell; Cambridge, Mass.: MIT Press.

Samuelson, P. A. (1971). Ohlin was Right. *Scandinavian Journal of Economics*, 73, 365–84.

8
Bundled International Factor Mobility

Wilfred J. Ethier

The international movements of productive factors, like the international trade of commodities, are restricted in diverse ways. This particular area of international economic policy has long interested Max Corden, and he has made important contributions to it (see, for example, Corden, 1967, and Corden, 1974, ch. 12). International factor movements might be subjected to taxation, or not allowed at all (a prohibitive tax). Or the conditions might be of a quite different sort. Very often, the factor movement must coincide with some other international transaction. I refer to factor movements restricted in this way as cases of *bundled* factor mobility.

The bundling requirement might be imposed explicitly by one of the governments involved, or it might be the implied consequence of the set of policies in place. An important example of the latter is afforded by the immigration policies of many countries. The immigration of unskilled labor is often severely restricted or prohibited outright, while workers who possess desirable skills are admitted freely. Thus, labor may move only if bundled with human capital (see Ethier, 1986). Analysis of this situation would constitute a distinct approach to the 'brain drain.'

Direct investment, by contrast, is often subjected to explicit bundling requirements. Host countries often impose entry conditions that require foreign firms to bring in (tangible and intangible) assets. Indeed, bundling may be central to the reason why direct investment takes place in the first place. The model of Helpman and Krugman (1985, ch. 13) is in effect such a special case of bundled factor mobility. This illustrates that bundling requirements might well reflect basic technical limitations to factor mobility, in addition to policy restrictions.

Sometimes the bundled factor movements are in opposite directions. Such *reverse bundling* occurs between countries which restrict capital mobility while allowing the temporary migration of unskilled labor. Guest workers frequently remit a significant part of their earnings abroad. Such international payments are in practice virtually impossible to control, even when other types of capital flows are effectively limited. Thus a capital flow in one direction is bundled with a labor flow in the other.

Our complex world also offers many examples of *composite bundling*, with a factor movement tied to a commodity flow, in the same or reverse direction. Direct investment, for example, is often made conditional on export performance. For recent treatments of the economic issues involved, see Herander and Thomas (1985) and Rodrik (1986).

As these examples suggest, bundling is pervasive–perhaps more the rule than the exception. Also, there is a good deal of diversity in the forms it takes. I will therefore inquire in this paper into what general conclusions one might draw, also examining bundling in general terms in the context of familiar special models of international trade.

1 GENERAL FORMULATION

Consider first a general two-country trade model with n goods and m factors. A particular bundling restriction can be represented by an m-dimensional vector b_i whose components, normalized in some way, represent the proportions in which the respective factors are required to migrate. Positive entries denote immigration and negative entries emigration. Thus, a policy of free immigration of factor j would be represented by a vector whose jth entry is unity; and, with all other entries zero, a reverse bundling policy would require a vector with both positive and negative components; and so on.

A country's migration policy can be described by the set of all allowed b_i. The rest of the world presumably has its own migration policy. But actual movements must be consistent with *both* policies: if Europe prohibits the export of human capital while the United States prohibits the immigration of labor without human capital, neither factor will in fact be allowed to move. Thus a particular policy in one country will be effective only if it corresponds to an opposite policy on the part of the other country. It is therefore sufficient to confine attention to the set of all effective home country policies. This set can be represented by the matrix b, whose rows consist of all the effective home policies. (In the special case of free mobility of all factors, b would consist of $2m$ rows, with m rows forming the $m \times m$ identity matrix and the remaining m rows the negative of this.)

Let the (row vector) k denote the actual level of activity subject to the various bundling restrictions. Thus kb equals the m-dimensional vector of actual net immigration into the home economy. Home production can be represented by the scalar y, where

$$y = f(p, v + kb). \tag{1}$$

Here, p denotes the vector of commodity prices prevailing at home, v the home endowment vector, and f is a standard national product function. If asterisks denote variables pertaining to the rest of the world.

$$y^* = f^*(p^*, v^* - kb). \tag{2}$$

Let w and w^* denote respective equilibrium factor prices in the two countries. It is necessary in equilibrium that the bundle of factors represented by any effective policy b_i earn an aggregate reward in the home (host) country at least as great as it could have earned abroad:

$$(w - w^*)b_i \geq 0. \tag{3}$$

If the policy b_i simply allows the free mobility of some particular factor, (3) reduces to requiring that that factor's reward be the same at home as abroad. More complex policies require the factor prices in the two countries to stand in linear relations to each other, but do not imply equalization of individual rewards. Several significant results can be established in this general framework.

2 FACTOR PRICE SUB-EQUALIZATION (I)

Suppose the available technology is the same at home as abroad. The fact that countries often bundle factor inflows in proportions useful to themselves suggests that the case where a policy b_i coincides with the technique actually used in some home production sector is of particular interest. So suppose that the policy is in fact identical to the technique actually used in sector i. Then the vector w of home factor prices solves the problem:

$$\begin{aligned} &\text{minimize } wb_i \\ &\text{subject to: } c_i(w) \geq p_i \end{aligned} \tag{I}$$

where $c_i(w)$ and p_i denote, respectively, the cost function and the value of a unit of output in sector i. Because the two countries share the same technology, w^* must also satisfy the constraint in (I), provided that the goods produced in sector i are freely tradeable: otherwise the home i sector would not be able to compete in world markets. But then (3) implies that w^* actually solves (I). If the solution is unique, we must therefore have $w = w^*$.

Thus, with internationally identical technology, the following result holds:

A bundling requirement identical to the technique actually employed in some home sector results in factor price equalization of the relevant factors, with freely traded outputs.

The result is important because it gives circumstances under which the bundling requirement is innocuous: abolishing the requirement to allow free migration would have no effect.

This general result can be exploited further in a particular context. Suppose, for example, that the production structure is that of the specific factors model: each of the n sectors produces one good and employs two factors, one specific to itself and one mobile among all the sectors. Thus $m = n + 1$.

A bundling requirement identical to the technique in one sector therefore involves the mobile factor and one specific factor. Thus, under the assumptions of the above result, the reward of the (intersectorally) mobile factor will be equalized across countries. But then the reward of each specific factor must also be equalized: otherwise the country with the higher reward for any such factor would necessarily have higher costs for the respective good and therefore could not produce it, preventing the market for that specific factor from clearing.

Thus the specific factors model yields the following additional result:

Free trade in goods and the bundled movement of two factors equalize all factor prices, provided that the bundle is the technique in some sector.

This follows even though no factor is individually mobile internationally, factor endowments are not restricted to be relatively similar across countries and, most surprisingly of all, the sector whose technique equals the bundling requirement need not be operated in both countries. Bundled factor mobility and free trade in goods produces the same result as would unconstrained international mobility of the internally mobile factor plus free trade in goods, or as would (*if* relative endowments were sufficiently similar) the unconstrained international mobility of a specific factor plus free goods trade.

The location of world production need not be the same in these three alternative cases. But that does not matter, as long as tastes do not change when factors migrate. The shifting across countries of the sector whose technique equals the bundling requirement would be an example of bundled mobility and would produce no other effects: thus the equilibrium location of that production is indeterminate. There might easily be cases where a country exports a relatively scarce factor, bundled with a relatively abundant one, but there is no significance to such cases.

3 FACTOR PRICE SUB-EQUALIZATION (II)

The case where the bundling requirement coincides with the actual host country technique is of special interest, but it is by no means of exclusive interest. So it is worth pointing out that the first result can be extended to a wider class of requirements. Suppose that the bundling requirement b_i can be expressed as a non-negative linear combination

$$b_i = \sum_j \alpha_j a_j$$

where $\alpha_j \geq 0$ and the a_j denote techniques used in some sectors of the home economy. Then home factor prices w must solve the following problem:

$$\begin{aligned} &\text{minimize } wb_i \\ &\text{subject to: } c_j(w) \geq p_j, \text{ all } j. \end{aligned} \qquad \text{(II)}$$

The earlier argument can now be repeated. Thus,

Any bundling requirement that can be expressed as a non-negative linear combination of techniques actually used in the host country implies international equalization of the rewards of the factors included in that bundle.

4 THE HOS MODEL

Turn now to the implications of bundling in the familiar 2×2 Heckscher–Ohlin–Samuelson model. Consider the effect of introducing the possibility of bundled factor movements into an initial equilibrium with free trade in goods but no international factor movements. Figure 8.1(a) shows isocost curves corresponding to both goods. If both countries produced both goods, factor prices in each country would be as indicated at point E (the figure is drawn without factor intensity reversals), and there would be no role for international factor movements. So suppose that home equilibrium is given by point H, so that the home economy produces only good 1 and its endowed capital–labor ratio is indicated by the slope of the isocost curve at H, and that the foreign economy is at point F. (The argument to follow would not be affected if one of the countries produced both goods, if both countries produced the same good, or if there were factor intensity reversals.) To simplify matters, suppose that international commodity prices are undisturbed by migration between the home and foreign economies (as would be the case if they were embedded in a large world with free trade in goods), so that the isocost lines will not move about.

Now suppose that bundled mobility is introduced. There is no need to restrict the type of requirements in any way, so consider all possibilities in which both factors move in the same direction. Note first that the straight line connecting points H and F defines a bundling requirement for which nothing happens: at initial factor prices, the implied bundle is worth the same in both countries. The factor proportions in this bundle are illustrated by the ray OT in figure 8.1(b). More capital-intensive bundles than this are worth more in the foreign country than in the home country and so would induce home emigration, whereas requirements with more labor-intensive bundles would induce home immigration. We shall confine our attention to the latter case, as the roles of the countries simply reverse otherwise.

There are now two possibilities, depending on whether the required bundle is more or less capital-intensive than the foreign economy is initially. Suppose it is more capital-intensive. Then the bundled factor movement from the foreign country to the home country will cause both countries to become less capital-abundant. Factor prices in the two countries adjust, as indicated in figure 8.1(a). This continues until a line with a slope reflecting the bundling requirement can connect the points showing both countries' factor prices. This is true when factor prices are as indicated by points H' and F' respectively in figure 8.1(a).

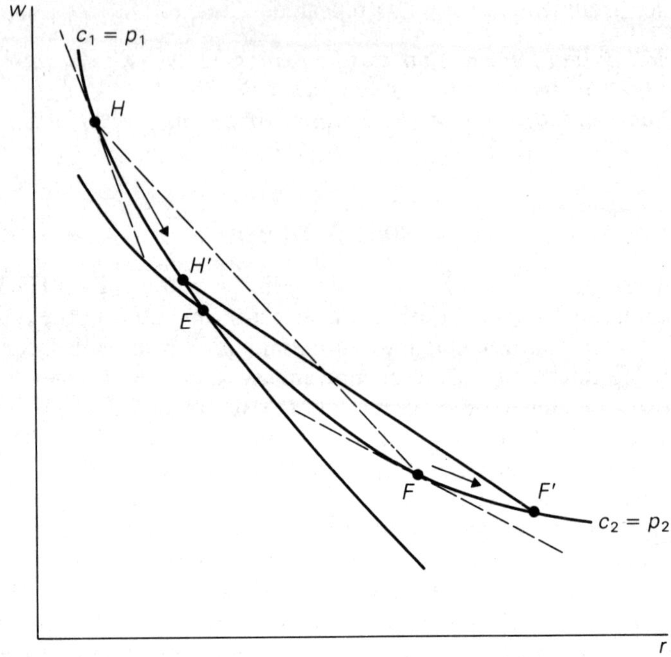

Figure 8.1(a)

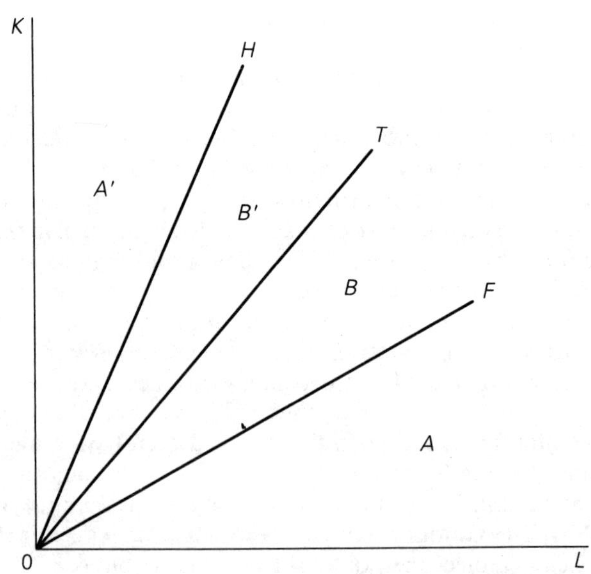

Figure 8.1(b)

Note that H' cannot possibly coincide with F': bundled factor mobility will not lead to factor price equalization in this case. Indeed, the introduction of such mobility might even cause factor prices to move further apart! This is in sharp contrast to the free mobility of either factor (that is, bundling requirements represented by a horizontal or a vertical line), which must produce factor price equalization.

Suppose now that the required bundle is less capital-intensive than the foreign economy. Then the induced factor movement causes the home economy to become less capital-abundant, as before, but the foreign economy now becomes more capital-abundant. Factor prices in the two countries move closer together, and a new international equilibrium cannot be established until factor prices are actually equalized.

The possibilities that bundled mobility allows in the HOS model are summarized in figure 8.1(b). The rays *OH* and *OF* depict initial relative factor abundances at home and abroad. Any bundling requirement can be represented by a ray through the origin. Requirements in zones *A* and *B* induce immigration into the home economy, while requirements in A' and B' induce emigration abroad. Policies in *A* and A' produce factor price equalization, so that bundled mobility is here equivalent to the unfettered mobility of either factor (represented by the two axes, respectively). Policies in *B* and B', on the other hand, cause factor prices in the two countries to move in the same direction and do not permit them to converge. The general principle is as follows:

> *Bundling requirements that are not linear combinations of the initial factor abundances of the two countries will result in factor price equalization, and those requirements that are such linear combinations can not do so.*

5 INTERNATIONAL DIFFERENCES IN TECHNOLOGY

Consider next what can be said once we drop the assumption of internationally identical technologies. Figure 8.2(a) depicts factor price frontiers *P* and P' for the home and foreign economies corresponding to international commodity prices in an equilibrium with no international factor mobility. Continue to assume that international factor movements have no effect on international commodity prices. Then point *E* shows what factor prices would be in the two countries with free international mobility of both factors, provided that the countries' joint endowment ratio lies between the slopes of the two frontiers at *E* (otherwise commodity prices would have to change to maintain equilibrium).

The common tangent to both frontiers is drawn through points *G* and *g*. This is an interesting special case. It shows a possible equilibrium corresponding to a bundling requirement set equal to one country's actual relative factor abundance. The equilibrium contrasts sharply with that given by point *E*; now factor prices remain unequal but instead factor proportions are equalized by migration! The international differences in factor prices in effect neutralized the international differences in technology. Of course, this is a very special case. It can happen only if world endowments are just in the proportion indicated by the common tangent. But it is an interesting boundary case for bundling requirements set equal, in equilibrium, to the relative factor abundance of the host country. Any such requirement more capital-intensive than that of G–g would require factors to move out of the home country (i.e., the country that is relatively capital abundant, in the sense of having a higher w/r ratio, in the G–g equilibrium). This is because a line steeper than that through G and g but still tangent to the home factor price frontier would necessarily fall entirely below the foreign factor price frontier. Similarly, any such requirement more labor-intensive than that of G–g would require factors to move into the home country.

Consider now the effects of a bundling requirement, coinciding wth actual home relative abundance, resulting in immigration of both factors into the home country. Let the initital (before-migration) home equilibrium be given by point H in figure 8.2(a). To result in immigration, the bundling requirement initially imposed must be sufficiently labor-intensive to intersect the foreign factor price frontier, as is in fact the case with the straight line drawn through H in the figure. Thus the home country initially has the higher wage–rental ratio; that is, it is relatively capital-abundant in the price sense. Furthermore, the initial foreign equilibrium must be on the segment F'–F'' of the foreign factor price frontier.

What happens next depends upon exactly where the initial foreign equilibrium is. Point F in the figure is the critical point. If the foreign equilibrium just happens to be there, the foreign capital–labor ratio corresponds to the home one, and therefore to that of the bundling requirement. Both factors emigrate from the foreign country until it ceases to exist; point H becomes the world equilibrium. But this is a knife-edge situation. If the initial foreign equilibrium is between F' and F, the foreign economy initially possesses a higher capital–labor ratio than that of the bundling requirement. Thus the emigration makes the foreign economy more capital-abundant: foreign factor prices move along the factor price frontier towards point F'. Since the home immigration does not alter factor proportions there, home equilibrium remains at H. The new equilibrium is reached when foreign factor prices have adjusted to point F'. Thus in this case bundled factor mobility causes factor prices to move more closely together, but not to coincide. Note that the foreign economy, with the lower wage–rental ratio, also had the higher capital–labor ratio: a factor abundance ranking on a price basis *contradicts* one on a quantity basis.

If the initial foreign equilibrium is instead between F and F'', the foreign economy possesses a lower capital–labor ratio than the home and than the bundling requirement. And a factor abundance ranking on a price basis *coincides* with one on a quantity basis. In this case the factor movement renders the foreign economy more labor-intensive. Foreign factor prices move towards point F'', and the new equilibrium is attained when they arrive there.

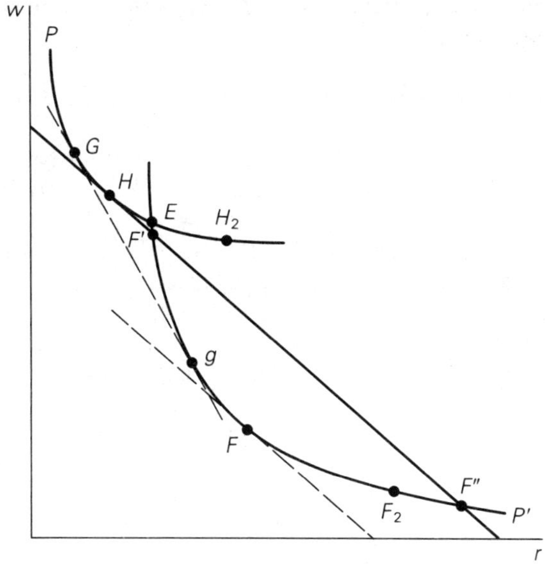

Figure 8.2(a)

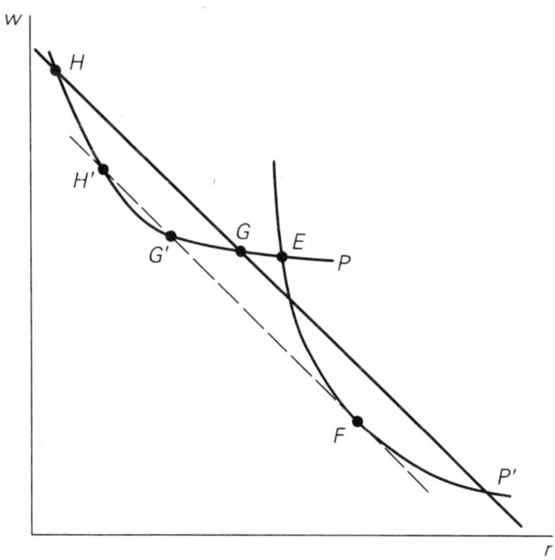

Figure 8.2(b)

Bundled factor mobility has caused factor prices in the two countries to move apart. The general conclusion appears to be as follows:

Bundled factor mobility subject to a requirement reflecting host country factor proportions produces (partial) factor price convergence when the pattern of relative factor abundance on the price basis contradicts that on the quantity basis, and it causes factor prices to move further apart in the opposite case.

(Note that capital–labor ratios in the two countries move further apart in both cases.)

It is of some interest that this conclusion is reversed if the host country sets its building requirement equal to factor proportions in the *foreign* country. This is illustrated in figure 8.2(b), where point F indicates factor prices abroad with no factor mobility. Suppose the home country becomes the host with a bundling requirement as indicated by the slope of the foreign factor price frontier at F. If the initial home equilibrium is at a point such as H in figure 8.2(b), where the home country is relatively capital-abundant in both the price sense and the quantity sense, migration moves home equilibrium to H', so that factor prices (and capital–labor ratios) converge internationally. If, instead, the initial home equilibrium is at a point such as G, where the price and quantity rankings differ, migration will drive factor prices apart (although capital–labor ratios still converge).

This indicates that restricting the bundling requirement to coincide with an initial capital–labor ratio is a substantive limitation. Recall also that, with similar technology, the relation of the bundling requirement to initial capital–labor ratios in the two countries was crucial. So it should now come as no surprise to see that arbitrary bundling requirements can produce quite different results from those seen thus far. For example, if in figure 8.2(a) the initial home and foreign equilibria were at H_2 and F_2 respectively, migration would drive factor prices apart, even though the bundling requirement is not a weighted average of the capital–labor ratios in the two countries.

6 REVERSE BUNDLING

Consider now a reverse bundling requirement, where the two factors must migrate in opposite directions. Such a requirement can be represented by a line of positive slope in the factor–price plane, as is illustrated in figure 8.3. Point H denotes the initial home equilibrium (the term 'host country' clearly becomes ambiguous with reverse bundling). With internationally identical technology, any reverse bundling requirement that induces migration will result in factor price equalization, and so will be equivalent to unrestricted migration of either factor. Suppose as in figure 8.3, that technology differs across countries. If the initial foreign equilibrium is below the bundling line drawn through the initial home equilibrium, as would be the case if the home and foreign equilibria were at H and F respectively, labor would move into the home economy and capital into the foreign. Home factor prices would move down the home factor price frontier, and foreign prices would move up the foreign frontier, until they both were on the same bundling line. Obviously, wages in the two countries must move closer together, but whether

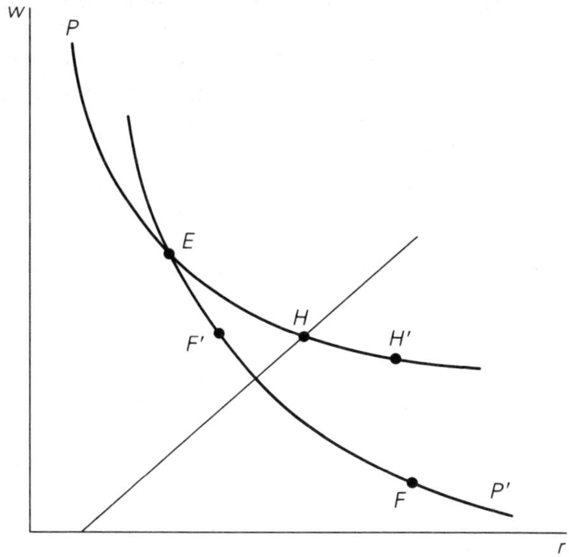

Figure 8.3

rents do so depends upon the exact positions of the initial equilibria and upon the shapes of the frontiers. If instead the initial home equilibrium were at H' and the initial foreign one at F', labor would flow into the foreign economy and capital into the home one, until the two countries were again on a common building line. In this case it is the rents that must move closer together and the relative wage movement that is ambiguous. In each case, one factor price must converge internationally while the other may or may not.

7 WELFARE IMPLICATIONS OF BUNDLING POLICIES

Though detailed normative treatments of policy choices are best left to other occasions, an elementary general principle can be stated easily enough. Let the expenditure function $e(p, u)$ denote the minimum national expenditure necessary at prices p for the home country to attain a specified welfare level u. Then

$$e(p, u) = f(p, v + kb) - wkb \tag{4}$$

if the home country is the host for the bundled factor movement kb. Consider the welfare consequences of a change db in the bundling requirement. From (4),

$$(\partial e/\partial u)du = f_v d(kb) - wd(kb) - (dw)kb = -(dw)kb \tag{5}$$

if international prices p and home factor ownership v do not change, since $w = f_v$.

Now (3) implies that, for each individual bundling requirement b_i, $(dw)b_i + (w - w^*)db_i = 0$, if some of each factor remains in each country after the change, and if foreign factor prices are not affected. Thus $(dw)(kb) + (w - w^*)k(db) = 0$, so that (5) becomes

$$(\partial e/\partial u)du = (w - w^*)k(db).$$

Thus a policy change db will improve the national welfare of a small host country if and only if

$$(w - w^*)k(db) > 0. \tag{6}$$

That is,

> *A change in bundling requirements will benefit the host country if the change, on average, increases mostly the immigration of those factors paid a relatively high reward in the home country.*

The condition is perhaps counterintuitive, and holds because in equilibrium domestic factor rewards must be such as to pay a migrating bundle of factors the same that it could earn abroad.

8 CONCLUDING REMARKS

This paper has investigated, in a very preliminary way, the pervasive practice of bundled international factor mobility, that is, factor movements that must coincide with some other international transaction. The analysis focused on two questions: When will bundled mobility tend to equalize factor prices across countries, and What are the welfare consequences of a change in bundling requirements? I think that these are clearly the appropriate places to start: the factor price equalization issue basically asks when bundling matters and when it does not, and welfare analysis must be central to any discussion of economic policy. The general nature of the results allows them to apply directly to composite bundling, which I have not explicitly considered. Further possible extensions should be obvious enough. Nevertheless, I suspect that bundled factor mobility is one of those topics, like trade under uncertainty, that soon demand a focus on particular applications rather than on general properties.

REFERENCES

Corden, W. Max (1967). Protection and foreign investment. *Economic Record*, 43, 209–32.

Corden, W. Max (1974). *Trade Policy and Economic Welfare*. Oxford: Oxford University Press.

Ethier, Wilfred (1986). International trade theory and international migration. In Ismail Sirageldin and Oded Stark (eds), *Migration Theory, Human Capital and Development*. Greenwich, Conn.: JAI Press.

Helpman, Elhanen and Krugman, Paul (1985). *Market Structure and Foreign Trade*. Cambridge, Mass.: MIT Press.

Herander, Mark G. and Thomas, Christopher R. (1985). Export Performance and Export–Import Linkage Requirements. Unpublished paper.

Rodrik, Dani (1986). The economics of export-performance requirements. Unpublished paper.

9

Tariffs and Subsidies under Oligopoly: The Case of the US Automobile Industry

Avinash Dixit

1 INTRODUCTION

The theory of trade and tax policies with regard to imperfectly competitive industries has made great advances in recent years. Some new reasons for policy intervention, and variants of old ones, have been identified. The clearest statement of the market failures and the appropriate policies can be found in Eaton and Grossman (1986). They offer a threefold classification. (1) When prices of home goods remain above marginal cost in the home market, there is social gain to narrowing this gap by increasing sales. This can be done by means of antitrust policies or subsidies. (2) When home firms fail to collude among themselves in their export activities, our country stands to gain by restricting exports to achieve such collusion, and can do so by means of an export tax. This is a variant of the standard optimum tariff argument. (3) When foreign firms earn pure profits, our country can gain at their expense if we can capture some of this profit. The proper instrument for this purpose depends on the nature of the oligopolistic conduct. Where the firms are competing in our own market, a tariff can serve this profit-shifting aim.

As is often the case in economic research, empirical work has lagged far behind these theoretical advances. Much of the blame can be placed on the paucity and the unreliability of data. However, a good case can be made

My greatest debt is to Robert Feenstra, who pointed out some major flaws in the first draft of this paper and led me to better data sources. I am also grateful to Charles Berry, James Brander, Gene Grossman, Carl Shapiro and Robert Willig for useful discussions and comments, and to the National Science Foundation for research support under grant SES-8308536. The views expressed are my own, as is the responsibility for any remaining errors.

for using such data as we have, and obtaining a rough idea of the size of the problem and of the policy intervention that is called for. Proponents of protection and export promotion are already invoking the theory as a basis for their favored policies. It is important to know whether such arguments hold water.

In this paper I shall carry out an exploratory exercise of this kind. The US passenger automobile market is an obvious candidate for it. The number of firms selling in the market is small enough to raise suspicion of oligopoly. The firms are from many countries, and the rivalry between US and Japanese firms is particularly important. The industry has seen a major episode of protection, the so-called Voluntary Export Restraints (VERs). Most previous empirical work (e.g. Tarr and Morkre, 1984; Feenstra, 1984) assumed the industry to be perfectly competitive, and found sizable economic costs to the United States arising from this protection. Gomez-Ibanez et al. (1983) assume a particular and rather *ad hoc* model of imperfect competition to study the effects of VERs. It is of some interest to let the data tell us how close the market conduct is to being competitive, and what the policy implications of any departures from perfect competition are. In particular, it is of interest to know if policies can be designed that will bring economic gain, rather than cost, to the United States.

I shall focus on the most interesting aspect of this market from the trade policy standpoint, namely, the rivalry between US and Japanese firms. To conform with the available information about market demand, I shall assume that US and Japanese cars are imperfect substitutes for each other, but perfect substitutes within each nationality. For computational simplicity, I shall take the demand system to be linear, and the marginal costs to be constants. I shall model oligopolistic behavior as a Nash equilibrium with conjectural variations. The coefficients representing these conjectures are treated as parameters which measure the degree of competitiveness or implicit collusion in market conduct. Their values are determined from the data.

This model has some serious shortcomings (see Friedman, 1983, for a discussion). Of course, one does not have to believe that firms actually entertain such conjectures; the theory might serve as an adequate 'as if' representation of reality. However, since the model is used for policy analysis, the spectre of the Lucas critique arises. If the conjectures are not true behavioral parameters, their values can change as the policy is altered. In the case of quotas or VERs, Krishna (1984) shows that such is in fact the case even in a static context. The problem also arises with tariffs if the true model is a repeated oligopoly (see Davidson, 1984).

Unfortunately, there is no available alternative to the conjectural variations model that is at the same time logically more satisfactory and empirically as manageable. Therefore I shall use it, but will avoid the special problem of quantitative restrictions by choosing the years 1979 and 1980 for the study.

The years offer quite a contrast. In 1979 the market as a whole was buoyant, and the demand for large cars was particularly strong. In 1980 the market weakened, and there was a sharp shift of demand towards small cars.

The performance of US firms deteriorated, and Japanese import penetration grew. It would be interesting to see how this translates into differences in market conduct, and in the scope of trade policies.

For each year, the model is calibrated to reproduce the initial equilibrium where only the most favored nation (MFN) tariff applied to Japanese imports. The effects of alternative policies are then examined. Because the data on demand elasticities and marginal costs are poor and subject to error, sensitivity analysis over quite a wide range of parameters is also carried out.

One must be very cautious in drawing conclusions from such a crude and preliminary analysis. With this warning, the broad findings of the paper are as follows. The market was much more competitive in 1980 than in 1979. The case for strategic trade and antitrust policies was therefore weaker in 1980. For the central cases of parameter values, the optimal tariffs are moderate (5–8 per cent) in 1980, and larger (12–17 per cent) in 1979. For lower ends of the range of marginal costs, corresponding to a greater degree of implicit collusion in the market, even higher tariff rates can be justified. But the aggregate economic gains to the United States are quite small even when the tariff rates are large. In no case could tariffs add more than $225 million to US real income. It should also be stressed that I am neglecting the possibility of retaliation; therefore the figures for the gains from tariffs are overestimates, possibly grossly so.

The role of domestic antitrust policies is more significant than that of tariffs; they can contribute over $700 million dollars to US real income in some cases.

The plan of the paper is as follows. Section 2 describes the model. Section 3 discusses the data, and the nature of the initial equilibrium. Section 4 examines the implied optimal policies. Section 5 offers some concluding remarks, and suggestions for future work.

2 THE MODEL

Let the subscripts 1 and 2 denote US and Japanese cars, respectively. Other imports, mostly from Europe, are less important in comparison and are ignored. Writing p_1 and p_2 for the prices and Q_1 and Q_2 for the aggregate quantities, the demand functions are assumed to be

$$Q_1 = A_1 - B_1 p_1 + K p_1 \tag{1}$$
$$Q_2 = A_2 + K p_1 - B_2 p_2. \tag{2}$$

All the parameters are positive, and $B_1 B_2 - K^2 > 0$. The corresponding inverse demand functions are

$$p_1 = a_1 - b_1 Q_1 - k Q_2 \tag{3}$$
$$p_2 = a_2 - k Q_1 - b_2 Q_2. \tag{4}$$

Again, all the parameters are positive, as is $(b_1 b_2 - k^2)$. This demand system can be derived from an aggregate sectoral utility function

$$U(Q_1, Q_2) = a_1 Q_1 + a_2 Q_2 - \tfrac{1}{2}(b_1 Q_1^2 + b_2 Q_2^2 + 2kQ_1 Q_2). \qquad (5)$$

Then the consumer surplus C is given by

$$C = U(Q_1, Q_2) - p_1 Q_1 - p_2 Q_2. \qquad (6)$$

The marginal costs are assumed to be constants. The US unit production cost is denoted by c_1, and the Japanese unit cost of production and transport to the US market by c_2.

Only the United States is assumed to be active in policy. It has two instruments, an import tariff t in \$ per Japanese car, and a home production subsidy of s in \$ per US car. The effect of the latter is to reduce the private cost to US firms, and thereby bring the market price of US cars closer to the true social marginal cost. This lowers the domestic distortion. However, we do not normally think of solving the problem of monopoly by subsidizing the monopolist. There may be adverse distributional effects. If the government does not have independent and accurate information about the firms' costs, there will be important incentive effects as the firms overstate their costs, or add managerial slack with impunity. If the government cannot police price-fixing conspiracies well, then firms in an industry will have additional gains from cartelization, namely, the larger subsidies that the government then offers to achieve a lower price. For all these reasons, a subsidy as such may be poor policy. In our model it should be interpreted as an imperfect proxy for antitrust policy in its effect of price reduction.

If there were sizable exports of US cars, we would have to distinguish between a subsidy for home sales and a production subsidy. Fortunately for the analysis, this is not a significant issue.[1]

Now consider a typical US firm. Denoting its sales by q_1, its profit[2] is $(p_1 - c_1 + s)q_1$. When q_1 is chosen to maximize this, we have the first-order condition

$$p_1 - c_1 + s + q_1 dp_1/dq_1 = 0 \qquad (7)$$

where the derivative represents the firm's belief about the effect on its price if it sells another unit, taking into account its conjectures about the output responses of other firms. One can split this conjecture into components corresponding to the separate responses of home and foreign firms, but that is not necessary for my purpose. If each firm assumes that the others hold their outputs constant – that is, if the oligopoly is conducted along Cournot lines – then $dp_1/dq_1 = -b_1$. If conduct is more competitive – that is, if each firm believes its price is more nearly constant with respect to its output variations – then dp_1/dq_1 is negative but numerically smaller. In the limiting case of perfect competition, each firm assumes $dp_1/dq_1 = 0$.

Suppose there are n_1 US firms. Aggregating the first-order conditions over them, we have

$$p_1 - c_1 + s - Q_1 V_1 = 0 \tag{8}$$

where V_1 is the aggregate version of the conjectural variation parameter. It equals b_1/n_1 in the case of Cournot conduct. It is numerically smaller if the oligopoly is more competitive than that, and zero in the case of perfect competition.

The effects of the US firms' conduct on the market outcome are thus channeled through the single parameter V_1. However, intuition about the conduct is better served by looking at the matter from a different angle. The same market equilibrium would arise if there were $n_1^* = b_1/V_1$ US firms (allowed to be a non-integer for this purpose) behaving in a Cournot manner. Call n_1^* the Cournot-equivalent number of US firms, and compare this with the actual number. If $n_1 < n_1^*$ the actual conduct must be more competitive than Cournot; otherwise, less. An equivalent procedure is to find the equilibrium prices that would arise if the n_1 actual firms behaved in a Cournot fashion: if these prices exceed the observed prices the actual conduct must be more competitive than Cournot; otherwise, less. I shall carry out these tests for each of the years to be considered in the next section.

Similarly, for the Japanese firms, we have

$$p_2 - c_2 - t - Q_2 V_2 = 0. \tag{9}$$

The parameter V_2 can be interpreted in the same way.

The conditions (8) and (9) can be solved together with the demand equations (3) and (4) to obtain the equilibrium prices and quantities for any given policy configuration of s and t. Then we can calculate the consumer surplus as indicated above in (6). Total US welfare W is obtained by adding the profits of the US firms and the revenues of the US government, so

$$W = C + (p_1 - c_1 + s)\,Q_1 + (tQ_2 - sQ_1). \tag{10}$$

Distributional considerations can be captured by giving the components different weights; I will not consider this complication here.

This completes the specification of the model, and allows us to proceed to an examination of the optimal policies. Explicit expressions can be found, but they are not very informative in this context. Therefore I shall omit them, and consider only the numerical values for the particular cases at hand. Interested readers will find the algebraic details in a related theoretical paper (Dixit, 1986).

There are four policy configurations that are of particular interest. The first is the status quo, with the MFN tariff of 2.9 per cent applied to Japanese imports, and no significant antitrust measures (or proxy production subsidies) applied to US producers. Call the resulting welfare W_0. Next, suppose the

Table 9.1 Data and parameters

	1979	1980
Quantities (millions)		
Q_1	8.341	6.581
Q_2	1.546	1.819
Prices ($'000)		
P_1	5,951	6,407
P_2	4,000	4,130
Range of US costs c_1 ($'000)		
Low	5,000	5,700
Central	5,400	6,100
High	5,600	6,300
Range of Japanese costs c_2 ($'000)		
Low	3,000	3,400
Central	3,400	3,800
High	3,600	4,000
Range of total market elasticity		
Low	0.75	0.75
Central	1.00	1.00
High	1.50	1.50
Range of elasticity of substitution		
Low	1.50	1.50
Central	2.00	2.00
High	3.00	3.00

(Sources and calculations are explained in the text.)

subsidy is kept at zero but the tariff is chosen optimally, and write the welfare level as W_t. Third, suppose trade is free but the domestic antitrust policy, here represented by s, is chosen optimally. Suppose this yields W_s. Finally, let both s and t be at their jointly optimal levels; let the resulting welfare level be W_{ts}.

Once we obtain these figures, we can answer some questions of interest about trade policy. The first is the simplest: Are the tariffs that emerge from such economic optimization large in relation to the policies that are now in effect? The second is, How large are the economic welfare gains that are available from the pursuit of optimal policies? Here we must consider two cases separately, one where a domestic production subsidy or antitrust policy is not available, and the other where it is. In the first case, the gain from using an optimal tariff over the status quo is $(W_t - W_0)$. In the second case, the contribution of the optimal tariff over and above what is possible with the subsidy is given by $(W_{ts} - W_s)$.

In section 4 I shall carry out this program for each of the years 1979 and 1980, for ranges of cost and demand parameters suggested by the data. The next section sets the stage by examining the data sources and determining such ranges.

3 THE DATA

Table 9.1 summarizes the information on prices, quantities, costs and demand elasticities for each of the two years, obtained from statistical sources and the research literature. Here I shall explain the sources and the procedures in some detail.

The quantities are retail sales from a trade publication, *World Motor Vehicles Data*, and I have used the 1982 issue. The prices are unit values, the US ones being at the manufacturing level and the Japanese ones at the CIF import level. They are obtained from the *Summary of Trade and Tariff Information* (US ITC Publication 841, 1.11:6-6-49), dated June 1984.

Costs raise very difficult issues of measurement as well as interpretation. The main question of interpretation is the contribution of capital costs to marginal costs. A satisfactory treatment would require an intertemporal optimization problem. In years where the capacity constraint is binding, its shadow price will appear as a component of the marginal cost. This is quite difficult to do properly. It negates my year-by-year approach. Inflation, and the complexities of the corporate income tax, have to be handled. Finally, the data on capital and investment are hard to find and use at the required level of disaggregation. For all these reasons, I have chosen to neglect capital costs altogether. The cost figures used (comprising labor and material costs) should then be thought of as lower bounds for the actual costs. The implied mark-ups of the observed prices over these cost figures, and therefore the implied degree of monopoly in the market, should be thought of as upper bounds for the corresponding realities. The resulting role of trade policy is likewise an exaggeration. The extent of the bias will vary from one year to another; one would suspect capacity constraints to be more important, and therefore the bias to be greater, in 1979 than in 1980. All this should be kept in mind when interpreting the results in section 4.

Even labor and material costs are hard to measure and allocate accurately, and different sources give very different answers. I have used findings from alternative approaches to establish the range for sensitivity analysis.

Three approaches were available for US production costs. The first is based on the Census of Manufactures. The Industry Series publication MC82-I-37A gives annual ratios of payroll and material costs to the value of shipments for SIC category 3711 (Motor Vehicles and Car Bodies). One would ideally like to have the corresponding figures for category 37111 (Passenger Cars). However, nearly 70 per cent of the value of shipments of the former comes from the latter, so the error should be tolerable. The ratios are as follows:

1979: 85% 1980: 89%.

Using the earlier figures for unit values, we get unit costs:

1979: \$5058 1980: \$5702.

The second approach follows Abernathy et al. (1981). They estimate the total costs of production of a subcompact car in the United States in 1979 at $4875, of which $1485 comes from payroll costs and $2584 from component and material costs. (The two add to $4069, which is 85 per cent of the total, in conformity with the Census of Manufactures figure.) They state that the average Ford car is the equivalent in cost of 1.38 subcompacts. Assuming the same for the US industry as a whole, the cost figure for 1979 becomes $5615.

To get the figure for 1980 by this method, I applied the manufacturing wage index (100/92.2) to the payroll costs, and the wholesale price index (100/87.7) to the component and material costs. The indexes came from the 1983 issues of IMF's *International Financial Statistics*. The resulting cost figure for 1980 was $6289.

The third approach used profit figures from US company reports, aggregated in the US Department of Commerce publication, *The US Automobile Industry 1982*. The totals from operations (not subtracting depreciation and amortization, in conformity with our neglect of capital costs) were as follows:

1979: $8.3 billion 1980: $2.5 billion.

If all of this is attributed to passenger cars, we can use the quantity figures from USITC to get the operating profits per car:

1979: $980 1980: $380.

Subtracting these from the unit values, we have unit costs:

1979: $4971 1980: $6027.

These profits are overestimates, because in reality some of the profit is attributable to other operations of the same companies. Therefore the cost figures are underestimates. This reinforces the bias already built in by our omission of capital costs.

The ranges in table 9.1, for example $5000–5600 for 1979, were chosen to span the three approaches. The central cases, for example $5400 in 1979, were chosen slightly above the mean of the range, to make partial allowance for the downward biases discussed above. Even then, I suspect that the figures at the upper ends of the ranges are the more likely ones.

A similar variety of methods was used to estimate the delivered unit costs of Japanese cars to the US market. Abernathy et al. (1981) estimate the production cost advantage of a Japanese subcompact to be $1670 in 1979. This stems entirely from a labor cost advantage, part of which is embodied in the cost of purchased components. Katz (1980) estimates a smaller figure of approximately $1000, but Abernathy et al. claim that this neglects the contribution of purchased components. Toder (1978, p. 151) estimates the

Japanese cost advantage to be 16.8 per cent, which in 1979 translates into the still smaller figure of \$819 for a subcompact.

We have two estimates of freight costs, Katz's (1980) \$400 for 1979, and Toder's (1978, p. 153) \$650 for 1975. Toder's appears to have a firmer base in the schedules supplied by the Massport Authority, but freight to Boston from Japan probably greatly overestates the cost to the average US market point. If we take \$500 as a reasonable figure for 1979, the range of net delivered cost advantage for a Japanese subcompact goes from \$319 (Toder) to \$1170 (Abernathy et al.).

The subcompact-equivalent of our 1979 range of US unit costs is \$3600–4060. Combining with the range of the Japanese advantage, we have a minimum minimorum of \$2430 and a maximum maximorum of \$3741. I have taken a narrower range of 20 per cent (\$3000–3600), and the central case to be \$3400. The workings for 1980 are similar.

Turning to demand, Toder (1978) estimates a total market demand elasticity of about 1 and an elasticity of substitution between US and Japanese cars of about 2. These seem to be the most cited figures in the literature, and are used by others, for example Tarr and Morkre (1984). I shall take them to be central values, and use the ranges shown in table 9.1.

The parameters of the system (1)–(4) can be calculated using the actual prices and quantities and the assumed elasticities. This is the process of calibration. Consider the direct demand functions (1)–(2). There are five parameters to be determined. In any one year, substitution of the actual prices and quantities give us two relations among them. Further work is based on the elasticity information.

Since US and Japanese cars are being treated as imperfect substitutes, I shall interpret the total market elasticity as the effect of an equiproportionate rise in the price of the two on the corresponding (dual) quantity aggregate. Thus let

$$p_1 = P_{10} P, \quad p_2 = P_{20} P$$

where P_{10}, P_{20} are the initial prices, and P the proportional change factor. The dual quantity index is

$$\begin{aligned} Q &= P_{10} Q_1 + P_{20} Q_2 \\ &= (P_{10} A_1 + P_{20} A_2) - (B_1 P_{10}^2 + B_2 P_{20}^2 - 2KP_{10} P_{20}) P. \end{aligned}$$

The total market elasticity is then the elasticity of Q with respect to P, evaluated at the initial point $P = 1$. This given us the third relation among the parameters.

The elasticity of substitution is defined as

$$-d \log (Q_1/Q_2)/d \log (p_1/p_2).$$

Setting this equal to the assumed value gives us a fourth relation. However,

Table 9.2 Demand parameters in the central case

	1979	1980
Direct demand function		
A_1 (million)	16.682	13.162
A_2 (million)	3.092	3.638
B_1	1,557	1,182
B_2	730	814
K	231	241
Inverse demand function		
a_1 (thousand)	11,902	12,814
a_2 (thousand)	8,000	8,260
b_1 (10^{-4})	6.739	8.999
b_2 (10^{-4})	14.370	13.069
k (10^{-4})	2.132	2.663

(Notation and calculations are explained in the text.)

in general (1) and (2) define Q_1/Q_2 as a function of the vector (p_1, p_2), and not of the single ratio p_1/p_2. To have it so, at least locally at the initial point, the parameters must satisfy an additional condition, which turns out to be

$$P_{10}(A_1K + A_2B_1) = P_{20}(A_2K + A_1B_2).$$

This is the fifth relation, which completes the required set.

The values of the demand parameters are not directly very informative, but for completeness I have shown in table 9.2 the sets for the central cases of elasticities and for each of the years 1979 and 1980.

Economically more interesting information is to be had by computing the implied conduct. As explained in section 2, this can be done by comparing the actual prices with those that would prevail if the actual firms behaved in a Cournot manner, or by comparing the Cournot-equivalent number of firms corresponding to the actual conduct with the actual numbers. Since actual US firms are not identical, we need the right proxy for their number. This is as usual the numbers equivalent of the US firms' Herfindahl index of concentration, but its value changes a great deal according to whether we take each US company or each division to be the appropriate non-cooperative profit-maximizing unit. In the absence of any clear reason to select one, I have shown the calculations on both bases.

The results for the central cases of costs and elasticities are in table 9.3. We see that the conduct in 1980 was a lot more competitive than Cournot whether we use the company basis or the division basis for the United States. Using the latter, the actual prices fall halfway between those that would arise under Cournot and Bertrand behavior. The outcome is a lot less competitive

Table 9.3 Market conduct in the central case

	1979	1980
Numbers equivalents of Herfindahl indices		
US (company basis)	2.250	2.077
US (division basis)	6.931	6.679
Japan	4.040	4.034
Cournot-equivalent firm numbers corresponding to actual prices		
US	10.201	19.291
Japan	4.443	10.336
US car prices ($'000)		
If actual firms behave Cournot		
US company basis	7,285	8,116
US division basis	6,178	6,974
Actual conduct	5,951	6,407
Bertrand conduct	5,400	6,100
Japanese car prices ($'000)		
If actual firms behave Cournot		
US company basis	4,127	4,520
US division basis	4,054	4,392
Actual conduct	4,000	4,130
Bertrand conduct	3,400	3,800

in 1979; if we use the division basis for the United States, then the Japanese firms are quite close to playing Cournot, and the US divisions are closer to Cournot than to Bertrand. On the whole, this confirms the impression that there was a greater degree of monopoly in the market, and therefore a greater role for strategic trade policy, in 1979 than in 1980.

4 THE RESULTS

Now we can carry out the various policy comparisons discussed at the end of section 2. This is done for the central cases of costs and elasticities, and the results are displayed in tables 9.4 and 9.5 for 1980 and 1979 respectively.

Let us begin with table 9.4. The last column shows the full optimum, where both a tariff and a subsidy are used optimally. The latter solves the domestic monopoly problem, and makes the US price equal to cost. Once this is done, the tariff has a relatively small role of profit-shifting. The optimal tariff of $211 per Japanese car means an ad valorem rate of 5.5 per cent. This is nearly twice as large as the MFN tariff, but still quite moderate when contrasted with historic rates or the ones often talked about in recent policy debates in the United States.

Table 9.4 Policy calculations for the central case, 1980

Variable	Unit	MFN tariff	Optimum tariff	Optimum subsidy	Optimum tariff & subsidy
t	\$/car	100	298	0	211
s	\$/car	0	0	368	325
p_1	\$	6,407	6,409	6,057	6,100
p_2	\$	4,130	4,309	4,030	4,222
Q_1	million	6.581	6.622	6.971	6.967
Q_2	million	1.819	1.673	1.817	1.670
Japan profit	\$b	0.600	0.353	0.418	0.352
US profit	\$b	2.021	2.045	2.267	2.264
US consumer surplus	\$b	24.840	24.512	27.392	26.758
Tariff revenue	\$b	0.182	0.499	0	0.353
Subsidy cost	\$b	0	0	2.564	2.264
Total US welfare	\$b	27.042	27.058	27.094	27.111
Gain over MFN	\$m	0	16	52	69

When a subsidy is not available, the tariff indirectly serves the function of reducing the domestic distortion: a higher tariff means greater sales of US cars, which is a welfare gain since the price exceeds the marginal cost. At the same time, however, the analogous trade distortion is worsened. For a linear demand, the former effect is the more important; Eaton and Grossman (1986) examine the general case. Of course, the primary role of the tariff in this context is to shift the profits away from the Japanese firms. Now the optimum tariff rate is 7.8 per cent, which is quite sizable. The decline in the volume of Japanese imports from 1.82 to 1.67 million is impressive, and in these terms the tariff is more restrictive than the VERs were.

More important than tariff rates or import volumes are the dollar values of the economic gains to the United States. Table 9.4 shows these to be quite small. When a subsidy is not available, for example, the optimal tariff confers an aggregate gain of only \$16 million over the MFN tariff. As usual, there are much larger redistributions concealed behind the small aggregate. US firms' profits go up by \$24 million, and US government revenue by \$317 million, while US consumer surplus goes down by \$328 million. Japanese firms' profits decline by \$247 million. Similarly, when a subsidy is available, using the tariff yields an additional aggregate welfare gain of only \$17 million, but there is a net swing in government revenue of over \$650 million.

When a subsidy to domestic production is the only available instrument, it has the direct role of reducing the domestic distortion as well as the indirect role of capturing foreign profits by squeezing their demand. We see that the two functions combine to yield an optimum subsidy that takes the domestic price a little below the marginal cost. The reason is a familiar one: for the first bit of subsidy beyond this point, the domestic deadweight burden from

Table 9.5 Policy calculations for the central case, 1979

Variable	Unit	MFN tariff	Optimum tariff	Optimum subsidy	Optimum tariff & subsidy
t	\$/car	100	570	0	408
s	\$/car	0	0	670	611
p_1	\$	5,951	5,956	5,341	5,400
p_2	\$	4,000	4,381	3,882	4,216
Q_1	million	8.341	8.421	9.263	9.249
Q_2	million	1.546	1.269	1.491	1.261
Japan profit	\$b	0.928	0.522	0.574	0.514
US profit	\$b	4.596	4.685	5.668	5.651
US consumer surplus	\$b	27.912	27.332	33.456	32.456
Tariff revenue	\$b	0.155	0.724	0	0.514
Subsidy cost	\$b	0	0	6.209	5.651
Total US welfare	\$b	32.663	32.741	32.914	32.970
Gain over MFN	\$m	0	78	251	307

driving price below marginal cost is of the second order, while the gain from profit capture is of the first order. The use of a subsidy alone produces an aggregate welfare gain over MFN trade of $52 million. This is not very much either, but is quite a lot more than the contributions of the tariff. In this sense, and recalling that the subsidy was intended as a modeling proxy for antitrust policy, it appears that, for the US auto industry in 1980, trade policy was less important than antitrust policy, and the absolute importance of either was not large.

In 1979 the market outcome was more monopolistic (see table 9.5). This shows up in the policy results. The optimum tariff is 16.8 per cent when a subsidy is not available, and 12 per cent when used in conjunction with an optimal subsidy. The import quantity reductions are large enough to make the US industry's and labor unions' mouths water. However, the aggregate welfare gains are still quite small. When no subsidy is used, an optimal tariff yields $78 million more than the MFN tariff. When an optimal subsidy is available, the further contribution of the tariff is only $56 million. Once again, domestic antitrust policy on its own is considerably more important: the optimum subsidy on its own yields a welfare gain of $251 over MFN trade. However, even this figure is not impressive enough to make it a major policy issue. After all, it is only a little over a dollar per capita.

I said before, and would like to emphasize again, that all these conclusions are very preliminary and tentative. It would take a much more ambitious research project, with much better theory and data, before we could have reliable results. The best I can do at this point is to perform sensitivity analyses with the material available. I have done so for both years, and over the ranges of costs and elasticities shown in table 9.1. To save space, I shall

Table 9.6 Sensitivity analysis for costs, 1979

c_1	c_2: 3000	3400	3600
5000	918 647	655 388	509 245
5400	841 676	570 408	420 259
5600	798 691	525 418	372 266

US welfare comparisons:

(i) $c_1 = \$5000$ and $c_2 = \$3000$:

Gain from optimum tariff over MFN tariff: $221 million

Gain from optimum tariff and subsidy over optimum subsidy alone: $133 million

(ii) $c_1 = \$5600$ and $c_2 = \$3600$:

Gain from optimum tariff over MFN tariff: $26 million

Gain from optimum tariff and subsidy over optimum subsidy alone: $24 million

show the results for only one such exercise, and mention the others briefly.

Table 9.6 shows the effects of changing costs on the optimal tariffs in 1979 per Japanese car. Each box corresponds to the indicated combination of US and Japanese costs. Of the two numbers in each box, the upper left-hand number shows the optimal tariff when no subsidy is available, and the lower right-hand number is the optimal tariff when an optimal subsidy is also used. For a given US cost figure, the higher the Japanese cost, the lower are the tariffs. For a given Japanese cost, higher US costs correspond to lower tariffs when a subsidy is not used, but to higher ones when it is. In theory, the formulas for the optimal tariffs involve the cost parameters c_i as well as the conjectures V_i. In the exercise conducted here, a change in costs entails a recalibration of the model and therefore a change in the conjectures. The net result is not easily predictable by intuition. But on the whole, higher costs are associated with more competitive conduct and thus with lower tariffs, as we see by scanning the table from north-west to south-east.

The clearest conclusion from table 9.6 is that tariff rates are highly sensitive to costs. Therefore the design of good policies makes it essential to have accurate cost information. This is an important point to remember when we think about future research. Next, for the low end of the cost range, and therefore at the high end of the range of implied degree of monopoly in the market, the tariff rates are really large, sometimes over 30 per cent. However, even in the most extreme case the aggregate US welfare gains from the use of tariffs are not large. In the case of the top left-hand corner in table 9.6, the gain from an optimum tariff over the MFN tariff is $221 million, and the contribution of the tariff when the subsidy is also available is only $133 million. It should also be borne in mind that the cost figures I used are biased downward, and the lower ends of the ranges are not very likely to be relevant.

The sensitivity of tariff rates to costs in 1980 is similar. The rates are much less sensitive to variations in demand elasticities in either year. Two offsetting influences are at work. Inelastic demand on its own is conducive to greater market power. But, to be consistent with the observed prices and costs, an inelastic demand entails more competitive conduct. It is fortunate that the net effect is small, because the estimates of these elasticities are even less reliable than those of costs.

5 CONCLUDING COMMENTS

I am painfully aware of the many shortcomings of this work. Probably the most serious is the degree of aggregation. It is important to distinguish large and small US cars. Second, it would be a great improvement to have the demand parameters estimated by systematic econometrics, instead of calibrating them using each year's prices and quantities and outside estimates of elasticities. Third, capital costs need to be better handled both in the theory and the empirical work. Fourth, the labor costs are assumed to be true resource costs, while in the United States a portion should be attributed to monopoly rents. Doing so would alter the social benefit calculation. Fifth, conjectural variations are not a very good basis for the theory of oligopoly, and a better and workable alternative should be sought. Finally, the functional forms (linear demand and constant marginal cost) should be improved upon. As I have said repeatedly, this exercise is intended as no more than a tentative exploration into the empirics of trade policy under oligopoly. I am working on some of the extensions mentioned above, and hope others will be stimulated to do better.

Let me conclude on a personal note. Like most theorists, or more so, I am usually motivated by logical or technical puzzles. Max Corden has often given me salutary reminders that I should pay at least as much attention to the practical or policy significance of the issues. He has done so in conversations and, even more importantly, by the example of his own work. I am delighted to express my gratitute by dedicating to him this quasi-empirical contribution. I hope he won't think that I have gone too far in following his advice!

NOTES

1 In 1981 the United States exported about 469,000 cars to Canada and imported about 564,000 from there. This is best seen as a production rationalization

arrangement. All other US exports of complete cars amounted to only 66,000 units, most of them large luxury cars sold to oil-producing countries. US exports of chassis and components are similarly concentrated in its trade with Canada (sources: World Motor Vehicles Data and USITC).

2 This omits costs that are fixed for the purpose of the production decision being considered here. However, the question of how to apply this criterion in practice is a difficult one. More on this point later.

REFERENCES

Abernathy, William J., Clark Kim B. and Kantrow, Alan M. (1981). 'The new industrial competition.' *Harvard Business Review*, 59, 68–82.

Davidson, Carl (1984). 'Cartel stability and tariff policy.' *Journal of International Economics*, 17, 219–37.

Dixit, Avinash (1986). 'Anti-dumping and countervailing duties under oligopoly. Princeton University, working paper, August 1986.

Eaton, Jonathan and Grossman, Gene M. (1986). 'Optimal trade and industrial policy under oligopoly.' *Quarterly Journal of Economics*, 101, 383–406.

Feenstra, Robert C. (1984). 'Voluntary export restraints in US autos, 1980–81: quality, employment and welfare effects.' In Robert Baldwin and Anne Krueger (eds), *The Structure and Evolution of Recent US Trade Policy*. Chicago: University of Chicago Press.

Friedman, James W. (1983). *Oligopoly Theory*. Cambridge: Cambridge University Press.

Gomez-Ibanez, Jose A., Leone, Robert A. and O'Connell, Stephen A. (1983). 'Restraining auto imports: does anyone win?' *Journal of Policy Analysis and Management*, 2, 196–219.

Katz, Abraham (1980). Statement of the Assistant Secretary of Commerce for Economic Policy before Hearings of the Subcommittee on Trade of the House Ways and Means Committee. In *World Auto Trade: Current Trends and Structural Problems*, Serial 96–78. Washington, DC: US Government Printing Office.

Krishna, Kala (1984). 'Trade restrictions as facilitating practice.' Harvard Institute of Economic Research, Discussion Paper no. 1119.

Tarr, David G. and Morkre, Morris E. (1984). *Aggregate Costs to the United States of Tariffs and Quotas on Imports*. (Bureau of Economics Staff Report.) Washington, DC: Federal Trade Commission.

Toder, Eric J. (1978). *Trade Policy and the US Automobile Industry*. New York: Praeger.

10

Market Access and Competition in High Technology Industries: A Simulation Exercise

Paul Krugman

This paper reports on the results of a simulation of the effects of protectionism in a numerical model of international competition. The industry modeled has some of the features of 'high technology' sectors such as semiconductors or computers. Although the parameters are intended to be plausible, the model is not based on empirical data. Thus the analysis is intended as a suggestive dry run of a technique which may in future be used to estimate the impact of trade policy in actual industries, based on real data. The results for the example studied here are sufficiently striking to suggest that such empirical application is a high priority.

Concern over US competitiveness in high technology industries has been growing in recent years. The source of the public concern lies in the widespread belief that such industries are of special strategic importance to the economy as a whole, an issue which will not be addressed here. Within this larger issue, however, there has been considerable dispute over the sources of changing competitive advantage in these industries. US firms have repeatedly charged that closed access to foreign markets, especially Japan, puts them at a disadvantage not only in the Japanese market but in the United States and third markets as well. Such a claim makes no sense in the context of conventional trade theory, but high technology industries clearly do not fit the assumptions of conventional theory at all well.

Recent advances in the theory of international trade have shown that, when the assumptions of traditional models of trade are lifted, some of the traditional policy conclusions can be substantially altered. In imperfectly competitive markets, export subsidies can raise profits by more than the amount of the subsidy, because of their deterrent effect on foreign competition (Brander and Spencer, 1985). If firms' marginal cost is decreasing in cumulative output owing to learning effects, protection of the home market acts like an export subsidy (Krugman, 1984a). If tariffs drive foreign firms out of competition, they may actually lower prices at home and raise them abroad (Venables, 1985a). These heterodox conclusions seem in principle to open the door to a much more activist trade policy stance than is usually advocated by professional economists.

The predominant reaction to these developments has, however, been one of caution. Discussions of application of the new concepts to trade policy have been marked by skepticism about their practical importance. The moral of a number of papers, including work by Dixit (1984, 1985a), Dixit and Grossman (1984), Eaton and Grossman (1983) and Krugman (1983, 1984b, 1985) has been that, while the new models of trade policy represent an intellectual advance, the possibilities for gains from active home trade policy and losses from active foreign trade policy suggested by this work are not important enough to warrant a modification of the usual economists' position on trade policy. This position is that, although there are respectable arguments for policy activism, the potential gains from such activism are small and the potential costs from trade conflict large, so that free trade is the best policy – even if other countries do not abide by it. This is a view that I continue to share; it must be recognized, however, that there is little evidence about the actual importance of the 'anti-classical' effects suggested by recent theory.

In this context, the results of the simulation exercise reported here are quite disturbing. A numerical model, whose parameters do not lie outside the ranges that case studies of high technology industries would indicate are reasonable, leads to very strong anti-classical conclusions. Home market protection by one country sharply raises its firms' market share abroad; if the protection is anticipated, it has so strong an effect in promoting entry of domestic firms and deterring entry of foreign firms that it converts what would have been a 50 per cent share of the world market under free trade to complete domination of that market under protection. Perhaps even more surprising, this export success is not purchased at the expense of domestic consumers. In fact, home market protection actually lowers the price at home while raising it abroad. Thus, in this example protectionism turns out to be a consummately successful predatory policy. The other country is better off responding to this protectionism in kind than doing nothing, even though the resulting trade war leaves both countries worse off than they would have been under free trade.

It may be that, once this model is modified to serve as a more adequate representation of actual industries, these results will turn out to have been misleading. An important recent paper by Dixit (1985b) on the automobile industry suggests that there, at least, the imperfect competition argument for trade activism is a quantitatively weak one. At the very least, however, this paper should serve as a goad to researchers to set about operationalizing recent trade theory.

The paper is in three parts. Section 1 sets up the basic model, and explains how it works. Section 2 then describes and compares three simulations: a 'baseline' case in which trade is free, a case in which one country reserves its home market for domestic firms, and a 'trade war' case in which both countries ban imports. Finally, section 3 discusses the implications of the results and suggests directions for further work.

1 THE MODEL

Assumptions

Consider a product which may be sold in two national markets, Home and Foreign. This product may be produced in either country, and we assume, to sharpen the analysis, that neither country has any inherent cost advantage in production. Costs, however, are assumed to fall over time. The basic idea is that of a product cycle: the product is introduced; costs fall as production experience is gained; then the product becomes outmoded and is replaced. Thus the simulation is a play of a one-time competition over a fixed period.

At any point in time total demand in each market is a decreasing function of the price in that market. The shape of the demand curve will unfortunately turn out to be important for the results; I will assume that it is linear, and express demand in inverse form:

$$p = A - Bz \tag{1}$$

$$p^* = A - Bz^* \tag{2}$$

where z, z^* are total sales in the domestic and foreign markets per unit time. Note that, for the purposes of the simulation, it is assumed that Home and Foreign have equal market sizes.

In each country total deliveries to the market per unit time are the sum of deliveries by domestic and foreign firms. We have

$$z = nx + n^*y \tag{3}$$

$$z^* = nx^* + n^*y^* \tag{4}$$

where

n = number of Home firms
n^* = number of Foreign firms
x = shipments per unit time by Home firms to the Home market
y = shipments per unit time by Foreign firms to the Home market
x^* = shipments per unit time by Home firms to the Foreign market
y^* = shipments per unit time by Foreign firms to the Foreign market.

In writing the condition this way, we have implicitly assumed that all firms based in a given country are identical; this will in fact be assumed to be true.

Turning now from the demand to the supply side, each firm has two kinds of costs: production costs, which depend on the total volume of production, and transport and distribution costs, which we will assume are incurred only on shipments to the other nation's market. Transport and distribution costs per unit will be taken to be fixed throughout the product cycle. Production costs per unit will be taken as given *at each point in time*. Thus the momentary profit condition will be

$$v = px + (p^* - t)x^* - c(x + x^*) \tag{5}$$

$$v^* = (p - t)y + p^*y^* - c^*(y + y^*) \tag{6}$$

where v, v^* are profits per firm in each country, t is the per-unit transport cost and c, c^* are per-unit production costs. However, production costs fall with cumulative output. Specifically, we have

$$c = K^{-e} \tag{7}$$

$$c^* = K^{*-e} \tag{8}$$

where K, K^* are cumulative firm output to date. That is,

$$dK/dt = x + x^* \tag{9}$$

$$dK^*/dt = y + y^*. \tag{10}$$

Finally, we need to specify the objectives of firms. In general, we would expect firms to maximize the present discounted value of profits. Following Spence (1981), however, we will assume that the product cycle is short enough that discounting does not matter, so that firms simply maximize the integral of profits over the cycle:

$$V = \int_0^T v\,dt \tag{11}$$

$$V^* = \int_0^T v^*dt. \tag{12}$$

Without loss of generality, we will set T, the length of the product cycle, equal to 1.

Equilibrium at a Point in Time

It is clear that, in the situation described by our model, firms will not simply maximize short-term profits. Instead, they will adopt a longer-run view, recognizing that increased output today lowers costs in the future. We will analyze this forward-looking behavior in a moment. The outcome of the problem is however clear: at any point in time, firms will maximize not profits but an expression (a Hamiltonian) which puts a shadow price on additions to their cumulative output:

$$H = v + q(x + x^*) \tag{13}$$

$$H^* = v^* + q^*(y + y^*). \tag{14}$$

Leaving the determination of the shadow prices q and q^* on one side for a moment, let us therefore analyze equilibrium *given* the shadow prices.

What we will assume, following Brander (1981) and Brander and Krugman (1983), is that at each point in time firms adopt a Cournot assumption about each others' behavior in each market separately. That is, each firm takes as given not just the level of each of its rivals' total output, but the division of that output between domestic shipments and exports. Based on this assumption, each firm then chooses its own levels of domestic and export shipments. In other words, this is a model of Cournot behavior with market segmentation.

As pointed out in the Brander and Brander–Krugman papers, the normal consequence of this kind of behavior is mutual interpenetration of markets – cross-hauling of the good. The reason is summarized by the phrase 'reciprocal dumping.' If firms in each country have the same (q-inclusive) marginal cost, and transportation costs are not too high, each country's firms will take part of the other country's market. The *average* revenue on exports will be no higher than on domestic sales, and marginal costs of exporting will be higher because of transport costs, so that this may seem an unprofitable activity. What sustains it is the fact that in equilibrium firms have a smaller market share abroad than at home, and thus perceive themselves as facing a higher elasticity of demand for exports than domestic sales. This makes *marginal* revenue on exports higher than on domestic shipments; in equilibrium, market shares are such as to make firms just willing to absorb transportation costs.

Foreign firms will sell in the Home market provided that in the absence of such sales the Home price would exceed Foreign marginal cost plus transport cost; that is,

$$A/(n+1)+(c-q)n/(n+1)>c^*-q^*+t.$$

If this condition is not satisfied, we will have $y=0$ and will analyze the Home market as an ordinary symmetric Cournot oligopoly. If the condition is satisfied, the equilibrium can be shown to be the following:

$$z=\{A(n+n^*)-n(c-q)-n^*(c^*-q^*+t)\}/D \qquad (15)$$

where

$$D=B(n+n^*+1)$$

$$x=\{A-Bz-(c-q)\}/B \qquad (16)$$

$$y=\{A-Bz-(c^*-q^*+t)\}/B. \qquad (17)$$

Note that, if the marginal costs of firms are equal ($c-q=c^*-q^*$), Foreign firms will have smaller sales in the Home market than Home firms, because of transportation costs; what the equilibrium conditions insure is that y is sufficiently smaller than x that the difference in marginal revenue offsets the difference in marginal cost.

A symmetric set of conditions applies in the Foreign market. Home firms will export to that market provided that the autarky price would exceed $c-q+t$; if they do export, the equilibrium conditions will be exactly parallel to those for the Home market.

This analysis shows how to determine production and trade given q and q^*, the shadow prices on experience. The next step is to show how these are determined.

Equilibrium over Time

In analyzing the determination of the shadow prices, we must confront the issue of strategic behavior. Do firms follow 'open-loop' strategies, in which they set their whole path of outputs taking other firms' output paths as given; or do they follow 'closed-loop' strategies, in which they assume that other firms revise their plans based on their observation of our output path? In the latter case additions to experience will yield a return not only because of their direct effect in lowering future costs of production, but also because of their *strategic* effect in deterring competitors over time. As Fudenberg and Tirole (1983) have argued, the closed-loop analysis is more satisfying as a characterization of rational behavior – though whether it is more realistic is less clear. Furthermore, the closed-loop outcome can be significantly different from the open-loop outcome.

None the less, for the purpose of this exercise we will assume that firms follow open-loop strategies. The reason is simplicity and convenience; as Spence (1981) showed, and as we will see in a moment, the open-loop case with no discounting has a very straightforward and easy solution. Extension to the closed-loop case will be a subject of future research.

Suppose, then, that each firm takes other firms' output paths as given. Its own output path will then maximize profits. This means that the marginal gain from an addition to experience is simply the reduction in costs along this optimum path. Thus, for a firm in Home we have, for the shadow price of experience at time t,

$$q = -\int_t^T (x+x^*)(\partial c/\partial K)\,ds. \tag{18}$$

It immediately follows that at time T, the end of the product cycle, $q=0$. A more surprising result, however, is the following: the rate of change of q exactly equals the rate of change in c. That is,

$$dq/dt = (x+x^*)(\partial c/\partial K) = dc/dt. \tag{19}$$

What this implies for the outcome is that the shadow price on experience falls at exactly the same rate as production costs, so that the true marginal cost on which short-run decisions are made, $(c-q)$, remains constant. More precisely, firms should act throughout the product cycle as if their marginal cost were equal to their actual production cost *at the end of the cycle.*

This clearly simplifies the description of the equilibrium considerably. Although firms are solving a dynamic problem, in fact prices, outputs and trade will remain stationary through the product cycle. Only costs change. Firms 'forward-price' at the beginning of the cycle, setting marginal and perhaps average revenue below marginal production cost in order to move down the learning curve, then reap the rewards later; the special feature of the setup here is that this process actually leads to a flat path of the price.

The analysis here also clearly suggests a computational procedure. Start with guesses at terminal c and c^*. Compute the implied pattern of production and trade, based on the fact that firms set marginal revenue equal to terminal cost throughout the cycle. Find the cumulative output which results, recompute c and c^*, and iterate until convergence.

Entry

Our discussion so far has taken the numbers of firms n and n^* as given. In modelling entry, we will assume that potential entrants are able correctly to anticipate post-entry profitability. We will also assume that all entrants have an equal chance at the starting line, so that no one is able to engage in strategic moves to deter entry. The result will be that as many firms will enter as are able to earn positive profits.

Because the number of firms in each country must be an integer, this assumption means that there will in general be some positive economic profits being earned. As it turns out, however, these profits are quite small.

2 SIMULATIONS

Parameter Values

The assumed parameter values for the simulations are as follows: $A=3.5$; $B=0.5$; $t=0.35$; $e=0.3$. They are not based on empirical data, but some reasoning went into the choices, and this should be described briefly.

First are the parameters of the demand curve in each country, A and B. These were chosen after some experimentation in an attempt to produce both a reasonable demand elasticity and a plausible trade volume in the baseline case. The actual implied elasticity in our simulations is somewhat low, at 0.67.

One might have expected that it would be reasonable to assume constant elasticity demand rather than linear, and to impose a plausible value directly. In Cournot models, however, constant elasticity demand leads to complex and sometimes perverse behavior. The reason is that constant elasticity demand fails to obey the 'Spencer condition' that each firm's marginal revenue be decreasing in other firms' output. Experiments with the constant elasticity form here confirmed the importance of that condition; the results of simulations were complex and difficult to give any meaningful interpretation.

The transport cost t was also chosen to produce a plausible baseline outcome. Given the numbers on marginal cost reported below, the value chosen may seem quite high; we know that transport costs are quite low on manufactured goods, perhaps especially so on high value-to-weight products such as high technology devices. The transport cost variable is however intended to capture more than literal costs of shipping. It also conceptually includes distribution costs, difficulties of communication between suppliers and users, increased uncertainty about delivery lags and so on. It is arguable that in high technology industries, where uncertainty is presumably high, these invisible costs could be substantial.

The remaining parameter is the slope of the learning curve. The business strategy literature of the 1970s, led by the Boston Consulting Group, commonly suggested learning curves of 20–30 per cent. The widespread applicability of this concept has since been called into question, but the high technology industries still seem to be characterized by definite learning effects. In semiconductors, where the evidence seems most clear-cut, a learning curve slope of 28 per cent has been estimated (Office of Technology Assessment, 1983). Thus, the 30 per cent slope assumed here, while not reasonable for the average industry, is not unrealistic for innovative industries with short product cycles.

Obviously, these parameters are not the result of careful research. Thus we must repeat that the simulation results that follow are indicative of what *can* happen, not of what must happen. The case was not, however, constructed in order to make a point; the strong results below were a surprise to the researcher and indeed were contrary to my prejudices.

A Baseline Simulation

The first simulation reported here is a baseline case of free trade in each country. The results of the simulation are of course symmetric between the countries, and are reported in tables 10.1 and 10.2.

The first step in this simulation exercise is to determine the number of firms in each country. To do this, we construct a grid of alternative values of n and n^* and for each pair solve the model using the iterative procedure described above. We then look for an entry equilibrium, defined as a combination of n and n^* in which all firms earn positive profits, but where any additional firm that entered would find itself earning negative profits.

Table 10.1 shows the relevant portion of this grid. Clearly, three firms in each country is an equilibrium. If another firm, either Home or Foreign, were to enter it would find the market sufficiently crowded that it would not cover its costs.

Table 10.2 presents some summary statistics about the (3,3) equilibrium under free trade. Since the two countries are symmetrical in this case, only one column of numbers is given. The price, output, consumer surplus and total welfare numbers are meaningful only as bases from which to measure the changes in subsequent simulations. However, the import share of

Table 10.1 Profitability and entry under free trade

No. of Home firms	No. of Foreign firms: 2	3	4
2	0.4194 0.4194	0.2008 0.1948	0.0953 0.0707
3	0.1948 0.2008	0.0365 0.0365	−0.0124 −0.0250
4	0.0707 0.0953	−0.0250 −0.0124	−0.0776 −0.0776

Note: For each pair of numbers of firms, the number on the upper right represents profits per Foreign firm, the number on the lower left, profits per Home firm.

Table 10.2 Baseline (free trade) results

Profits per firm	0.0365
Import share	0.2853
Price	1.4038
Output	4.1924
Consumer surplus	4.3939
Welfare	4.5034

28.5 per cent is interesting in itself; in this example reciprocal dumping leads to a substantial volume of trade.

One-sided Protectionism

The next set of simulations examines what happens when one country, here assumed to be Home, follows a protectionist policy. A variety of activist policies could be studied in this model; here we assume that the policy is a simple one of denying Foreign producers any access to the Home market.

The effects of such a policy on competition can be thought of in two stages, although these will not be the actual dynamics. First, for given numbers of domestic and foreign firms in the market, the protection would give domestic firms an advantage which would be reflected both in higher profitability and higher output. Second, the shift in relative profitability will encourage more entry by domestic firms, less by foreign. To understand the effects, then, it is useful to begin by examining what would happen if the number of firms in the market were the same as in the free-trade case. This will turn out not to be an equilibrium; thus we then turn to determination of the number of entrants and the characteristics of the entry equilibrium.

Table 10.3 shows what would happen if three firms from each country were to enter the industry despite Home's protectionist policy. The results

Table 10.3 Protection of Home market (3 × 3 cases)

	Home	Foreign
Profits per firm	0.4505	−0.0956
Import share	0	0.5229
Price	1.4793	1.4611
Output	6.1737	1.9456
Consumer surplus	4.0833	4.1572
Welfare	5.4348	3.8702

Table 10.4 Profits and entry under Home market protection

	No. of Foreign firms			
	0	1	2	3
No. of Home firms				
3	n.a. 0.8581	0.1160 0.5816	−0.0079 0.4774	−0.0956 0.4505
4	n.a. 0.3330	−0.0453 0.1918	−0.1174 0.1368	−0.1755 0.1308
5	n.a. 0.0808	−0.1141 0.0004	−0.1584 −0.0322	−0.1987 −0.0365
6	n.a. −0.0517	−0.1374 −0.1008	−0.1613 −0.1211	−0.1859 −0.1270

are in line with the theoretical analysis in Krugman (1984a). By shifting domestic scales from Foreign to Home firms, the protectionist policy raises cumulative output of Home firms and lowers that of Foreign. This lowers the relative marginal cost of Home production, leading to a substantial increase in the Home share of Foreign sales as well – that is, import protection has served as export promotion as well. This export expansion is achieved to some extent at the expense of Home consumers, who must pay a higher price than they would have done under free trade. This consumer loss is, however, more than offset by a gain in profits of Home firms – in the manner of Brander and Spencer (1985), this trade policy has the effect of shifting rents from Foreign to Home firms.

This 3 × 3 outcome is, however, clearly not an equilibrium if firms expect the protectionist policy. The rent-shifting effects of the policy have, in table 10.3, led to sharply increased profits by Home firms and losses on the part of Foreign firms. Thus we would expect that more Home firms and fewer Foreign firms would in fact enter this market.

Table 10.5 Protection of Home market (5 × 0 case)

	Home	Foreign
Profits per firm	0.0808	n.a.
Share of imports	0	1
Price	1.2990	1.5490
Output	8.3039	0
Consumer surplus	4.8443	3.8063
Welfare	5.2481	3.8063

Table 10.4 shows how per-firm profits depend on the number of firms in each country. The result is very striking: with the Home market closed to Foreign firms, the equilibrium market structure shifts from one containing three firms from each country to one containing five Home firms and no Foreign firms. Restriction of access to the domestic market turns out to lead to Home domination of the entire world market.

In this a Pyrrhic victory? Surprisingly, it is not. Table 10.5 reports the implications of this 5 × 0 market structure. Comparing this with the free trade equilibrium in table 10.2, we note the following:

1 The Home market price is *lower* with protection than with free trade, because of larger firms and increased competition in the Home market. This means that domestic consumers actually gain from protection. Domestic consumer surplus rises; this is reinforced by a small increase in profits, so that the sum of consumer and producer surplus rises substantially.
2 The Foreign price rises, because all of the good must now be imported and must incur transport cost. Foreign consumers lose, and this effect is reinforced by the loss of the small profits that Foreign firms would have earned under free trade. So Foreign welfare is unambiguously reduced.

The implication is that Home's protection is a highly successful predatory policy, not only increasing its sales and market share but also improving its welfare by any measure.

These results are not entirely unexpected. Theoretical analysis of the effects of tariffs in a segmented market model, carried out by Venables (1985a, 1985b), has already shown that, with free entry, such policies will lower prices at Home while raising them abroad. What is surprising is to see the results come out so strongly for such a simple policy.

Trade War

If protection is such a successful predatory policy, we might expect one country's protection to be imitated by the other, out of a spirit of either

Table 10.6 Trade war

Profits per firm	0.0714
Share of imports	0
Price	1.500
Output	4.000
Consumer surplus	4.000
Welfare	4.2857

Table 10.7 Welfare levels under alternative policies

	Foreign policy	
	Free trade	Protection
Home policy		
Free trade	4.5034 4.5034	5.2481 3.8063
Protection	3.8063 5.2481	4.2857 4.2857

emulation or revenge. Our final simulation considers the effects of a trade war in which each country denies the other access to its market.

Eliminating trade reduces competition in each market, and raises the profitability of any given number of firms. In our example this turns out to make it profitable for one more firm to enter in each country, so that we now have a four-firm oligopoly in each. These oligopolies are symmetric, so table 10.6 reports only one set of numbers.

The elimination of trade reduces output per firm, raises the price, leaves consumers worse off, and reduces total welfare. An alternative way of saying this is to say that free trade is beneficial in this model. This is in line with the result, reported in Brander and Krugman (1983), that, even in the case of seemingly pointless 'reciprocal dumping,' free entry insures that the favorable effects of trade on competition and scale outweigh the losses arising from transportation cost. A trade war, then, leaves both countries worse off than free trade.

An equally important comparison, however, is with the situation of one-sided protectionism. If we compare table 10.6 with 10.5 we discover a crucial point: *Foreign is better off if it matches Home's protection than if it does not*. By protecting its market, Foreign not only recaptures some monopoly profits that would otherwise have been lost, but actually lowers its price relative to one-sided protection.

What this means is that the structure of the policy problem for the two governments is in fact that of a Prisoner's Dilemma. Table 10.7 shows how the sum of consumer and producer surplus in each country depends on the choice to protect or not to protect. Both countries are better off with free trade than with a trade war, yet each country has an incentive to protect regardless of what the other country does.

3 IMPLICATIONS

Summary

In this paper we have considered the effects of protection in a numerical model designed to capture some of the distinctive aspects of competition in high technology industries. The specific policy considered was a complete closure of access by foreign firms to the domestic market. The results were strikingly anti-classical. For the specific example considered, we found that:

1. Protection by one country unambiguously improves its welfare at the other country's expense. Creation of a domestic market 'safe haven' for national firms leads to a domination of the foreign market as well; the effect is actually to *lower* domestic prices and thus make domestic consumers better off, as well as shifting some small economic rents from Foreign to Home firms.
2. Retaliation in kind by the other country leaves it unambiguously better off than it would be if it pursued free trade while the first country was protectionist. When both countries close their markets to foreign competition, however, both are worse off than under free trade. The policy problem therefore has the structure of a Prisoner's Dilemma, where self-interested behavior by both countries leads to a mutually undesirable outcome.

Problems with the Analysis

This paper presents an example, not an empirical study. In assessing the example, it is important to be aware of the problems which limit its generality. These may be grouped under two headings: technical problems, and empirical questions.

The basic technical problem with the analysis is the way it models the process of competition. At a minor level, the assumption of a zero discount rate is unrealistic, though some simulation experiments suggest that for short product cycles this does not matter too much. More important is the question of open-loop versus closed-loop. There is some question whether a closed-loop, subgame perfect analysis is actually more realistic than the simple analysis here – it may be making too many demands on the calculation abilities of firms. It will be desirable, however, to recast the analysis in this form, if only to see how sensitive the results are to the choice.

We should also note that the Cournot assumption about short-term competition is motivated by convenience rather than evidence. As Eaton and

Grossman (1983) have shown, in some contexts the assumption about strategy variables in imperfect competition can unfortunately make quite a lot of difference.

Perhaps even more important than these conceptual difficulties, however, is the fact that the parameters used here are based on loose appeals to plausibility rather than empirical evidence. The obvious next step is to try to fit a model along the lines of this one to real data.

The moral of this paper, then, is not that protection of high technology industries is necessarily a policy that works to the national advantage. The point is, instead, that we cannot dismiss this possibility *a priori*, and that it is therefore urgent that we move to develop empirical analysis which can tell us more about the facts.

REFERENCES

Brander J. (1981). Intra-industry trade in identical commodities. *Journal of International Economics*, 11, 1–14.

Brander, J. and Krugman, P. (1983). A 'reciprocal dumping' model of international trade. *Journal of International Economics*, 15, 313–21.

Brander, J. and Spencer, B. (1985). Export subsidies and international market share rivalry. *Journal of International Economics*, 18, 83–100.

Dixit, A. (1984). International trade policy for oligopolistic industries. *Economic Journal*, 94, supplement, 1–16.

Dixit, A. (1985a). How should the US respond to other countries' trade policies? Paper prepared for the conference, US Trade Policies in a Changing World Economy, held at University of Michigan, March, 28–29. 1985.

Dixit, A. (1985b). Optimal trade and industrial policies for the US automobile industry. Mimeo.

Dixit, A. and Grossman, A. (1984). Targeted export promotion with several oligopolistic industries. NBER Working Paper no. 1344.

Dixit, A. and Kyle, A. (1985). The use of protection and subsidies for entry promotion and deterrence. *American Economic Review*, 75, 139–52.

Eaton, J.and Grossman, G. (1983). Optimal trade and industrial policy under oligopoly. NBER Working Paper no. 1236.

Fudenberg, D. and Tirole, J. (1983). Learning by doing and market performance. *Bell Journal of Economics*, 14, 522–30.

Krugman, P. (1983). Targeted industrial policies: theory and evidence. In Federal Reserve Bank of Kansas City, *Structural Change and Public Policy*. Kansas City: FRBKC.

Krugman, P. (1984a). Import protection as export promotion. In H. Kierzkowski (ed.), *Monopolistic Competition and International Trade*. Oxford: Oxford University Press.

Krugman, P. (1984b). Foreign industrial targeting and the US economy. *Brookings Papers on Economic Activity*, 77–121.

Krugman, P. (1985). Strategic sectors and international competition. Paper prepared for the conference, US Trade Policies in a Changing World Economy, held at University of Michigan, March 28–29, 1985.

Office of Technology Assessment (1983). *International Competitiveness in Electronics*. Washington: US Congress.

Spence, A. M. (1981). The learning curve and competition. *Bell Journal of Economics*, 12, 49–70.

Venables, A. (1985a). Trade and trade policy with imperfect competition: the case of identical products and free entry. *Journal of International Economics*, 19, 1–19.

Venables, A. (1985b). International trade, trade and industrial policies, and imperfect competition: a survey. Mimeo.

11

Product Quality, Intra-industry Trade and (Im)perfect Competition

Rodney E. Falvey and Henryk Kierzkowski

1 INTRODUCTION

The decade or so since the publication of Corden's *Theory of Protection* and *Trade Policy and Economic Welfare* has seen significant advances in both the positive and the normative treatments of differentiated products and imperfect competition in pure trade theory. The purpose of this paper is to construct a model of international trade in differentiated products which is capable of explaining both the pattern and the volume of trade in these products, but which does not involve imperfect competition, economies of scale or consumer taste differences.

The recent outburst of writings on imperfect competition and international trade has been triggered off by an apparent inability of traditional trade models to explain the coexistence of intra- and inter-industry trade flows.[1] In addition, while both the Ricardian and the Heckscher–Ohlin models suggest that, the less similar countries are, the more trade there should be, the evidence suggests that trade volumes tend to be larger between similar countries. It is probably fair to say that a consensus has recently emerged that the explanation of intra-industry trade requires the construction of new models which differ, sometimes drastically, from the old ones.

Almost without exception, these models rely on imperfect competition to explain intra-industry trade flows, with factor endowment differences remaining only as a basis for the coexisting inter-industry trade. Imperfect

We would like to thank Alan Deardorff, Avinash Dixit, Christopher Findlay, Elhanan Helpman and John Sutton for comments on an earlier draft. Research on this paper was done while the authors were visiting the Research School of Pacific Studies at ANU. They wish to express their thanks and gratitute to Max Corden for providing excellent research conditions.

competition stems from the existence of economies of scale in the differentiated product industry. With fixed costs to be borne, only a limited number of producers can survive in equilibrium; but this number is large enough so that free entry ensures that no pure profits are made in the long run. Chamberlinian monopolistic competition replaces perfect competition.

A second building block of the new genre of trade models is the specification of the demand side. Two alternative approaches prevail. One originates in the Dixit–Stiglitz model of monopolistic competition in the closed economy and has been extensively used by Krugman, among others. Individuals value variety *per se* and are only too happy to consume all differentiated goods being offered. Any new variety entering the market can be assured of finding its place in the consumer's budget. The number of products is limited by the fact that the differentiated product industry produces under conditions of economies of scale. Trade increases the number of varieties available, thus making consumers better off.

The alternative approach to modelling demand for differentiated goods harks back to the classic Hotelling formulation of the location problem. Goods demanded by consumers embody different characteristics, and different groups of individuals have their most preferred 'packages' of characteristics. Unlike the Dixit–Stiglitz formulation, an individual does not value variety in itself and buys only one type of the differentiated good. Diversity of tastes then gives rise to a demand for variety at the *aggregate* level. Once again, international trade extends the menu of goods available in a single country beyond those supplied by its domestic producers.[2]

Both these variety and characteristics approaches represent cases of horizontal product differentiation. A further alternative to taste modelling, namely vertical differentiation, has received less attention.[3] Chamberlin (1933) was clearly aware of this type of differentiation and accordingly distinguished between product improvement or deterioration (vertical product differentiation) and product change (horizontal product differentiation). Lancaster (1980b, pp. 27–8, 220–2) offers insight into the alternative formulations of demand for differentiated products, and argues that vertical product differentiation becomes most relevant when consumers have different incomes or endowments and products are indivisible. Explaining his emphasis on horizontal differentiation, he observes that:

> For most of the analysis it has been assumed that there is a uniform density of consumers and a uniform distribution of income (or welfare, if demand is fully compensated) over the spectrum. If this is interpreted to represent an *equal* distribution of income over individuals, then there is no scope for vertical differentiation. (Lancaster, 1980b, p. 221).

Leaving aside the question of divisibility, it is clear that a significant element in explaining vertical product differentiation will be unequal incomes. The distribution of income plays a negligable role, if any, in most international trade models.[4] In contrast, it becomes a central feature of the analysis developed in this paper. While retaining the traditional assumption that consumers have identical tastes, we assume that each individual demands only one type of differentiated product and that, given relative prices, this 'preferred variety' is determined uniquely by the individual's income; as his income changes, so does his preferred quality. Since the aggregate income of a society is not equally distributed, there is, at any point in time, an *aggregate* demand for a variety of differentiated goods.

On the supply side, we assume that production takes place in two sectors, one of which produces a single homogeneous output and the other a multi-quality product. Further, in keeping with well established tradition, we assume that constant-returns-to-scale technologies prevail in both sectors. If we were also to assume identical technologies across countries, then the presence of more 'goods' than 'factors' in the differentiated product sector could combine with factor price equalization to yield a trade pattern in terms of qualities (though not factor services) that is completely indeterminate. If the trade pattern is not to remain a matter of chance, either technology differences must appear somewhere in the model, or factor endowments must be sufficiently dissimilar to force specialization in free trade.[5] Given that rather large endowment differences would be necessary for this purpose, we have chosen the technology alternative (where differences need not be great) and for simplicity have assumed that technology differences are confined to the homogeneous product sector.[6]

Bhagwati (1982, p. 175) has also observed that technology differences may be required if one is to end the indeterminancy in the trade pattern in differentiated products that pervades the current literature. He argues that, 'if we want to introduce the notion of "similar" products, with different nations trading such products to one another, we really have to give up the Heckscher–Ohlin assumption that all firms, and nations, share identical know-how *ex ante*.' The Bhagwati–Feenstra (1982) 'biological' approach to trade in similar products then assumes that each nation's firms develop technological advantages in particular sub-ranges of products that are related to national characteristics such as tastes, climate and so on, and therefore tend to specialize in their production under free trade. Such an approach, while more specialized, is consistent with the type of framework developed below.

The remainder of the paper is as follows. The next section develops our model and determines its autarky equilibrium. Section 3 then considers the general properties of the free trade equilibrium. Perfect competition and constant returns to scale are consistent with two-way trade in differentiated products, provided some basis for intra-sectoral cost differences exists between the two countries. Here this basis is provided by technology differences elsewhere in the economy, a feature which also implies a determinate pattern of trade. Section 4 examines the connection between income differences and trade volumes in this structure, with particular reference to the 'Linder Hypothesis'. Because the range of vertically differentiated products demanded depends on the income distribution, changes in, say, factor endowments and technology affect the range of products both supplied and demanded. Our conclusions occupy section 5.

2 A MODEL OF VERTICAL PRODUCT DIFFERENTIATION

Let sector Y produce the homogeneous product and sector X a continuum of differentiated products referred to as *qualities* and indexed by $s(0<s<s_m)$. We assume that each economy is endowed with fixed stocks of two homogeneous resources – capital (K) and labour (L) – and that capital is specific to the differentiated product sector. The homogeneous product sector is thus modelled along Ricardian lines, while the differentiated product sector is of the Heckscher–Ohlin type.[7] Each quality is assumed to require a fixed capital–labour ratio in its production, and for simplicity we adopt the normalization that production of a unit of quality s requires one unit of labour and s units of capital. Despite the lack of substitution between factors at the individual quality level, this sector's aggregate capital–labour ratio will vary as the quality mix of its output varies.

Perfect competition in production is assumed throughout, yielding competitive profit conditions

$$1=bw \quad \text{and} \quad p(s)=w+sr \tag{1}$$

where w, r and $p(s)$ are the wage to labour, rental on capital and price of quality s, respectively, in units of Y, and b is the number of units of labour required per unit output of Y. The corresponding full employment conditions are

$$bY+X=L \quad \text{and} \quad \int sX(s)ds=K \tag{2}$$

where X and Y denote the total outputs of the two sectors, and $X(s)$ is the output of quality s. On the demand side, we assume that all consumers have the same underlying preferences but consume different qualities for the same reason that they consume different quantities of products: namely, their incomes differ. Each consumer's welfare depends on the quantities of the two goods (x and y) and the quality of the differentiated product (s) that he consumes. We assume preferences can be represented by a utility function $U(x,q,y)$, where $q=sx$ is the total number of 'quality units' consumed by this individual, and that this function is non-negative, continuous, quasi-concave and increasing in its arguments.

The output of the X sector then effectively has two separate dimensions – quantity (x) and quality (q) – with the consumer being free to select independently the amounts of each he will consume (through the choice of x and s). Given constant returns to scale and perfect competition, any demand that covers costs can be assumed to be met, at least in the long run.

The typical consumer's problem then is to maximize $U(x,q,y)$ subject to his budget constraint

$$I=(w+sr)x+y=wx+rq+y \tag{3}$$

where I is this individual's income. The solution will yield implicit demand functions for s, x and y, as functions of income and relative (factor) prices. In particular, increases in income can be expected to increase the demands for both outputs and the quality of the differentiated product, assuming that none of the three is inferior.

Fortunately, this rather unwieldy demand structure can be simplified by moving to the derived demands for 'factor services'. With a finite number of factors but a continuum of qualities, one expects considerable simplification to follow from concentrating on factor markets. In particular, while the individual's budget constraint (3) is nonlinear in terms of X-sector output, it becomes linear when converted to his underlying demands for quantity (x) and 'quality' (q). Given our assumptions on input use, these demands convert directly into implicit demands for 'labour' and 'capital' services, respectively.

To ease aggregation, we further suppose that preferences can be represented by a Stone–Geary type function of the form[8]

$$U(x,q,y)=(x-x_0)^{\alpha}\ (q-q^0)^{\beta}\ (y-y^0)^{\Upsilon} \tag{4}$$

where (x_0, q_0, y_0) can be interpreted as a 'subsistence' consumption bundle, and for convenience we assume $\alpha+\beta+\Upsilon=1$. Let $I_0=wx_0+rq_0+y_0$. Then the corresponding utility-maximizing demands can be derived as

$$\begin{aligned} x(I)&=x_0+(\alpha/w)\ (I-I_0)\\ q(I)&=q_0+(\beta/r)\ (I-I_0)\\ y(I)&=y_0+\Upsilon\ (I-I_0). \end{aligned} \tag{5}$$

The interpretation of (5) is straightforward. Each consumer implicitly meets his subsistence, then allocates his remaining (discretionary) income proportionately over the three 'goods'.

Aggregating the implicit factor demands across individuals and substituting the results into (2) yields

$$N(rq_0-\beta I_0)+\beta(wL+rK)=rK$$

where $wL+rK$ is total income and N is the total number of income earners in the economy. Rearranging, this can be written as

$$w(L-N\ell_0)=r(1-\beta)\ (K-Nk_0) \tag{6}$$

where $k_0=q_0$ and $\ell_0=x_0+by_0$ is the total individual subsistence labour requirement. Converting this expression to a 'per capita' basis by defining $k=K/L$ and supposing $L=N$, one has

$$\frac{w}{r}=\frac{(1+\beta)}{\beta}\ \frac{(k-k_0)}{(1-\ell_0)}\equiv m\ \frac{k_e}{\ell_e}. \tag{7}$$

The autarky equilibrium wage–rental ratio therefore depends on 'tastes' (via m) and the 'effective' or 'discretionary' capital–labour endowment ratio (k_e/ℓ_e). Equations (1) and (7) can be used to illustrate the effects of effective endowment and technology differences on autarky factor prices.

$$\hat{w} = -\hat{b}; \qquad \hat{r} = -\hat{b} - (\hat{k}_e - \hat{\ell}_e). \tag{8}$$

A technological advance in the homogeneous product sector ($\hat{b}<0$) raises both the wage and rental rates (in terms of Y) in equal proportions. A decrease in the effective capital–labour ratio also raises the rental on capital.

Equation (8) permits the prediction of the effects of endowment and technology differences on relative autarky prices. Using (1), we have for any quantity s that

$$\hat{p}(s) = \theta_L(s)\hat{w} + \theta_K(s)\hat{r}$$

where $\theta_L(s)$, $\theta_K(s)$ are the factor cost shares. Substituting from (8) yields

$$\hat{p}(s) = -\hat{b} - \theta_K(s)\,(\hat{k}_e - \hat{\ell}_e). \tag{9}$$

A technological advantage in the homogeneous product leads to higher relative prices (costs) of all differentiated products, but relative prices within the X sector remain unaffected. The latter are affected by differences in effective per capita endowments, however. A larger effective capital–labour ratio reduces the relative prices of the higher qualities (since $\theta_k(s)$ rises with s at a given factor prices). So a relatively capital-abundant country will tend to have not only lower prices for differentiated products in general, but also a price differential that widens as one moves up the quality spectrum.

On the basis of these autarky price differences, one would make the following (*ceteris paribus*) trade pattern predictions:

1 A country with a superior technology in the homogeneous product will tend to export Y and import X.
2 A country that is relatively labour-abundant will tend to export Y and import X, particularly the higher qualities of X where the autarky price differences are greatest.
3 Conversely, a country that is relatively capital-abundant will tend to export X, particularly the higher-quality X products, and import Y.

But to determine the actual pattern of intra-industry trade itself, one needs to examine the free trade equilibrium more closely.

3 FREE TRADE EQUILIBRIUM

As noted earlier, our model combines Ricardian and Heckscher–Ohlin components, implying that trade will reflect differences in both factor endowments and technologies.

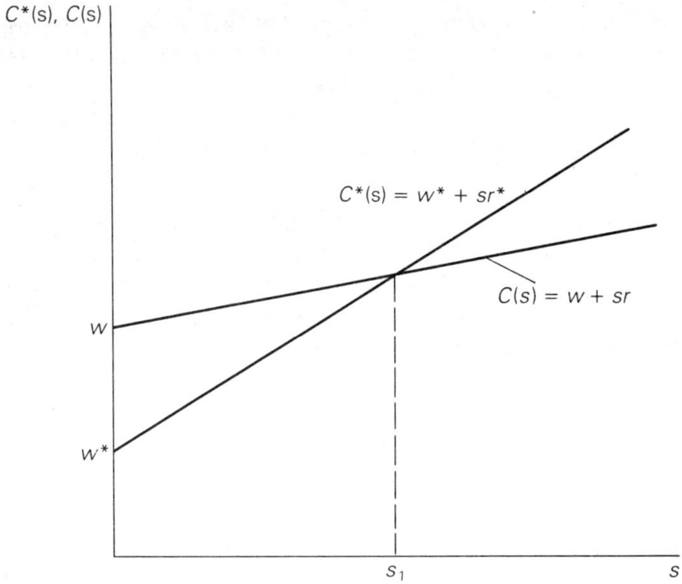

Figure 11.1

Suppose the home country has a technological advantage in production of the homogeneous good (i.e., $b<b^*$). Then if both countries produce Y in free trade, the home wage rate (in terms of Y) must exceed the foreign wage rate. If home capital also had a higher rental, then the foreign country could underprice the home country in all differentiated products. Full employment of the home capital stock therefore requires that $r<r^*$, giving home producers a cost advantage at the higher-quality end of the differentated products spectrum.

This equilibrium is illustrated in figure 11.1, where foreign producers are assumed to have lower costs ($C^*(s)<C(s)$) over the range of qualities below the 'marginal quality' (s_1), and home producers have the lower costs above that.[9] The price configuration facing consumers in both markets then has the following form:

$$p(s)=\begin{cases} w^*+sr^* & s\leq s_1 \\ w+sr & s\geq s_1 . \end{cases} \tag{10}$$

With this price structure, consumers in each country will divide into two groups. Those with high incomes will buy the higher-quality products of the home country, and those with low incomes will buy the lower-quality foreign products. To demonstrate this, consider a consumer of either nationality (we assume common world tastes) with an income of I and preferences as reflected in (4). His most preferred home-produced quality yields a welfare level of $V(I)=U_0(I-I_0)/w^{\alpha}r^{\beta}$, where U_0 is a constant.[10] If instead he were to select from the foreign production range, his welfare level would be $V^*(I) = U_0(I - I_0^*)/w^{*\alpha} r^{*\beta}$. Consumers would then opt to purchase home (foreign) produced qualities when $V(I) > (<) V^*(I)$. This allows one to determine a marginal income level (I_1) at which any consumer would be indifferent as to the source of his preferred differentiated product; that is,

$$I_1 = \frac{I_0 - BI_0^*}{1 - B} \tag{11}$$

where $B = (w/w^*)^\alpha \ (r/r^*)^\beta$. Since $I_0 - I_0^* = \{(w + s_0 r) - (w^* + s_0 r^*)\}$, $x_0 > 0$,[11] where $s_0 = q_0/x_0$ is the lowest quality that will meet subsistence, $B < 1$ in equilibrium (relative rentals adjusting to ensure this). As

$$\frac{dV(I)}{dI} = \frac{1}{B} \frac{dV^*(I)}{dI} > \frac{dV^*(I)}{dI},$$

it is clear that those individuals with income less than I_1 will purchase qualities inferior to s_1 from the foreign market, while those with incomes greater than I_1 will purchase qualities superior to s_1 from home producers.

An interesting outcome is that, even with a continuous distribution of income in each country, a continuum of qualities that can potentially be supplied and constant returns to scale in their production, there will be a 'gap' in the range of qualities actually produced and demanded, coinciding with that area of the quality spectrum where one country's production ceases and the other's begins. This is a consequence of the direction and discreteness of the shift in the 'marginal cost of quality' (down from r^* to r) at s_1, and the correspondingly discrete differences in the quality and quantities demanded from the two countries by individuals at the margin.[12] Let the marginal income earner's purchases at home be denoted x_1, q_1, y_1, and his alternative purchases abroad be x_1^*, q_1^*, y_1^*. Then from (5) and (11) we have, after manipulation, that

$$x_1 - x_1^* = \frac{\alpha(I_1 - I_0^*)}{w} \left(B - \frac{w}{w^*} \right) < 0 \tag{12}$$

$$y_1 - y_1^* = \Upsilon(I_1 - I_0^*)(B - 1) < 0$$

and hence $q_1 - q_1^* > 0$, since $V(I_1) = V^*(I_1)$.

Given the difference in relative prices, consumers substitute away from relatively expensive labour services towards relatively cheaper capital services in the home market. Despite the continuity in incomes, there will be measurable differences in the varieties exported by the two countries.

4 TRADE VOLUMES AND RELATIVE INCOMES

This section focuses on the relationship between relative incomes and the volume of trade. This relationship is of interest since it serves to differentiate two competing explanations of the trade pattern (particularly in manufacturers). The traditional Heckscher–Ohlin theory suggests that, since trade is generated by differences between countries (in endowments specifically), its volume should increase as countries become less similar. So should income differences, indirectly implying a positive relationship, if any, between income differences and the volume of (inter-industry) trade. The alternative approach developed by Linder (1961, ch. III) argues that in manufacturing a country's range of potential exports (and imports) is determined primarily by its internal demand, so that countries with similar demand structures will potentally trade more. Linder further suggests that similarity of average income levels can be used as an index of similarity of demand structures, implying a negative relationship between per capita income differences and trade volumes, *ceteris paribus*.

Our model is in many respects an amalgam of these two approaches. By emphasizing the link between the quality of product demanded and an individual's income, we have captured an essential aspect of the demand side of Linder's model (1961, pp. 98–100). We retain a traditional supply side, however, with comparative advantage based on technology or endowment differences. Linder himself does not attempt to develop a general explanation of the source of comparative advantage (p. 105), but expects trade in manufacturers to be characterized largely by monopolistic competition arising from economies of scale and variety-specific technological and managerial advantages (p. 102).[13] The influence of factor proportions on relative costs remains present, but is now just one determinant among many (p. 104). Our framework should therefore indicate the importance of the demand aspects of Linder's model to his prediction that trade propensities will be larger between countries with similar per capita incomes.

Given identical tastes, there are three underlying sources of country dissimilarity: factor endowments, technologies and patterns of factor ownership (income distributions). We begin with countries initially differing in a single respect (that generating any trade) and then examine how widening the differences between them affects both income levels and trade volumes. We also assume constant and identical populations throughout, so that all variables can be considered on a per capita basis.

There are three cases of interest.

1 *Identical endowments and technologies:* In this case factor prices, endowments and hence per capita income will be identical across countries. This, combined with identical tastes, indicates no basis for trade. Income distributions could differ radically, implying that the ranges and distributions of differentiated products produced and consumed would differ, but each country would be capable of meeting its own demands at the common prices.

2 *Identical technologies but different endowments:* Suppose that $k > k^*$, but that this endowment difference is not so large as to force specialization. We are then essentially in a Heckscher–Ohlin world in which factor price equalization accompanies free trade and the intra-sectoral trade pattern is indeterminate. The relatively capital-abundant home country will be a net

exporter of differentiated products (embodied capital services), but the specific qualities traded are indeterminate and so therefore is the value of trade.[14]

One can measure the equilibrium value of home exports of capital services and how this changes as countries become 'less similar', but it should be noted that this may provide an imperfect index of changes in the volume of trade. The results here are familiar: the greater the dissimilarity in endowment ratios, the greater the difference in per capita incomes and the greater the per capita volume of trade in capital services. Increased income dissimilarities from this source are therefore accompanied by increased trade volumes.

To infer something about the likely pattern of trade, one would need further information on the income distribution. The relatively capital-abundant country has the higher per capita income, and hence, with (say) symmetric unimodal income distributions that differ only in their means, widening endowment differences will move the income distributions in the two countries further apart, reducing their range of overlap.[15] One would then anticipate a tenency for the exports of the 'richer' (relatively capital-abundant) country to become more concentrated in the lower-quality products demanded by the 'poorer' country. In extreme cases, the low qualities exported by the rich country may cease to be consumed at home.

3 *Identical endowments but different technologies:* Suppose the home country has a superior technology in the homogeneous product sector, so that $w > w^*$. In this case factor prices are not equalized and the technologically advanced (high-wage) country exports high-quality products and imports low-quality products as above. This case is more complex than case 2 above.

Let M, M^* and M_y^* denote home expenditure on foreign-produced qualities, foreign expenditure on home-produced qualities and foreign expenditure on imports of the homogeneous product, respectively, all measured in units of Y. The balance of trade constraint is $M = M^* + M_y^*$, so that, assuming M_y^* is positive, the total volume of trade is M, the volume of intra-industry trade is M^* $(= \min(M, M^*))$ and the volume of inter-industry trade is $M - M^*$ $(= M_y^*)$. Using (5) aggregated across individuals, we can write

$$\begin{aligned} M &= \{(W_0^* + R_0^*)G + (\alpha+\beta)JF\}N \equiv AN \\ M^* &= \{(W_0 + R_0)\bar{G}^* + (\alpha+\beta)J^*\bar{F}^*\}N^* \equiv A^*N^* \end{aligned} \tag{14}$$

where $W_0 = wx_0 - \alpha I_0$ and $R_0 = rq_0 - \beta I_0$; $J = w + rk$ and $J^* = w^* + r^*k^*$ are the per capita incomes in the two countries; and G and F measure the proportions of the total home population and aggregate home income, respectively, made up of consumers with incomes no greater than the marginal income (I_1).[16] Thus, GN is the number of home consumers with incomes below the margin and FNG is the total income held by these consumers. Foreign parameters are defined analagously, with $\bar{G}^* = 1 - G^*$ and $\bar{F}^* = 1 - F^*$. Given our assumptions on tastes, the relevant properties of the income distributions are captured by these cumulative density functions. We assume that the latter are differentiable in r, k and w.

In principle, (14) is consistent with many patterns of trade depending on technology, endowment and income distribution differences. To isolate their individual influences we begin with an initial equilibrium in which the two countries are as similar as possible, excepting of course their technologies (and hence their factor returns). We therefore add the following assumptions:

1 The two countries have identical factor endowments (eliminating any traditional 'endowment' basis for trade).
2 In the free trade equilibrium, the per capita (and hence total) incomes in the two countries are equal ($J = J^*$). In combination with assumption 1, this requires that $(w - w^*) = (r^* - r)k$.
3 The two countries have identical income distributious (i.e., $F = F^*$ and $G = G^*$).
4 There is no subsistence requirement on the homogeneous product. This is convenient since it implies that $W_0 + R_0 = \Upsilon I_0$ and $W_0^* + R_0^* = \Upsilon I_0^*$.

With these assumptions, the trade pattern is also determined. Identical incomes and distributions imply that the two countries have equal per capita expenditures on the homogeneous product of $E_y = \Upsilon\{J - (I_0^* G + I_0 \bar{G})\}$ (using home notation for common values). The home output of homogeneous products will exceed the foreign output, however, for two reasons. First, home employment in the differentiated product sector is smaller, because the home sector uses higher capital–labour ratios in all its products and the two countries have identical capital stocks. With identical labour forces, this leaves more home labour to be employed in the other sector. Second, home labour is more productive in the homogeneous product sector (i.e., $b < b^*$). Thus $M_y^* > 0$, and $M > M^*$ in this initial free trade equilibrium, as one would expect, given that our assumptions have essentially neutralized the effects of all other variables on the trade pattern.

Underlying the relationship between incomes and trade volume(s) are differences in our three 'parameters' (endowments, technologies and income distributions). With per capita incomes initially equal, any parametric change that does not affect incomes equally will create an income 'differential'. To eliminate the resulting ambiguity as to the direction of parametric changes that actually result in a 'greater divergence' in per capita incomes, we consider only changes whose net effect is to increase the home income relative to the foreign. This recognizes the presumption that, with identical endowments, the home country's superior technology should, if anything, give it the higher per capital income.

Any parametric change will have two effects: an *impact effect* (at constant capital rentals), followed by a *secondary effect* (arising from the induced changes in capital rentals required to restore equilibrium in the capital markets). Letting z denote a general parameter, we have that[17]

$$\frac{dJ}{dz} = J_z + J_r \frac{dr}{dz}$$

and

$$\frac{dA}{dz} = A_z + A_r \frac{dr}{dz} + A_r^* \frac{dr^*}{dz} \tag{15}$$

with analagous expressions for foreign variables. In each case, the first term denotes the impact effect, and the remaining terms the secondary effects.

Since most variables influence these expenditure relationships through similar channels, we examine a few in detail and then simply apply the same terminology and assumptions to the rest. Consider A_r, which captures the effects of a *ceteris paribus* change in the home capital rental on home per capita expenditure on foreign differentiated products. From (14), this can be written as

$$A_r = (1-\Upsilon) FJ_r + \{\Upsilon I_0^* G_r + (1-\Upsilon) JF_r\}.$$

An increase in the home rental then has two types of effect on A. First, there is a positive *income effect*, since home per capita income has increased ($J_r = k > 0$) and a fraction ($(1-\Upsilon)F$)[18] of the induced expenditure increase is allocated to imports of differentiated products. Second, there are *distributional* (*or substitution*) *effects*, which result from the induced changes in the distribution of home incomes (G and F). *A priori*, both G_r and F_r have ambiguous signs. For a given margin (I_1), the increase in capital incomes can be expected to increase the proportion of individuals with incomes above the margin and hence to reduce expenditures on the lower-quality imports. But the increase in r also raises the marginal income and hence raises the proportion below the margin for a given distribution. Taking both effects together, the sign of A_r is ambiguous. However, it seems plausible that, unless there is a mass point in the two distributions at the existing marginal income, the income effect will dominate, and hence an increase in r will be associated with increased home per capita expenditures on imports.

Similarly

$$A_r^* = (1-\beta) Gq_0 + \{\Upsilon I_0^* G_r^* + (1-\Upsilon) JF_r^*\}.$$

In this case the overall sign remains ambiguous. While the income effect is unambiguously positive (reflecting the increase in the cost of foreign subsistence), the distributional effects are unambiguously negative. (An increase in r^* has no effect on home incomes, but does reduce the marginal income, thereby redistributing home consumers towards domestic products.) With no reason to suppose that either effect will necessarily dominate, the sign of A_r^* is truly ambiguous. However, its magnitude is also likely to be relatively small, and we assume its influences can be neglected below.

In the same fashion, one can show that $A_{r^*}^*$ is unambiguously positive (both the income and distribution effects work towards increased foreign per capita expenditures on home differentiated products, with a rise in foreign incomes and an increase in the cost of foreign products), while A_r^* is ambiguous but likely to be small.

We are interested in the effects of parameter changes on the following per capita variables: income differences ($J - J^*$), total trade (A), intra-industry trade (A^*) and inter-industry trade ($A - A^*$). We are also interested in the *range* of qualities traded. The latter requires a knowledge of the maximum and minimum income levels in the two countries, and how these are affected by changes in endowments and technologies. While there are many possibilities, it seems plausible to suppose that the minimum income in each country depends (primarily) on its wage rate, while the maximum income is more heavily influenced by per capita capital income (rk).[19] To simplify the derivations, and to maintain a clear sense of increasing inter-country differences, we consider opposite (offsetting) parameter changes in the two markets.

Let us consider each parameter in turn.

Capital/Labour Endowment Differences

Consider a simultaneous increase in k and decrease in k^* such that, at the initial factor prices, $rdk = -r^*dk^*$. The impact effects on per capita incomes are then equal in magnitude but opposite in sign. The impact effects on the trade measures are obtained from

$$A_k = r(1-\Upsilon)F + \{\Upsilon I_0^* G_k + (1-\Upsilon) JF_k\}$$

and

$$A^*_{k^*} = r^*(1-\Upsilon)\bar{F}^* + \{\Upsilon I_0 \bar{G}^*_{k^*} + (1-\Upsilon) J^*\bar{F}^*{}_{k^*}\}.$$

An increase in k has a positive income effect on A but negative distributional effects (G_k and F_k are both negative). Assuming, as above, that the income effect dominates, $A_k > 0$. An increase in the foreign endowment ratio tends to increase foreign per capita imports on both counts, so $A^*_{k^*}$ is unambiguously positive.

Given that the home (foreign) country specializes in the production of high (low)-income products, the range of qualities traded is effectively determined by the minimum home income, which sets the lower limit on the range of home imports, and the maximum foreign income, which sets the upper limit on the range of foreign imports. The other limit is the common marginal income in each case. With factor prices as yet unaltered, our assumptions on extreme incomes imply that these endowment changes will have raised the home maximum income and reduced the foreign maximum income with both minimum incomes unchanged. The impact effect thus reduces the range of qualities traded.

Turning to the secondary effects, the capital market equilibrium conditions, expressed in per capita expenditure terms, are given by

$$E = (R_0\bar{G} + \beta J\bar{F}) + (R_0\bar{G}^* + \beta J^*\bar{F}^*) - rk = 0$$
$$E^* = (R_0^* G + \beta JF) + (R_0^* G^* + \beta J^* F^*) - r^*k^* = 0.$$

To derive the induced capital rental adjustments, we make the following assumptions on these excess demands: both net own-price effects are negative (E_r, $E^*_{r*} < 0$), both cross-price effects are positive (E_{r*}, $E^*_r > 0$), and equal increases in both rentals lead to excess supplies of both capitals (i.e., own-price effects dominate, so that $E_r + E_{r*} < 0$ and $E^*_r + E^*_{r*} < 0$). Again, this amounts to assuming that income effects dominate distribution effects in the otherwise ambiguous cases (specifically, E_r and E^*_r).

The impact effects of our endowment adjustment in the capital markets are now readily determined. At constant factor prices, the home supply of capital has increased and the foreign supply declined. This has been accompanied by what amounts to an income transfer from the foreign to the home country, whose impact effects on expenditure can be assumed to be approximately offsetting (given identical tastes and income distributions initially). The net result is then an excess supply of home capital and an excess demand for foreign, at the initial rentals. Under our assumptions, this leads to a decline in r and a rise in r^*. The secondary effects of these rental changes on relative incomes, trade volumes and the trade range work in the opposite directions to the impact effects in each case.

Although we therefore expect ambiguity in the total effects, some outcomes are clear. If the adjustments in rentals were to completely neutralize the impact of the endowment changes on per capita incomes, then rk and r^*k^* would be as initially. But even without income effects, demands would still change with the shift in the marginal income. Both rental changes tend to reduce I_1, yielding an excess demand for home capital and an excess supply of foreign. Capital rentals will not therefore adjust to this degree, implying a net increase in home per capita income and a net decline in foreign per capita income, thus 'widening the income gap'. In addition, with higher home and lower foreign maximum incomes, but no change in minimum incomes, there is a consequent reduction in the range of qualities traded.[20]

The total effects on trade volumes remain ambiguous. The increased home per capita income tends to raise A, but the lower marginal income tends to reduce it; similarly for A^*. Whether the impact or secondary effects dominate depends on the relative magnitudes of the income and distributional effects. If a presumption exists it might be that the impact effects will dominate. At least, this is true for relative incomes, in which case wider income differences would be accompanied by increased volumes of total and inter-industry trade, but a reduced volume of intra-industry trade and range of trade. In any event, there seems to be little reason to expect that per capita income differences induced by factor endowment differences will be reflected in *reduced* per capita total trade volumes.

Technology Differences

Consider a simultaneous decrease in b and increase in b^* such that $dw = -dw^* > 0$. Again, the impact effects on per capita incomes are equal in magnitude but opposite in sign. The impact effect on the home per capita trade volume is given by $A_w dw + A_{w*} dw^*$, where $A_w = (1-\Upsilon)F + (\Upsilon I_0^* G_w + (1-\Upsilon) JF_w)$ and $A_{w*} = \Upsilon x_0 G + (\Upsilon I_0^* G_{w*} + (1-\Upsilon) JF_{w*})$. One expects A_{w*} to be of the same order of magnitude as A_{r*} and hence negligible. If one assumes that the positive income effect of the increase in w dominates any possibly offsetting consequences of the ambiguous distributional effects, one has $A_w > 0$, and home per capita imports are increased. Similarly, taking A_{w*} as negligible and A^*_{w*} as positive, foreign per capita imports decline. Since these wage adjustments raise the home minimum income, they also reduce the range of trade.

The capital market adjustments can be determined as for the endowment change. Again, the income effects are approximately offsetting, but both wage changes tend to raise the marginal income level, switching expenditure from home to foreign capital services. This reduces the home rental and raises the foreign, generating secondary effects with the same signs as for the endowment change.

To determine the total effects, again suppose that r and r^* were to adjust sufficiently to leave per capita incomes unchanged. The initial wage rate changes and induced rental changes have opposing effects on I_1, so we may suppose that any resulting change in I_1 is also small. Then the only significant changes in the capital markets would be the decline in rk and increase in r^*k^*, implying that at these rentals there is an excess demand for home capital and an excess supply of foreign capital. Thus, as before, rentals will not adjust sufficiently to offset the impact effects on per capita incomes. Under our assumptions, the rise in w and decline in rk indicate a narrower income range at home, and conversely in the foreign country. The net effect on the range of trade is ambiguous, however, since both the minimum home and maximum foreign incomes have increased.

The total effects on trade volumes are again ambiguous. While the income effects are clear, the direction and magnitude of the effects of any change in the marginal income are unknown. If one is prepared to assume that the effects of the factor price adjustments on I_1 are approximately offsetting, however, then the income effects will dominate and the total effects will have the same sign as the impact effects, but with reduced magnitudes. In this case a wider 'technology gap' would imply wider income differences accompanied by increased volumes of total and inter-industry trade, but a reduced volume of intra-industry trade.

Income Distribution Differences

In this framework, shifts in the income distribution can have no impact effects on per capita incomes, and impact the trade volumes only to the extent that incomes and individuals are shifted from one side of the margin to the other. Similarly, any induced change in capital rentals will depend on the shifts in demand for capital services from the two sources.

Consider, for example, equal but opposite shifts about the margin in the two income distributions – say, $dG = -dG^* > 0$, $dF = -dF^* > 0$. These offsetting changes leave the demands for capital unaffected and hence induce no changes in capital rentals. The total effect thus leaves per capita incomes unchanged, but increases A and A^*. Total trade increases, as does intra-industry trade, and inter-industry trade declines slightly ($d(A-A^*) = -\Upsilon(I_0 - I_0^*)dG$).

This example illustrates that the trade volume depends on how income is distributed at any given income level. Some distributions will imply more trade than others. However, there is unlikely to be any predictable relationship between income distribution differences and trade volumes. Similar arguments apply to the range of trade.

5 CONCLUSIONS

Our aim in this paper has been to establish a structure in which intra- and inter-industry trade coexist, without relying on the existence of increasing returns to scale or imperfect competition. This is not intended to deny that increasing returns and imperfect competition are important considerations for trade theory, particularly intra-industry trade; but they do not appear to be prerequisites for the existence of such trade, and as yet they have contributed little by the way of direct explanation for its pattern. In part, the latter may be attributable to concentration on horizontal rather than vertical product differentiation. Vertical product differentiation allows the production of various qualities to be allocated among countries on the basis of 'comparative advantage' in the usual way. Such an allocation can occur because different qualities can reasonably be presumed to differ in their factor input requirements. The same will not necessarily be true for horizontally differentiated products, as their factor input requirements are unlikely to differ greatly, implying either that all varieties will be produced in the same location, or that the allocation between locations will be essentially arbitrary. Thus, while economies of scale explain why any variety will be produced in only one location, the don't specify which location. Either production locations are arbitrary and immaterial, or they are determined by relative costs in the traditional fashion.

The model constructed above has relied wherever possible on familiar components. Clearly, the approach is not tied to these simplifying assumptions, but they do allow its main features to be highlighted with a minimum of distraction. Unequal incomes were introduced as a way of generating demands for a variety of vertically differentiated products. By translating these product demands through the underlying implicit input demands into the factor markets, one can apply familiar techniques (such as aggregation via an indirect utility function).

It is important to distinguish the roles that technology (Ricardian) and factor endowment (Heckscher–Ohlin) differences play in our framework. With identical technologies, factor endowment differences lead to a predictable pattern of inter-industry trade. The relatively capital-abundant country will be a net exporter of embodied capital services. But with more products than factors, the mixture of qualities that this will involve cannot be specified *ex ante*. Intra-industry trade may or may not occur. Technology differences then provided a way of determining a precise pattern of intra-industry trade in differentiated products. To be sure of generating and explaining two types of trade, one appears to need two independent explanations for trade.

Two further points. First, despite the assumed continuity of incomes, 'gaps' appear in the range of differentiated products demanded, coinciding with changes in the location of production. This implies that vertically differentiated products from particular locations will be 'distinguishable', in terms of both quality and price, and that models of the Armington (1969) type, which differentiate products by their locations of production, may represent a useful empirical approximation.

Finally, the relationship between the trade volume and income differences in this model appears to be a multi-dimensional one. In this structure, as in the monopolistically competitive trade models, the Linder hypothesis – that trade will be more intense between countries with similar per capita incomes – would seem to be restricted to intra-industry trade and the range of products traded.

NOTES

1 For the main ideas the reader is referred Lancaster (1980a), Helpman (1981), Dixit and Norman (1980), Falvey (1981), Brander (1981), Kierzkowski (1984) and Krugman (1979).
2 These alternative approaches are surveyed in Helpman (1984) and Kierzkowski (1985).
3 An exception is Shaked and Sutton (1984).
4 Mayer (1984) uses the distribution of factor ownership (income) to explain the determination of tariff rates through majority voting.
5 Deardorff (1984) and Helpman (1984) are examples of the latter approach. An alternative, though less appealing, approach is to use transport costs to determine the pattern of trade; see Hong (1970) and Krugman (1980).
6 Recall that an indeterminate pattern (but not level) of intra-industry trade is a feature of the existing models of trade in differentiated products. Since the role of technology is not our main interest here, technological differences are taken in their simplest (Ricardian) form. This also has the advantage that, because the Ricardian structure is so familiar, it is relatively straightforward to disentangle the role of technology from the other features of our framework.
7 These and the other simplifying assumptions that follow are intended to maintain trade theory's traditional emphasis on simplicity of structure by using as many familiar features as is feasible.
8 More generally, one could assume an indirect utility function over implicit factor demands in Gorman Polar Form (see Woodland, 1982, ch. 6). This would avoid the assumption of fixed 'discretionary expenditure' shares that is implied by (4), but otherwise would alter little of what follows. In (4), $U(x,q,y)$ is what

Blackorby, Boyce and Russell (1978) refer to as an 'affinely homothetic function', that is, one that is homothetic to a point that is not (necessarily) the origin. This non-homotheticity is necessary to ensure that relative prices do not determine a unique optimal quality for all consumers independent of their income (i.e., if $x_0 = q_0 = 0$, then $s = q/x = (\beta/\alpha)\ (w/r)$, which is independent of income). Further, to ensure that consumers with higher incomes buy higher-quality products (i.e., that $\partial s/\partial I$ is positive), we require that $\beta w x_0 > \alpha r q_0$ at all times.

9 Deardorff (1983) uses a similar diagram to explain trade patterns in a multi-country Heckscher–Ohlin model with a continuum of products.

10 In fact, $U_0 = \alpha^\alpha \beta^\beta \Upsilon^\Upsilon$.

11 This assumes identical subsistence bundles in the two countries. If 'subsistence' is to some extent socially determined, one would expect the lower-income (wage) foreign country to have lower subsistence requirements, so that this inequality would be preserved. In any event, it is important to note that we implicitly assume that 'subsistence requirements' *cannot* be satisfied in a separate location from the rest of consumers' purchases; otherwise, there would be only one subsistence expenditure $I_0^* = \min\ (I_0, I_0^*)$.

12 The budget constraint facing each consumer is convex in the quality dimension as a result of the nonlinear price schedule (11). This feature, in combination with the concave utility function, results in an intermediate range of consumption bundles not being demanded.

13 This supply-side structure is of course the focus of the monopolistic competition models of Krugman, *inter alia*.

14 One could appeal to transport cost minimization to obtain a specific trade pattern.

15 For non-unimodal distributions, this range of overlap may expand or contract of course; see Economides (1984), for an instance.

16 Let $n(I)$ denote the number of individuals whose incomes equal I. Then $n(I)/N$ is the proportion of individuals with income I, and $n(I)\ (I/NJ)$ is the proportion of total income held by individuals with income I. Aggregating, one has

$$G = \int^{I_1} \frac{n(I)}{N}\, dI \quad \text{and} \quad F = \int^{I_1} \frac{n(I)I}{NJ}\, dI.$$

17 Subscripts denote the appropriate partial derivative; e.g., $A_r \equiv \partial A/\partial r$.

18 Note that the proportion of income spent on products from any specific source is not constant in this model, owing to changes in I_1 etc. This mitigates the restrictiveness of the constancy of α, β and Υ.

19 Alternatively, one might assume that both extreme incomes move in the same direction as per capita income.

20 One would have the same outcome if extreme incomes moved in the same direction as average income.

REFERENCES

Armington, Paul S. (1969). The theory of demand for products distinguished by place of production. *International Monetary Fund Staff Papers*, 16, 159–78.

Bhagwati, Jagdish, N. (1982). Shifting comparative advantage, protectionist demands, and policy response. Chapter 6 in J. N. Bhagwati (ed.), *Import Competition and Response*. Chicago: University of Chicago Press for the National Bureau of Economic Research.

Blackorby, Charles, Boyce, Richard and Russell, R. Robert (1978). Estimation of demand systems generated by the gorman polar form. A generalization of the S-branch utility tree. *Econometica*, 46, 345–63.

Brander, James A. (1981). Intra-industry trade in identical commodities. *Journal of International Economics*, 11, 1–14.

Chamberlin, E. H. (1933). *The Theory of Monopolistic Competition*. Cambridge, Mass.: Harvard University Press.

Deardorff, Alan V. (1983). The directions of developing countries trade: examples from pure theory. University of Michigan, mimeo.

Deardorff, Alan V. (1984). An exposition and exploration of Krueger's trade model. *Canadian Journal of Economics*, 17, 731–46.

Dixit, Avinash and Norman, Victor (1980). *Theory of International Trade*. Cambridge: Cambridge University Press.

Economides, Nicholas (1984). Do increases in preference similarity (across countries) induce increases in trade? *Journal of International Economics*, 17, 374–81.

Falvey, Rodney E. (1981). Commercial policy and intra-industry trade. *Journal of International Economics*, 11, 495–511.

Feenstra, Robert C. (1982). Product creation and trade patterns: a theoretical note on the 'biological' model of trade in similar products. Appendix to chapter 6 in J. N. Bhagwati (ed.), *Import Competition and Response*. Chicago: University of Chicago Press for the National Bureau of Economic Research.

Helpman, Elhanan (1981). International trade in the presence of product differentiation, economics of scale and monopolistic competition: a Chamberlin–Heckscher–Ohlin approach. *Journal of International Economics*, 11, 305–40.

Helpman, Elhanan (1984). Increasing returns, imperfect markets, and trade theory. Chapter 7 in R. W. Jones and P. B. Kenen (eds), *Handbook of International Economics*, vol. 1. Amsterdam: North-Holland.

Hong, Wontack (1970). The Heckscher–Ohlin theory of factor price equalization and the indeterminacy in international specialisation. *International Economic Review*, 11, 328–33.

Kierzkowski, Henryk (ed.) (1984). *Monopolistic Competition and International Trade*. Oxford: Oxford University Press.

Kierzkowski, Henryk (1985). Models of trade in differentiated goods. In D. Greenaway (ed.), *Current Issues in International Trade*. London: Macmillan.

Krugman, Paul R. (1979). Increasing returns, monopolistic competition, and international trade. *Journal of International Economics*, 9, 469–79.

Krugman, Paul R. (1980). Scale economies, product differentiation, and the pattern of trade. *American Economic Review*, 70, 950–9.

Lancaster, Kelvin (1980a). Intra-industry trade under perfect monopolistic competition. *Journal of International Economics*, 10, 151–75.

Lancaster Kelvin (1980b). *Variety, Equity and Efficiency*. Oxford: Basil Blackwell.

Linder, Staffan B. (1961). *An Essay on Trade and Transformation*. New York: John Wiley.

Mayer, Wolfgang (1984). Endogenous tariff formation. *American Economic Review*, 74, 970–85.

Shaked, Avner and Sutton, John (1984). Natural oligopolies and international trade. In H. Kierzkowski (ed.), *Monopolistic Competition and International Trade*. Oxford: Oxford University Press.

Woodland, Alan (1982). *International Trade and Resource Allocation*. Amsterdam: North-Holland.

12
Intermediate Goods, Export Taxation and Resource-based Industrialization

Ronald Findlay

The concept of effective protection, which is one of Max Corden's best-known contributions to our field, reminds us of the significance and special character of the role of intermediate goods in international trade. Until recently this is a topic that has been curiously neglected in trade theory. Our typical practice of defining domestic production possibilities *independently* of imported intermediate inputs cannot, as Lionel McKenzie (1954) long ago pointed out, handle such a simple and obvious fact as that England's main export for many decades after the Industrial Revolution – cotton textiles – could not have been produced domestically at all in the absence of imports of raw cotton. This points to the need for an addition to the tool kit of trade theory, a simple model that focuses directly on the role of exports and imports of raw materials in exchange for finished goods – in other words, a 'vertical' as opposed to a 'horizontal' view of the pattern of international exchange in terms of final goods alone.[1]

My purpose in this paper is to present such a model in terms of some simple diagrams of the sort that I hope Max, as an afficionado of trade geometry, will like.[2] After constructing the model, I will apply it to a fascinating episode in the economic history of England, which I first became aware of when Carlos Diaz Alejandro and I visited Max at Nuffield in the autumn of 1975. One of the books on economic history from the Nuffield library that I read during my monastic sojourn was the brilliant monograph on the medieval English wool industry by Eileen Power (1941). In discussing Edward III's tax on exports of raw wool, implemented to finance the start of the Hundred Years War, she pointed out that, while the tax had led to a sharp reduction in exports of raw wool, it had stimulated the domestic woolen cloth industry, which had received 'most *effective protection*' from the export tax on its essential intermediate input. I showed Max the quote, and teased him about having been anticipated on effective protection by Eileen Power. During that same visit Max and Dorothy took Carlos and me on a memorable trip through the Cotswolds, where we visited the little town of Chipping Campden, a famous center for the medieval wool trade. We talked about economic history as a source of problems for trade theory, and Max said that we should have 'Cliotheoretics' along with Cliometrics. I verbally sketched a model that Max encouraged me to write up. He may have been joking, but here, ten years later, is my joint offering to Max, Clio and the muse of economics, whoever she may be.

1 THE MODEL

The economy consists of two sectors, one producing a raw material denoted R, and the other a final product, F, which uses R as an input. The production function for the raw material is

$$R = R(L_R, T) \tag{1}$$

where L_R denotes labor engaged in the production of the raw material and T is land, in fixed supply. We assume that R exhibits constant returns to scale, and diminishing returns to labor. The production function for the final output is

$$F = F(L_F, R_F) \tag{2}$$

where L_F and R_F are the inputs of labor and raw material into the production of the final output. We suppose that F also exhibits constant returns to scale, and that L_F and R_F are smoothly substitutable for each other, above a certain minimum level for each.

The constraints on the inputs are that

$$L_R + L_F = \bar{L} \tag{3}$$

$$R_F + R_E = R \tag{4}$$

where $\bar{L}$ is the fixed supply of labor available to the economy and R_E is the export of the raw material. The sole consumption good is the final output F, and thus, whatever imports are obtained in exchange for R_E will consist of the final good itself. In the absence of foreign trade, R_E will of course be zero.

Figure 12.1 immediately indicates the solution in the absence of foreign trade possibilities. The distance OO' measures $\bar{L}$, the fixed amount of labor available to the economy, with L_R measured from O and L_F from O'. The curve OR indicates the output of R as a function of L_R, from (1). The production function (2) is indicated by isoquants with origin at O', showing inputs of L_F and R_F necessary to produce any specified level of output.

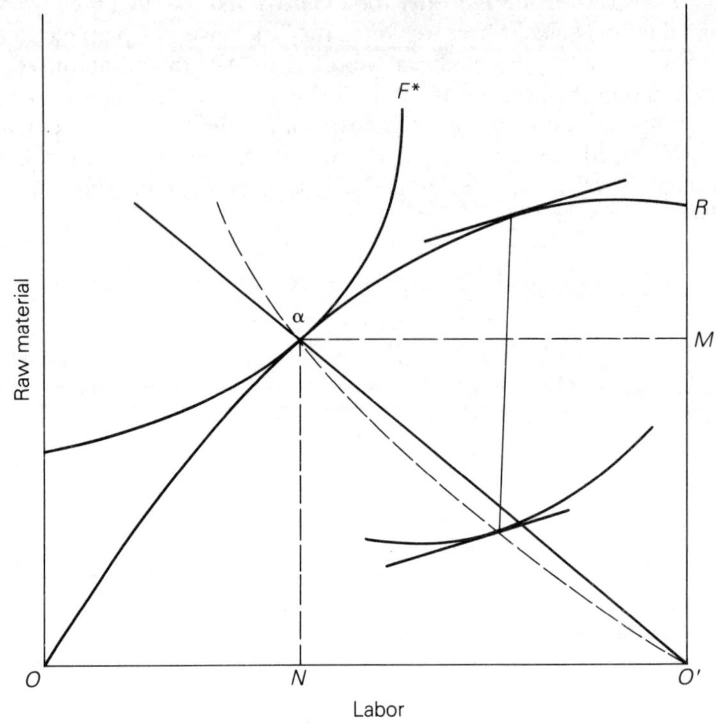

Figure 12.1

Consider the point α on OR, at which it is tangent to the isoquant F^*. The point α determines L_R as ON, L_F as $O'N$ and R as $O'M$. This is the pattern of resource allocation that results in F^* being the *maximum* output of F that is attainable, given technology and the total labor input available. The slope of OR at α is the marginal physical productivity of labor in the raw material sector, while the slope of F^* at α is the marginal rate of substitution between L_F and R_F in the sector producing final output. The marginal products of R_F and L_F are uniquely determined by the ratio of these variables to each other, indicated by the slope of the ray $O'\alpha$, because of the assumption of constant returns to scale in the F-sector. The relative price of the raw material in terms of the final output will be equal to the ratio of the marginal products of labor in the F-sector and the R-sector, respectively.

All these relations follow from profit maximization by price-taking producers. This results in

$$P_R \frac{\partial R}{\partial L_R} = w \tag{5}$$

$$P_F \frac{\partial F}{\partial L_F} = w \tag{6}$$

$$P_F \frac{\partial F}{\partial R_F} = P_R \tag{7}$$

where P_R and P_F are the nominal prices of R and F and w is the nominal wage. From these conditions it follows that

$$\frac{\partial R}{\partial L_R} = \frac{\partial F}{\partial L_F} / \frac{\partial F}{\partial R_F} \tag{8}$$

which is the tangency condition holding at the point α in figure 12.1. We also see that

$$p \equiv \frac{P_R}{P_F} = \frac{\partial F}{\partial R_F} = \frac{\partial F}{\partial L_F} / \frac{\partial R}{\partial L_R}. \tag{9}$$

National income, denoted Y, can be seen to equal

$$Y = F - \frac{P_R}{P_F} R + \frac{P_R}{P_F} R = \frac{w}{P_F}(L_R + L_F) + \frac{r}{P_F} T = F \tag{10}$$

where w/P_F and r/P_F are the real wage and rent per unit of land, measured in terms of final output. When F is equal to F^*, all other variables in (10) are at their corresponding unique equilibrium values.

We can now extend the analysis to an open economy. In order to do this, consider figure 12.2. It shows, for any given level of F, the maximum amount R_E, which from (4) is equal to $(R - R_F)$, that is attainable by the economy. In other words, it is the maximum surplus of R over the requirements for the given level of F. Clearly, when F is at zero the maximum possible R_E is equal to the output of R corresponding to the entire labor force being assigned to the raw material sector, measured by the distance $O'R$ in figure 12.1. When F is equal to F^*, the maximum amount of R_E is zero. The curve RF^* shows the maximum value of R_E for any value of F between zero and F^*.

How is the frontier RF^* derived? For each specified level of F, locate the corresponding isoquant in figure 12.1. We must then maximize R_E, subject to R_F and L_F being on this specified isoquant. It is easy to see that R_E is maximized subject to this requirement when the vertical distance between OR and the isoquant is maximized, that is, when the slope of OR is equal to the slope of the isoquant at a point vertically below it. As we reduce F^* toward zero, the corresponding maximized value of R_E rises from zero to the maximum attainable level indicated by $O'R$ in figure 12.1, when the entire labor force is allocated to the R-sector.

The dashed curve $O'\alpha$ in figure 12.1 is the locus of all such 'efficient points' on each F-isoquant. At any point on this locus the slope of the F-isoquant

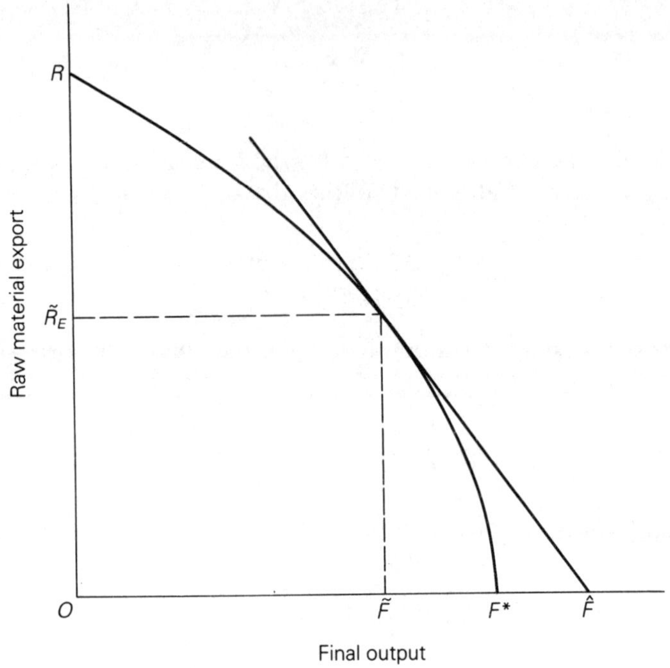

Figure 12.2

passing through it is equal to the slope of OR at the point vertically above it. The ratio of R_F to L_F rises along $O'\alpha$ as we move from O' to α, indicating that the marginal productivity of labor in the F-sector is rising and that of the raw material is falling.

To any given value of the price ratio p, the corresponding supplies of F and R_E will be indicated by the point on RF^* in figure 12.2 at which its slope is equal to the value of p, that is, where the marginal rate of transformation of F into R_E is equal to p. As the relative price of the raw material is increased, the supply of R_E increases and the supply of F falls. Whatever the parametric value of p, it is clear that the marginal productivity conditions (5)–(7), and hence (8)–(9), always hold, ensuring that production is indeed on the 'efficient' frontier RF^* in figure 12.2, corresponding to the dashed locus $O'\alpha$ in figure 12.1. Production of F is maximized at F^*, corresponding to the lowest possible value of p, the relative price of the raw material.

So far we have varied p only parametrically. Its value in the open economy now has to be determined. To do this, suppose, for simplicity, that the foreign country is completely specialized on the production of the final good, in other words that it lacks the natural resources necessary for domestic production of the raw material. Given its technology and labor force, there will be a negatively sloped demand curve for the home country's export of the raw

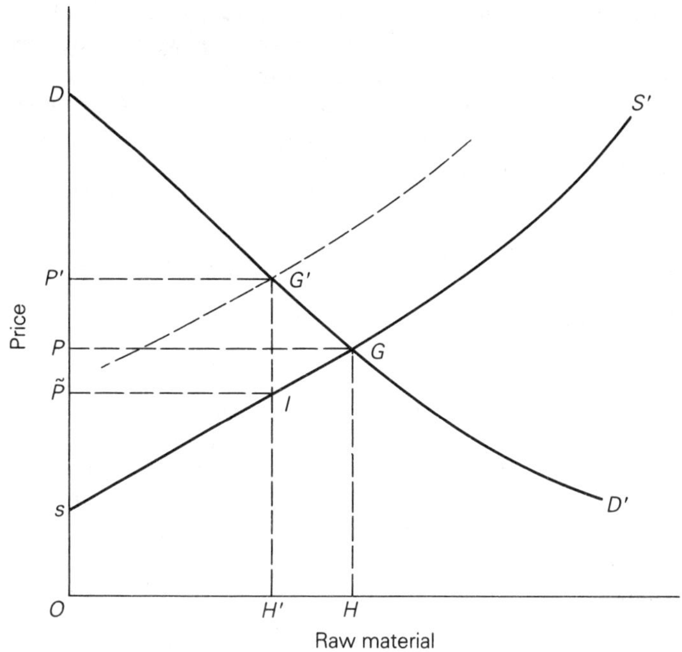

Figure 12.3

material, as depicted by the DD' curve in figure 12.3. The positively sloped curve SS' is the home country's supply curve for R_E, derived in the manner described in the previous paragraph. Intersection of the two curves at G determines the equilibrium value OP of the terms of trade between raw materials and final output and the level of raw material exports as OH. The rectangular area $OPGH$ is the value of final goods imports obtained by the home country, while the triangular area DPG is the national income (value added) of the foreign country.

In figure 12.2 the equilibrium solution is depicted by production levels $\tilde{F}$ and $\tilde{R}_E$ corresponding to the point on RF^* where its slope is equal to OP. Imports of F are equal to the difference between total consumption $O\hat{F}$ and production $O\tilde{F}$. The 'gains from trade' can be measured physically by the distance between OF^* and $O\hat{F}$. By reducing domestic output of F from F^* to $\tilde{F}$ and exporting the $\tilde{R}_E$ obtained as a result, the home economy is able to increase its consumption of the final good to $\hat{F}$ from F^*.

Finally, we may note the strong implications for income distribution of the export possibilities for raw materials. The marginal product of land rises in terms of the raw material, since more labor is now employed in that sector. Since the price of the raw material rises in terms of final output, the rent per unit of land must therefore go up in terms of final output as well, so landowners are clearly better off. The marginal product of labor falls in terms of raw material, since more labor is employed in the *R*-sector with the supply of land unchanged. Reduction of the output of the *F*-sector, movement along the locus $O'\alpha$ towards O', can be seen to result in a lower ratio of R_F to L_F, and hence to a fall in the real wage in terms of final output as well. Thus labor is worse off as a result of the export of the raw material. Stolper–Samuelson therefore holds in this model.

2 THE MEDIEVAL ENGLISH WOOL TRADE

Our mental image of the British economy these days is of the once-mighty 'workshop of the world,' pioneer of the Industrial Revolution, which, after reaching its 'climacteric' in the 1890s, gradually lost ground to the competition from Germany and the United States, sliding into the lower ranks of the contemporary industrial powers. We very seldom think of Britain's earlier economic history, when the country was a raw material exporter on the 'periphery' of the late medieval European economy, with its flourishing industrial centers in Flanders and northern Italy. It is to this period that I would like to apply the model of the previous section.

The writings of Eileen Power, M. M. Postan (1973, 1975) and E. M. Carus-Wilson (1967) have informed us of the extent to which this late medieval English economy prospered on the basis of the production and export of raw wool, derived from the fleece of what are estimated to have been up to 18 million sheep at the peak of this era. We all know that the Chancellor of the Exchequer sits on the Woolsack: as Postan puts it, the 'majesty of England,' and not just the Chancellor's posterior, rested on this foundation for several centuries. King Richard I may have had the heart of a lion, but his ransom when he was captured on his return from the Crusades was paid in the wool from 6 million sheep. This late medieval English economy underwent a transformation from exporting raw wool to 'resource-based' industrialization that increasingly absorbed these wool supplies as intermediate inputs for the domestic woolen cloth industry.[3] This 'import substitution' phase was followed by eventual export of woolen cloth, which was a leading export until displaced by cotton textiles based on *imports* of raw cotton during the Industrial Revolution.

According to an old historical fable, related by Postan (1973, p. 216), this transformation was achieved at one stroke by King Edward III in the 1330s, by restricting the export of raw wool and inviting Flemish weavers to England to develop a woolen cloth industry on the basis of the formerly exported raw material. Shades of 'economic nationalism' and 'industrialization by invitation,' which we usually associate with the developing countries of today! As Postan says, the truth revealed by this tale is the fact that Edward III, urgently needing revenue to finance the war that he was waging against the French (the start of the so-called Hundred Years War), placed a heavy tax on the export of raw wool. This naturally reduced the domestic price of the raw material in England, providing the 'most effective protection' to the cloth industry that Eileen Power referred to. The Flemish weavers, on the other hand, faced a higher price for the imported input, thus giving them an incentive to relocate production in England. As Postan observes, the important question is not why the Flemish weavers were invited but why they accepted.

The economies of England and Flanders, according to Postan (p. 213), were joined together in a 'natural symbiosis,' with the latter country being one of the 'wonder stories of medieval economic history.' Indeed, the factors that Postan cites, such as the peace and orderly government of the strong Counts of Flanders, the density of population and a lack of natural resources under the Flemish cities, seem very much like Hong Kong and Singapore in our own time.

The two 'countries' of our model thus conform reasonably well to the 'stylized facts' of the medieval economic system of the wool trade as described by Postan.

The effects of an export tax can be readily ascertained in the context of our model. For any given value of the terms of trade p, the domestic relative price of the material will now fall to $(1-t)p$ where t is the rate at which raw material exports are taxed. This will induce a movement along RF^* in figure 12.2, which results in an increase in F and a reduction in R_E, since the gross output of R falls while the domestic demand R_F rises. Assuming that all of the tax revenue is spent on the final good, this reduced amount of R_E at each p will be the supply of exports. In terms of figure 12.3, this means that the supply curve of raw material exports has shifted to the left, resulting in an improvement in the terms of trade from OP to OP' and a fall in the domestic relative price of the raw material from OP to $O\tilde{P}$. The area $\tilde{P}P'G'I$ in figure 12.3 represents the proceeds of the export tax.

Thus, production and employment in the R-sector decline, while both increase in the F-sector. The volume of raw material exports declines from OH to OH' in figure 12.3, on account of both the fall in R and the rise in R_F; but the relative price of these exports in terms of the final output has risen. The foreign country has a lower volume of raw material imports at a higher price in terms of final product and so is clearly worse off as a result of the imposition of the export tax.

The 'welfare' effects of the export tax on the home country depend upon the level of the tax. Since the country clearly has a degree of monopoly power in its external trade, the familiar 'optimum tariff' argument applies to the case of an export tax as well, because of the symmetry between taxes on imports and on exports. The optimum export tax in this model is the level that maximizes domestic consumption (private plus government) of the final product. Denoting domestic consumption of the final product as F_c, the problem is to

$$\max F_c = F(R_E) + p(R_E)R_E \tag{11}$$

where $F(R_E)$ is the level of domestic production, which varies inversely with the level of R_E as depicted in the frontier RF^* in figure 12.2, and $p(R_E)R_E$ is the level of imports of the final good. From the first-order condition for a maximum, we have the well-known monopoly solution.

$$-\frac{dF}{dR_E}=p(1-1/\eta) \tag{12}$$

where η is the elasticity of foreign demand for the raw material, so that (12) can be interpreted as the equality of domestic marginal cost of raw material exports with the marginal revenue arising therefrom. The level of the optimum export tax, denoted τ, is readily obtained from the condition that the *domestic* price ratio, $(1-\tau)p$, will be equal to each side of (12), yielding

$$\tau=\frac{1}{\eta}. \tag{13}$$

Domestic consumption of the final good increases with the level of the export tax up to τ, at which its maximum is reached. It declines thereafter, reaching the autarky level F^* when the export tax becomes prohibitive.

National wefare, as reflected in domestic consumption of the final good, is not however likely to have been the objective of a fourteenth-century monarch. Maximum revenue is a likelier consideration. We can accordingly assume that the export tax is set so as to

$$\max\ V=\{p^D(R_E)-p^S(R_E)\}R_E \tag{14}$$

where V is government revenue, p^D is the demand price for raw material exports, paid by the foreign country and corresponding to the terms of trade, and p^s is the supply price of raw material exports, corresponding to the *domestic* price ratio, the difference between the two prices constituting the tax itself. The first-order condition for a maximum of (14) can be expressed as

$$\frac{R^S}{p^D}=\frac{(\eta-1)}{\eta(1+1/\sigma)} \tag{15}$$

where σ is the elasticity of domestic supply of the raw material. The maximum revenue export tax, denoted θ, is therefore

$$\theta=1-\frac{R^S}{p^D}=\frac{(1+\eta/\sigma)}{\eta(1+1/\sigma)}. \tag{16}$$

Since $\eta>1$, it follows that $\theta>\tau$; in other words, the rate of export tax that maximizes revenue will be *greater* than that which maximizes domestic consumption. Since the 'wedge' between p^D and p^S created by the export tax is greater in the maximum revenue case, it follows that p^D must be higher, and p^S and R_E lower, than in the case of maximum consumption. The foreign country will thus be even worse off under θ than under τ, since it will receive a more restricted level of raw material imports at a correspondingly higher price. The domestic production of the raw material will also decline even further under θ than under τ, but the output of the final good and domestic intermediate demand for the raw material will be further enhanced. Real wages will be correspondingly higher and rents lower. Domestic consumption of the final good may be higher or lower than under free trade, though of course less than under the 'optimum' export tax.

Thus the King's concern with revenue, intended to be used solely for the conduct of war, can nevertheless result in an alteration of the structure of relative prices so as to bring about a substantial degree of 'effective protection' for industrialization. The activities of kings, perhaps even more than those of Adam Smith's butchers and bakers, can cause the invisible hand to promote ends that were no part of their intention.

NOTES

1 See also Kemp and Ohyama (1978), Findlay (1979) and Sanyal and Jones (1982).

2 This model will be a development of an approach outlined in the third section of Findlay (1985).

3 See Roemer (1979) for an excellent discussion related to contemporary less developed countries.

REFERENCES

Carus-Wilson, E. M. (1967). *Medieval Merchant Venturers*. London: Methuen.

Findlay, R. (1979). Economic development and the theory of international trade. *American Economic Review*, 69, 186–90.

Findlay, R. (1985). Primary exports, manufacturing and development. In M. Lundahl (ed.), *The Primary Sector in Economic Development*. London: Croom Helm.

Kemp, M. C. and Ohyama, M. (1978). On the sharing of trade gains by resource-poor and resource-rich countries. *Journal of International Economics*, 8, 93–115.

McKenzie, L. W. (1954). Specialization and efficiency in world production. *Review of Economics Studies*, 21, 165–80.

Postan, M. M. (1973). *Medieval Trade and Finance*. Cambridge: Cambridge University Press.

Postan, M. M. (1975). *The Medieval Economy and Society*. Harmondsworth, Middx: Penguin Books.

Power, E. E. (1941). *The Wool Trade in English Medieval History*. Oxford: Oxford University Press.

Roemer, M. (1979). Resource-based industrialization in the developing countries. *Journal of Development Economics*, 6, 163–202.

Sanyal, K. and Jones, R. W. (1982). The theory of trade in middle products. *American Economic Review*, 72, 16–31.

13
The Importance of Economic Policy in Development: Contrasts between Korea and Turkey

Anne O. Krueger

In the early years of thinking about development, the majority of policy-makers and development economists were skeptical – to put it mildly – about the importance of the traditional 'neoclassical' analysis and policy prescriptions. In no field was this more true than international trade, where doubts were expressed about the rate at which developing countries could expand their exports (elasticity pessimism), the probable future of terms of trade for primary commodities and the ability of developing countries to experience satisfactory industrial growth in the absence of high walls of protection surrounding their infant industries.

Three phenomena proved that much of that skepticism was ill-founded. First, empirical evidence failed to support elasticity pessimism with regard to the terms of trade. Second, analytical developments revealed difficulties with a protectionist strategy even beyond those that had earlier been pointed out by advocates of free trade. Third, experience in developing countries that adopted protectionist strategies proved less satisfactory than had been anticipated, while those developing countries that adopted more outer-oriented trade strategies had performance that usually exceeded expectations.

Of the analytical developments that were important, development of the concept of effective protection was certainly key. In demonstrating that the same nominal tariff rate might imply very different rates of protection to value added for producers of different specific items, the concept served to underscore the infeasibility of a 'rational' protective structure: the only

I am indebted to Bela Balassa, Vittorio Corbo, Kemal Dervis, Kwang Suk Kim, Chong Nam, Julio Nogues, Sarath Rajapatirana and Rusdu Saracoglu for helpful comments on an earlier draft of this paper.

uniform effective tariff was a uniform nominal tariff, which, in turn, implied a zero rate of protection or uniform nominal tariffs and export subsidies once it was recognized that tariffs did not affect the prices of exportables.

Max Corden's seminal work on effective protection was a key element in the gradual shift in thinking about trade policy in relation to development. His emphasis, in both his teaching and his research, on the importance of trade policy, and his contributions to trade policy discussions, helped focus attention on the importance of these issues, and influenced both his colleagues and a generation of students. His careful, straightforward, analytical approach did much to clarify the issues and to speed the time when policies might shift.

Although good theory can inform policy decisions, it cannot by itself yield guidance as to the quantitative importance of those decisions. Moreover, most policies are implemented in an environment where myriad other changes are occurring simultaneously, and it is often difficult for the analyst, based on the experience of a single country, to infer the quantitative importance of a particular change. Hence, a variety of other methods of attempting to assess the quantitative importance of policy shifts are needed, none of which, in and of itself, can prove conclusive but which, through the weight of cumulative evidence, can permit firmer judgements to form.

One such method involves a comparison of countries with different policy regimes. An interesting pair is Turkey and Korea, the subject of this essay. Both started out, in the 1950s, with a legacy of highly restrictive trade policies and severe macroeconomic imbalances. Turkey maintained a broadly restrictionist trade strategy until 1980, whereas Korea shifted in the early 1960s. While all countries have unique circumstances that make any comparison subject to numerous qualifications, the similarities and differences between these two countries make an interesting case study that demonstrates the importance of trade policy, and therefore of Corden's contributions, in the development process. An essay on the contrasts between Turkish and Korean experience therefore seems an appropriate tribute to him.

Out of this contrast, the lesson that 'policies matter' emerges clearly. Any observer of developing countries in the 1950s would have concluded that, in almost all regards, Turkey had the more favorable development prospects. The Korean reforms of the early 1960s, however, led to a fundamental transformation of the economy. Although Turkey also undertook some necessary changes in policy in the late 1950s, the reforms centered only on immediate correction of macroeconomic imbalances, and did not encompass any overhaul of the incentive structure.

Section 1 provides background information on the economic structures and other circumstances of the two countries in the early 1950s. Section 2 then traces the evolution of economic policy over the 1960–85 period in the two countries, and a final section contrasts the economic performance of the two countries.

1 INITIAL SIMILARITIES AND DIFFERENCES

Pre-1953 Heritage

Comparison of any two countries, especially countries with widely disparate cultural and geopolitical backgrounds, is always hazardous. And, in some fundamental regards, the Turkish and Korean backgrounds are very different.

Although the Turks were always a distinct group, Turkey was the seat of the Ottoman Empire until the First World War, and emerged thereafter as an independent Turkish nation under the leadership of Ataturk.[1] Disassociation from the Ottoman rule brought with it (1) the declaration that Turkey was a secular state, (2) the introduction of Latin alphabet and (3) a conscious effort to 'modernize' and adopt political, legal and economic systems much more akin to those of Europe than to those associated with the Ottoman legacy. None the less, the vast majority of Turks are Muslim and cultural ties to the Middle East remain. One might even venture the generalization that Turkey was and is caught between Europe and the Middle East and confronts a challenge to find her own unique identity between those two large and dissimilar regions.

In the 1920s and 1930s, many of the institutions that would be important in the postwar years were established. For present purposes, concern must be limited to noting these developments that significantly affected growth in the post-1950 period. After an initial period of relatively *laissez-faire* policies in the 1920s and very low overall growth, the government rejected the philosophy and shifted to a policy of 'Etatism' in the 1930s. Although 'Etatism' as enunciated contained a large number of elements with important implications for policy (such as the view that there were no distinct economic interests and hence no recognition of any role or rights for particular groups such as unions or industrialists), the chief and lasting legacy was the establishment of a number of State Economic Enterprises (SEEs) which produced and marketed a variety of agricultural, mineral and manufactured commodities. Many of these SEEs produced manufactured goods that had previously been imported. High tariffs were established to protect the new enterprises. By the end of the 1940s, it is estimated that more than half of Turkish industrial production originated in SEEs. They produced, and continue to produce, a variety of import-substitute commodities, ranging from textiles, clothing and footwear to petroleum products, paper, fertilizer and steel. In most activities, there is also private production.

The 1920s and 1930s also witnessed a rapid expansion of Turkish schools, and an increase of educational attainments in Turkey. Even so, in 1950 about half of the male population over 14 years of age was illiterate.

Korea, by contrast, had a long history as a distinct nation prior to the twentieth century, but was occupied as a Japanese colony in 1910. Korea is situated between the two geographic giants of East Asia – China and Japan – just as Turkey is situated between Europe and the Middle East.

Although there is a Confucian tradition in common with the country's Asian neighbors, Koreans have been a distinct ethnic group and nation for many centuries. They have tended to be somewhat inward-looking throughout their history, except when invaded or occupied by one of the two large Asian powers.

During the 1920s and 1930s, considerable manufacturing activity developed in Korea under Japanese occupation, although much of it was in the north and was owned by Japanese who also constituted a very high fraction (probably 80 per cent) of the technical manpower. Under the Japanese, little emphasis was placed on educating Korean children, and such education as did occur was provided in the Japanese language; use of Korean and teaching of Korean language and culture were forbidden.

During the Second World War Turkey was not an active combatant, but none the less she was largely cut off from international markets. Inflation rose sharply, reaching peak rates of 92 and 74 per cent in 1942 and 1943 respectively (Hale, 1981, p. 69). Economic activity was stagnant owing in large part to the cutoff from international trade. As of 1946 Turkey was the poorest country in Europe, with the lowest per capita income and the highest rate of inflation. It is estimated that real GNP in Turkey grew at an average annual rate of about 2 per cent over the decade 1938–48.

Whereas the Second World War was a period of very slow growth for Turkey, it was a period of economic decline for Korea as the Japanese directed their efforts to the war. In 1945 the Japanese left, and the country was partitioned along the 38th parallel: the South and North got approximately equal land (and arable land) areas, but the South got 17 million people, contrasted with the north's 8.8 million. The result was that there were only 1309 square meters of arable land per capita in the South – the highest density of population in the world at that time. The Americans occupied what is now South Korea.

The north had been the source of most electric power and minerals, and a very high fraction of manufactured output of metal and chemical products, while the South had been predominant in textiles, processed foods and machinery. The economic disruption after the war and partition, therefore, was probably as great, if not greater, than that of some of the countries in which fighting had occurred. For example, it is estimated that, by 1948, production of textiles was only about 18 per cent of what it had been in 1939; machinery production stood at 40 per cent of its 1939 level, and overall manufacturing production was about 14 per cent of its 1939 level (Frank, Kim and Westphal, 1975, p. 26). The real economic dislocations were accompanied by a hyperinflation; the Seoul retail price index of 1949 was 123 times what it had been in June 1945.

Thus, Korea's wartime legacy was vastly worse than Turkey's, although both countries had immediate reconstruction problems and low incomes. Both countries were recipients of sizable amounts of foreign aid from the United States, starting in the immediate postwar years. But that is almost the only similarity, and even there, Korea received proportionately much more aid than Turkey. The events of the decade after the war ended in 1953 made the contrast much stronger, with everything apparently favoring Turkey's rapid growth and hindering Korea's.

For Turkey, US aid under the Point Four Program and then the Marshall Plan was directed largely toward the development of infrastructure and agriculture. The government established very high support prices for agricultural commodities, and, in addition, a sizable fraction of aid was allocated for the importation of tractors, and for the conversion of pastureland and forests in the Anatolean plateau into wheat-growing areas. Wheat production boomed at a time when world prices were high and European demand was rising rapidly. By the early 1950s, Turkey was the largest exporter of wheat in the world, exporting a net of 600,000 metric tons in 1953 and 950,000 metric tons in 1954 (Krueger, 1974, p. 43) while simultaneously building up domestic stocks.[2] The price supports translated rapidly into heavy budgetary costs, which were a major cause of inflationary pressure in the mid-1950s, but until 1953 these were offset by Marshall Plan aid and export earnings at favorable terms of trade. It is estimated that Turkish real GNP at 1961 prices rose 15 per cent of 1951, 8.5 per cent in 1952 and 11.2 per cent in 1953 – exceptionally rapid growth by any standard.

The Korean economy's evolution over the 1946–53 period falls into two parts. As already mentioned, aid receipts were channeled toward reconstruction efforts and attempts to mitigate the dislocations of partition. The US military occupation carried out a successful land reform program (see Mitchell, 1952, for an account), and in addition assisted with educational reforms that provided virtually universal primary education. Thus, although Korea's stock of manpower and new entrants to the labor force in the late 1940s were probably less well educated than the Turkish labor force, the educational reforms of the late 1940s laid a basis for rapid increase in educational attainments in later years.

Spurred by reconstruction activities and an inflow of aid, Korean output grew significantly until June 1950, although it probably did not re-attain the levels of the late 1930s. Per capita income figures are not available, but an unweighted index of production,[3] with 1946 = 100, stood at 171 in 1948 and 149 in 1949 (although items that probably had large weight in the index, such as rice, wheat and barley, were up only 20 per cent over their 1946 levels, while items such as nails and chinaware had increased 4 and 8.5 times, respectively).

However, whatever gains in output had been achieved by early 1950 were again lost with the outbreak of the Korean war, which lasted until mid-1953. During those years, the excess demand generated by wartime expenditures and by the demands of United Nations troops (including Turkish) intensified inflationary pressures. Meanwhile, the initial invasion of large parts of South Korea by the North was repulsed by UN troops, only to be followed by re-invasion, which was in turn followed by a final repulsion. The fighting destroyed much of the infrastructure that had been rebuilt in the late 1940s. When the war ended in 1953, the South Korean economy was once again severely dislocated.

Political and Geopolitical Situations

It would take this essay too far afield to sketch in any degree of depth the domestic and international political situations of the two countries over the decades after 1953. But a few brief observations are necessary.

First, the perceived threat from the North in Korea led to a degree of cohesion in the Korean body politic that might otherwise have been absent. There was a powerful imperative for economic development that arose not only because of low living standards but also because of rivalry with the North. This phenomenon may have permitted the government to pursue economic goals more singlemindedly than would otherwise have been the case, but it also had its costs: the large defense budget was one such cost. Second, because of these same concerns, Korean foreign policy was firmly based on alliance with the United States. The large aid inflows of the 1950s, and the continued US military presence, were consequences. Third, because of memories of the colonial era, Korea did not even have formal relations with Japan until 1965, when a formal treaty was signed, and Japan agreed to extend what were in effect reparations. At least until 1965, proximity to rapidly growing Japan was not a significant plus to Korea's growth, and the Japanese share of Korean trade fell up to 1965.

Although Turkish proximity to the Soviet Union is not the same as the Korean partition, Turkey's strategic location none the less also determined her international policy stance. Turkey has been a member of NATO and has supported the largest army of any European NATO country, receiving military as well as economic aid from the United States and Western European countries. In terms of both trade and aid, the United States and Western Europe were the dominant economies. Because of proximity as well as a commonality of religion and heritage, there were also strong links to the Middle East.

As to domestic politics, Turkish elections in 1950 brought Adnan Menderes to the prime ministership, and turned the Republican Peoples' Party (RPP), the recipient of the Ataturk heritage, out of office. This ended the era of single-party rule in Turkey. Ataturk, who had been a general, had left a strong legacy to the military, which regarded itself as the guardian of the nation and of Ataturk's tradition. Menderes was re-elected to office during the 1950s in an environment that was regarded as increasingly oppressive, and by the late 1950s there were charges of a rigged election. In 1960 the military intervened, and sponsored the writing of a new constitution which took effect in 1961, when elections were held and a civilian government was returned to office (with the RPP winning the 1961 election, and the Justice Party, the successor to the Menderes heritage, winning election in 1965). The military intervened once again in 1971, but again there followed a return to civilian government and democracy under the 1961 constitution. Starting in the mid-1970s, however, there were several years of increasing violence and a deteriorating economy, with excessive and unsustainable borrowing. The government seemed unable to resolve either the economic or the political issues, in part because neither of the two major parties could attain a majority in Parliament and had to enter into a coalition with one of several minority parties. In early 1980 the military once more intervened. This time a new constitution was written, partly with the intention of reducing the influence of the smaller parties, but also with a view to preventing a recurrence of some of the apparent excesses of the 1970s. When elections were held in 1983, the civilian government under Prime Minister Turgut Ozal was operating with somewhat smaller powers than had earlier elected regimes.

Thus, throughout the postwar period the Turkish military was a major presence in the country's political life. However, for the majority of time the government was democratically elected under a constitution.

The Republic of Korea was founded in 1948, and Seungman Rhee became president and remained in that office until 1960. The Rhee regime was aptly characterized as follows: 'Despite the existence of certain trappings of democracy, the Rhee regime was indubitably an authoritarian government . . .' (Mason, Kim et al., 1980, p. 44).

In 1960 a student revolution, with widespread support of other groups, led to Rhee's resignation. A one-year interim government (clearly democratically elected) was unable to maintain law and order, and was overthrown after about a year by a military coup. General Park Chung Hee became chairman of a military council which revised the constitution to permit more centralized government in the expectation that centralization would prevent the apparent excesses of the earlier government; elections were held in late 1963. Although the opposition received 53 per cent of the votes, it was badly fragmented and Park was elected president, with his party controlling 110 of 175 seats in the National Assembly. In subsequent elections Park was returned to office, first with a 'landslide victory' in 1967 (Mason, Kim et al., 1980, p. 51), which effectively endorsed the economic success of the regime, but then with smaller fractions of the total vote and more charges of voter irregularities. But the major turning point of the political process came after the 1971 presidential election, in which Park was elected for a third term. In 1972 the government, apparently alarmed by the reduced margin of victory of popular support, abruptly abolished the existing constitution and introduced a new one in which the procedure for electing the president was converted to an indirect one, thus paving the way for President Park's indefinite stay in power.

Park was assassinated in October 1979, after which there followed an interim period of about a year before General Doo-Hwan Chun became president. His government, which has ruled to the date of writing, announced that he would serve only one term as president, and held elections for the Assembly in February 1985, which were intended to lead up to an indirect national election in 1988 for determination of President Chun's successor.

Even during the period when President Park's office had clearly been won in a free and open election, all observers would agree that government and power in Korea was highly centralized. And, for periods including the late

1950s and from the late 1970s to the present, the government has been arguably authoritarian. Its basis of support, however, has been the challenge from the North and its ability to deliver a strong economic performance. Indeed, Mason, Kim et al. concluded that: 'As long as the possibility of aggression seemed real to a majority of the population, and as long as continued growth assured increased real incomes to both rural and urban communities, the legitimacy of the Park Government in Korea was widely accepted' (Mason, Kim et al., 1980, p. 56).

Structure of the Two Economies, mid-1950s

By the mid-1950s the Korean war was over and the reconstruction effort begun, while the initial period of rapid growth in Turkey had ended and the underlying macroeconomic imbalances were becoming increasingly evident. It is thus useful to contrast the economic structures of the two countries at that time as a starting point for later analysis.

Tables 13.1, 13.2 and 13.3 give an idea of some key magnitudes. The population sizes of the two countries were very similar, each in excess of 20 million (see table 13.1). Korea was by far the poorer country: by UN estimates, the only Asian countries with lower per capita incomes in those years were India and Burma. Turkey's estimated per capita income of $210 was considerably higher than Korea's, although well below that of the richer Latin American countries and lower than any other European country covered by the UN estimates at that time. Thus, although both countries were poor, Korean living standards were probably among the lowest in the world, while Turkey was probably at the lower end of the spectrum of 'middle-income' developing countries.

Table 13.2 gives some idea of the structure of production in both countries in the mid-1950s. As can be seen, both were predominantly agricultural: in Turkey 74 per cent of the population lived in rural areas, and agricultural output accounted for 41.9 per cent of national income.

Despite these similarities, there was and is an important difference: Turkey is relatively land-abundant, and Korea is land-scarce. Turkey is favored with a variety of climatic conditions, including: (1) the Mediterranean coast, where cotton, citrus, tree crops (especially olive trees) and fresh fruit and vegetables vie for rich land; (2) the Anatolean plateau, colder and with somewhat poorer soil, which probably has a comparative advantage in livestock and, to a lesser extent, wheat and other grains; and (3) the Black Sea region, where tobacco and hazlenuts are major crops. Turkey's resources are so large that one would expect her to be a net exporter of agricultural commodities throughout the development process: one foreign visitor aptly suggested that 'Turkey should be the California of Europe.' In addition to land, the country has large deposits of chrome, copper, coal, iron ore and a variety of other minerals. However, there is very little oil, and the country imports its entire supply.

Table 13.1 Comparative data on the Korean and Turkish economies, 1952–1954

	Population (million)	NNP (US$million)	Per capita income ($)
Korea	21.38	1500	70
Turkey	22.46	4717	210

Source: United Nations, *Per Capita National Product of Fifty-Five Countries: 1952–54*, Statistical Series E, no. 4, New York, 1957.

Table 13.2 Structure of output, Korea and Turkey, 1955

	Agriculture	Manufacturing	Construction	Other
Korea	44.8	11.2	3.0	41.0
Turkey	41.9	14.2[a]	5.8	38.1

[a] Includes all industry.
Sources: Korea: Bank of Korea, *National Income Statistics Yearbook, 1953–1967,* Seoul, 1968; Turkey: State Planning Organization, *First Five Year Plan, 1963–1967*, Ankara, 1964, p. 13.

Table 13.3 Structure of expenditures, Turkey and Korea, 1955 (% of GNP)

	Consumption	Investment	Government consumption	Exports	Imports
Korea	86.4	12.3	8.7	1.6	9.8
Turkey	74.0	14.0	15.0	4.3	6.6

Source: Krueger (1974, p. 12) and Bank of Korea, *National Income Statistics Yearbook*, 1953–1967, Seoul, 1968, p. 10.

Table 13.4 Composition of exports, Korea and Turkey, 1955[a]

	Total exports ($m)	Agricultural exports	Mineral exports (% of total exports)	Manufactured exports
Korea	17.6	23.4	51.6	25.0
Turkey[b]	305.0	75.3	15.7	9.0

Sources: Korea: Wontack Hong, 1976, tables A.11 and A.12); Turkey: Krueger, 1974, p. 182).
[a] The commodity classification may not be identical for the two countries.
[b] Turkish data are for 1956.

By contrast, Korea had the smallest amount of arable land per capita (and not necessarily good-quality land) of any country in the world in the 1950s. Although the country was a net exporter of rice to Japan in the 1930s, that export reflected the realities of colonial administration; once land reform was undertaken, Korea became a net importer of grains. Korean policy toward agriculture in the 1960s was one of relative neglect; in the 1970s policy shifted toward protection for domestic food production, largely on income

Table 13.5 Geographic distribution of exports and imports, 1955 (%)

	Korea		Turkey	
	Exports	Imports	Exports	Imports
United States	41.9	34.9	15.5	22.4
Japan	39.1	14.7	0.3	0.7
EC	0.7	19.7	43.1	38.1
Other Europe	–	2.1	5.3	5.8
Middle East	–	–	5.8	6.7
Other	18.3	28.6	30.0	26.3

Source: United Nations, *Yearbook of International Trade Statistics*, 1955.

distribution grounds. Korea is lacking in almost all mineral resources – minerals and oil are major import items.

Table 13.3 gives data on the structure of expenditures in the two countries in 1955. As can be seen, both had imports considerably in excess of exports; in Turkey's case, foreign aid and other capital flows represented 2–3 per cent of GNP in the 1950s. In the Korean case, however, domestic savings were very small, as foreign aid accounted for about 8 per cent of GNP, or four-fifths of 1955 investment.[4]

Table 13.4 presents data on the composition of exports and imports in the two countries. As can be seen, Turkey's exports were about 17 times larger in total value than were Korea's. Turkey's exports were predominantly agricultural, with cotton and tobacco the two leading agricultural export commodities. Even so, her exports of minerals (primarily chrome and copper) were three times as large as Korea's *total* exports. Other exports, which in table 13.4 are recorded as manufactures, constituted no more than 9 per cent of total exports. By contrast Korea's exports were so small that a percentage composition table almost does not make sense. However, what exporters there were primarily minerals, with some forestry products and some agricultural and fishery products (especially marine products) constituting the balance.

One final aspect of trade structure deserves at least brief mention: that is, the geographic pattern of trade. Table 13.5 gives data on the share of trading partners in Korean and Turkish exports and imports. As can be seen, the United States is important for both countries, but much more so for Korea. Reflecting their respective geographies, however, Japan was relatively more important for Korea (although the Japanese share of Korean exports fell by at least half over the subsequent decade) and Europe for Turkey. The large 'other' category for Turkey reflects the importance of bilateral trading arrangements (especially with Council of Mutual Economic Assistance – CMEA countries) in Turkey's exports in the mid-1950s.

In sum, there were remarkable similarities between the two countries. They were of approximately equal size in terms of population. Both were heavily agricultural and had low per capita incomes, although Korea's was considerably lower than Turkey's. Both had sizable military expenditure burdens and were recipients of military and economic aid. Both countries had periods of authoritarian rule and periods where the government was legitimized by relatively free elections, although on average the Korean government was considerably more centralized and authoritarian than the Turkish.

There were also significant differences. Turkey had by far the more generous resource endowment, both in terms of land per man in agriculture and in terms of other natural resources. And Turkey had the period from 1946 onward in which policies could focus at growth and efforts to raise living standards. Korea, by contrast, had been much more devastated by the political aftermath – partition and departure of the Japanese, and the Korean war – and was, in the mid-1950s, much less far ahead of the immediate postwar situation than was Turkey.

2 ECONOMIC POLICY REGIMES

Turkey's economic performance until 1955 was regarded as one of the most promising of any developing country, while Korea remained a war-devastated country. Over the following five years, both countries pursued rather similar economic policies, each with relatively unsatisfactory results. Those policies are the subject of the first part of this section. In the late 1950s each country embarked upon some needed policy reforms, although the centerpiece of the reform packages and the scope and extent of reforms differed vastly. Those reform packages are the subject of the second part of the section. In each case, the reform packages set the pattern for the economic policies that were pursued throughout the 1960s, which are discussed in the third part of this section. The fourth part then covers the reactions to the oil price increase of 1973, while the concluding part traces the shifts in economic policy in each country since 1980.

Policies in the late 1950s

Turkish economic policy in the late 1950s was shaped by the difficulties that arose out of the unsustainable and expansionary fiscal and monetary policies that had been pursued in the early 1950s; Korean economic policy was formulated in response to the exigencies of postwar reconstruction against the backdrop of heavy aid dependence. Interestingly, despite the difference in origins, the resulting policies and problems were remarkably similar. The difficulties in each instance manifested themselves in the balance of payments.

As already seen, Korea was heavily dependent on US aid and receipts from US military outlays to cover the import bill. Americans in effect borrowed Korean currency to purchase local goods and services and to provide US troops with domestic currency for local expenditures. At a later date, negotiations were then held covering the exchange rate at which the loan would be repaid in dollars. Inflation was rapid during the war period, when prices as reflected in the cost of living index rose at rates of 167, 402, 126 and 53 per cent in the years 1950–3, respectively.[5]

Despite that, the Korean authorities attempted to keep the nominal exchange rate constant in the expectation of higher dollar receipts for won loans. By the time the war ended, the exchange rate was thus already heavily overvalued. Frank, Kim and Westphal (1975, p. 32) estimate that, in 1965 constant won per US dollar, the official exchange rate (which had fluctuated between 180 and 250 in 1949) was only 55.6 won per dollar in August 1953 when the Korean war ended. Despite periodic devaluations, the real rate fluctuated between 55.7 and 154.8 in the years before 1960, and did not re-attain the 1949 level until the end of 1960. Thereafter, it was always well in excess of 200 1965 constant won per dollar.

In response to the pressures that arose on the balance of payments, the authorities took a number of measures. First, there were multiple exchange rates, with as many as eight different rates for different classes of transactions in the late 1950s. Second, there was extensive exchange control, including licensing of all imports, which were not permitted unless they were on a list of 'eligible' commodities. Finally, tariffs and surcharges were imposed on those commodities that were imported in an effort to contain excess demand. There were numerous changes in regulations, and the overall exchange regime was chaotic. Despite occasional efforts to provide some relief and incentives to exporters, the discrimination against exports and in favor of the domestic market was enormous. Among the consequences, there was considerable import substitution in consumer goods industries; in addition, corruption increased among those trying to obtain imports, which was a significant factor in the downfall of President Rhee. Needless to say, exports lagged badly as a consequence: even in 1960, Korean exports were only $33 million compared with $40 million in 1953, representing about 2.4 per cent of GNP.[6]

Underlying the erosion of the real exchange rate, of course, was macro-economic imbalance. Although annual inflation rates did not again reach 100 per cent after 1953, the consumer price index rose more than 20 per cent in every year until 1958, and as much as 66 per cent in 1955. At that time, these rates were among the highest in the world.

The origins of inflation lay in the government budget deficit and its financing. As a percentage of GNP, the budget deficit rose from 1.9 per cent in 1953 to a peak of 7.6 per cent in 1955 and remained at about that level until 1958. Once economic policy reforms began, it fell sharply. Budget deficits were financed largely through credit creation, as financial markets were almost nonexistent because of regulation. Nominal interest rates were controlled at very low levels throughout the period, and were negative in real terms until 1958 (see Kim and Roemer, 1979, p. 73).

The growth rate in Korea was lacklustre until 1960, despite the opportunities present in a reconstruction era for rapid growth. In 1960 real GNP is estimated to have been 589 billion won, compared with 422 billion won in 1953 – an increase of 39 per cent, or an average annual rate of less than 5 per cent (Bank of Korea, *National Income Statistics Yearbook, 1953/57*, p. 16).

Investment remained at about 10 per cent of national income, and foreign aid continued to finance the bulk of investment.

For Turkey, the origins of the macroeconomic difficulties lay in a decision to maintain an exchange rate of TL2.8 per dollar in 1946. This rate was manifestly unrealistic, given the Turkish inflation during the Second World War. But the boom in wheat exports, the ability to run down reserves that had earlier been accumulated and the availability of Point Four and Marshall Plan aid permitted maintenance of this rate for an extended period of time. When commodity prices fell sharply in 1953, the government reacted by imposing quantitative restrictions on imports – no importer was to receive permission to import more than a specified percentage of his preceding year's imports. From this point onward, excess demand for foreign exchange increased as inflation persisted, but was contained through a complex set of regulations.[7] The trade and payments regime became an extremely complex amalgam of multiple exchange rates with surcharges of different levels for different categories of imports, and export premia for specified exports, import licensing, tariffs, bilateral trading arrangements and export price checks (see Krueger, 1974, ch. 2 for a description).

There was little conscious 'industrialization' policy in Turkey during the 1950s, but the foreign trade regime none the less provided a highly protected domestic market to any domestic supplier of import-competing goods. The SEEs and private industry both increased their output fairly rapidly until 1956. Almost all of it was in consumer goods, just as in the Korean case. After 1956 the inability to obtain raw materials, intermediate goods and spare parts severely constrained the output of Turkish industry.

Even without inflation, foreign exchange difficulties would have been acute, but there were inflationary pressures arising out of the budgetary deficits incurred as a result of agricultural price supports and large public expenditures on infrastructure. The budgetary deficits were aggravated by the government's effort to suppress inflation by holding down the prices at which SEEs could sell their output. The consequence was large losses by these enterprises, which were financed by central bank credits, which further fuelled inflation.

Price controls led to significant discrepancies between official prices and market prices, so that inflation exceeded, and probably substantially so, the rate recorded in official price indices. Even those indices, however, record rates in excess of 20 per cent for the years 1955–7.

Economic Reforms of the late 1950s and early 1960s

In both Korea and Turkey, the economic policy stance of the mid-1950s was unsustainable without a significant change in some key parameters. For Korea, export earnings were stagnant, and growth could proceed only if that situation would change or if foreign aid could be expected to grow indefinitely. The United States had informed the government of its intention to reduce aid, which made prospects in the absence of policy change even bleaker. Moreover, the government budget was sufficiently imbalanced that the prospect would probably have been for an accelerating rate of inflation even if aid levels had been sustained in the absence of measures to adjust expenditures relative to income. Whereas for the Koreans it was recognition of the infeasibility of maintaining growth over the long run which prompted policy reform, for the Turks reforms were forced upon them by the imperatives of a balance of payments crisis.

Stated another way, in Turkey the option of changing the underlying parameters of economic policy with respect to protection was not considered. The role of state economic enterprises in the economy and the need for control of economic activity was unquestioned, and there does not appear to have been any significant group within Turkey advocating a significant shift in policies of control and regulation. A deep-seated suspicion of private economic activity and belief in the need for detailed regulation and control pervaded Turkish society. While there was opposition to the changes in Korea with dominant businessmen dependent on the restrictive trade regime and controls for their profits, the change in government in 1960 seems to have led to the formation of a consensus on the need for growth-oriented policies and an export orientation. Once begun, President Park's commitment to growth, and the highly visible success of the new policies, assured the maintenance of the strategy.

In the Turkish case, imports were financed by borrowing from abroad, on ever-worsening terms, until finally even suppliers' credits were unavailable to would-be importers. By the summer of 1958, harvests were left in the fields in the absence of gasoline to power the tractors and trucks to bring produce to the ports and markets, and many activities were running at far below capacity because of import shortages. Indeed, the situation could be described as having been critical for at least a year before that time, but the Menderes government resisted policy reforms until it became apparent that there would be no alternative.

The major Turkish policy reforms were carried out under the aegis of an IMF stabilization program in the summer of 1958. The centerpiece was a major realignment of the exchange rate (from TL2.8 per dollar to TL9 per dollar, although the change was implemented through surcharges on imports and subsidies on exports until it was legitimized in the summer of 1960). Other measures included credit and budgetary ceilings, an attempt to rationalize the import regime and a rescheduling of the debt. In addition, Turkey received a sizable credit to permit a resumed flow of imports. The intent of the government, if there was an intention other than to satisfy international creditors enough to be eligible for resumed lending and foreign aid, was to remedy the short-term macroeconomic imbalances.

Even the rationalization of the import regime took the form of instituting three semi-annual 'import programs': one program listed goods eligible for importation without quantitative restrictions (mostly raw materials and intermediate goods used in production where there was no domestic source of supply); another program listed quotas for imports of other commodities; yet a third listed commodities that were eligible for importation only under bilateral trading arrangements. Commodities not listed on any of these were not legally importable.

The inauguration of regular import programs, and especially a liberalized list, represented a significant improvement over the chaotic conditions that had prevailed when importers, even with valid licenses, had to queue at the central bank for six and even eight months in order to obtain a foreign exchange permit. None the less, the new system permitted the government to liberalize or restrict the trade regime in accordance with the dictates of foreign exchange availability and/or desires to protect domestic industry: shifting of commodities to the quota list, or removing them from any list, automatically heightened restrictions. And during the 1960s shifts of this sort were a major means by which domestic import substitution was encouraged. The import programs remained the basic instrument of protection for domestic industry throughout the following two decades. Once domestic production of an item had begun, imports of the import-competing good were placed on the 'Quota List'; when production was deemed 'adequate' to supply the domestic market, the item was removed entirely from the import lists, which meant that it could not legally be imported.

The Korean reforms started in 1957–8 with a first effort at macroeconomic stabilization and the introduction of some export incentives. Thereafter, the process of liberalization continued, and it continues to this day.[8] Cutbacks in expenditures permitted a sharp reduction in the rate of monetary expansion, and the rate of inflation plummeted from its 30–50 per cent range to virtually zero by 1959. In 1960 (after the student revolution), reforms of the trade and payments regime began. The initial effort was geared primarily at stimulating exports: the official exchange rate was adjusted (for the first time since 1955), and in addition tax rebates and a number of export subsidies were introduced to compensate for the bias against export activities that would otherwise have resulted from the tariff structure. After 1960, the real exchange rate for exporters was kept relatively constant.

Along with the increased incentives for exporting, the Korean government, through its policy pronouncements, assured exporters that those incentives would be maintained. Over the next several years these assurances were accompanied by a number of policy measures that gave them credibility. In the first place, the rates of export subsidies and tax incentives were adjusted periodically to insure that exporters did not lose when inflation was not offset by exchange rate changes. Second, procedures were developed so that exporters could import their needed raw materials and intermediate goods duty-free provided only that they re-exported these materials within a year; indeed, the provisions were sufficiently generous so that there was probably an element of subsidy in the scheme. Third, exporters were the only ones eligible to receive import licenses and were thus the recipients of whatever premia there were on imports (primarily consumer luxury goods). Finally, exporters were extended highly preferential treatment in receiving credit. Because of interest rate ceilings and credit rationing, the real interest rates applicable were negative, at least until 1965, and the value of credit was substantial.

Thus, the initial set of Korean reforms had two distinct parts: on the one hand, there was a major effort to realign monetary and fiscal policy in order to reduce the rate of inflation drastically; on the other hand, there was a huge shift in incentives away from import substitution and toward export promotion.

Turkey and Korea were similar in that (1) they both started with trade and payments regimes that were highly protective of import substitution activities and discriminated against exports; (2) they had relatively high rates of inflation (as seen from the perspective of the 1950s and 1960s) and attempted to reduce excess demand; (3) new governments in 1960 were, if anything, more committed to the economic programs and reforms than had been their predecessors.

They differed in three respects. (1) The Turkish reforms were driven by the exigencies of a balance of payments and debt crisis, whereas the Korean reforms were motivated largely by a commitment to economic growth through an export-oriented strategy, given that aid flows could not be expected to sustain the sort of growth of imports that would be essential for satisfactory overall economic development. (2) There was no real intent on the part of the Turkish authorities to alter the underlying incentive structure of the economy with regard to exportables and import substitutes. As pronouncements in the First and Second Five-Year Plans amply demonstrate, it was intended to develop industry as a leading sector through import substitution. (3) The Korean government recognized the role of incentives and was essentially pragmatic in its efforts to stimulate economic performance, whereas the Turks remained highly suspicious of private economic activity and remained committed to a policy regime based on direct controls.

Policies during the 1960s

In both Korea and Turkey, policy during the 1960s and 1970s really evolved in response to the perceived needs originating from the basic strategy that had already been decided upon. In Turkey, perceived needs originated largely in foreign exchange difficulties; in Korea, perceived needs were actions that would support the export drive.

In Turkey the initial results of the 1958 reforms were highly successful. The stabilization was accompanied by receipt of new credit which financed a resumed flow of imports; partly for this reason, but also because there was a good harvest, the initial response to the stabilization program was a substantial increase in output, combined with a sharp reduction in the rate of inflation (after an initial, once-and-for-all, increase in prices of products of the SEEs). Perhaps because of that, the Menderes government began to exceed the credit and budget ceilings agreed upon with the IMF by late 1959, and signs of inflation reappeared. In May 1960 a military coup removed Menderes from office; interestingly, among the first actions of the new government was the reinstatement of the stabilization program.

Throughout the 1960s Turkish inflation remained moderate, averaging just under 5 per cent annually over the decade. Economic policy was articulated in the First and Second Five-Year Plans, which set industrialization as a major goal, to be achieved through import substitution. Aid in support of Turkey's development plans constituted 2–3 per cent of GNP during most of the 1960s. The real exchange rate for traditional exports in 1958 prices, which had reached TL7.69 per dollar after the devaluation, fell to TL6.82 per dollar in 1963 and to TL5.45 per dollar by 1969. For non-traditional exports, some subsidies were given to offset part of the disincentive inherent in an appreciating real exchange rate, but none the less, the real rate in 1958 prices fell from TL9 per dollar in 1958 to TL7.18 in 1965 and to TL6.00 by 1969 (see Krueger, 1974, p. 187).

Exports responded to the significantly increased incentives which resulted from the more realistic exchange rate in the early 1960s. Turkish exports, which were \$396 million in 1953, had fallen to a low of \$247 million in 1958: they rose by over \$100 million in 1959, and reached a level of \$458 million in 1965. While this did not represent exceptionally rapid growth, the availability of aid in addition to export earnings led to a fairly comfortable balance of payments position, and the major motive for the import programs in the first half of the 1960s was to protect domestic industry.

By the mid-1960s, however, the cumulative effect of inflation at rates of 5 per cent against the backdrop of stable international prices was beginning to take its toll, and growth of export earnings slowed down markedly. The government attempted to mitigate the situation by providing export incentives, in the form of subsidies, for non-traditional exports, and these grew somewhat more rapidly in the late 1960s. However, export earnings from the traditional sources of foreign exchange – agricultural and minerals – stagnated. Meanwhile, the import content of planned investment and output in import-substituting industries generally exceeded expectations, so that demand for foreign exchange was rising rapidly.

With only slow growth in availability and more rapid growth in demand, the import programs became increasingly restrictive in 1966, 1967 and 1968. None the less, foreign exchange difficulties increased, so that by 1969 even those who had received import licenses under an Import Program were waiting six to eight months before they received their foreign exchange allocation from the central bank. In this environment, incentives for producing domestic substitutes of almost anything were very great: no competing imports were permitted; those products dependent on imported raw materials or intermediate goods had virtual monopoly positions as their shares of these materials were determined by the import licensing regime. As foreign exchange availability decreased, premia on import licenses rose, and growth rates fell in the late 1960s.

A devaluation in 1970 was aimed at providing more incentives for exports. In the short run it did so, but the authorities were unable to sterilize the inflow of funds associated with the remittances of repatriated workers (who had earlier held their funds abroad) and with reverse capital flight. As a consequence, inflation accelerated rapidly. Thus, despite the fact that exports rose from \$537 million in 1969 to \$1317 million in 1973, inflation as measured by wholesale prices rose from 5.6 per cent in 1970 to 19.8 per cent in 1973.

Whereas Turkish economic policy with regard to the relative incentives for exportable and import-competing production was driven largely by foreign exchange availability, Korean economic policy in the 1960s and early 1970s was determined largely by the desire to maintain the momentum of the export drive. Once the export incentives were in place, they were generally altered in order to maintain their constancy in real terms: the real effective exchange rate for exports hardly changed from 1960 to 1968, although the exchange rate itself was pegged in the early 1960s and floated after 1964, and the fraction of the real rate that originated in export incentives (including tax rebates, export subsidies and subsidized credit) varied widely. Over time, there was a trend toward greater reliance on the exchange rate, and less on individual incentive schemes, than had earlier been the case. Over time, too, the real effective exchange rate began to be adjusted in response to the degree to which export performance was deemed to be flagging or unsustainably rapid.

In support of this general thrust, however, further reforms were undertaken in the 1960s. In 1961 a major overhaul of the protective system was undertaken, as quantitative restrictions were largely replaced by tariffs. In 1964, budgetary reforms consolidated the government accounts and increased fiscal discipline, with the result that the inflation rate fell from about 30 per cent in 1963 and 1964 to 6 per cent in 1965 and remained under 20 per cent for the remainder of the 1960s; in the same year, financial reforms resulted in positive real interest rates to depositors for the first time in the postwar period and reduced the degree of subsidy in official lending rates. In 1967, imports were further liberalized, as the earlier positive list of imports was replaced by a negative list (one that specifically itemized those goods that could *not* be imported).

As mentioned earlier, US aid was phased out during the 1960s. Until 1966 Korean policy largely discouraged foreign investment and foreign borrowing. But with decreased aid flows, the government reversed its stance and began to encourage private capital inflows, initially in the form of bank lending. These inflows were carefully controlled, with the government deciding upon the aggregate amount of borrowing that would be permitted and reviewing individual applications for it. After 1970 somewhat greater encouragement was given also to direct foreign investment, although it has remained relatively small contrasted with borrowing.

In all of this effort, however, the export drive was central. Monthly joint meetings of government officials and businessmen were held, chaired by President Park, in which export performance, industry by industry, was reviewed. In cases where exports appeared to be lagging, inquiry was made as to the difficulties; in many instances officials were then directed to remove restrictions or otherwise facilitate performance. In the Korean system, government officials tried to keep low targets for their industries (because higher targets meant more work for them), and had every incentive to

Table 13.6 Estimated incentive levels in Korea and Turkey, 1968

(a) Korea: effective subsidy rates (%)

	For export	For domestic industry	Average
Agriculture, Forestry and Fabrics	−9.4	21.7	21.3
Processed Food	1.8	−19.6	−18.0
Beverages and Tobacco	12.6	−20.8	−19.5
Mining and Energy	2.7	4.5	4.1
Construction Materials	4.4	−12.9	−12.1
Intermediate Products I	26.0	−21.9	−15.7
Intermediate Products II	11.6	13.1	13.0
Nondurable Consumer Goods	4.1	−15.7	−11.2
Consumer Durables	1.5	23.6	19.5
Machinery	1.9	21.0	20.2
Transport Equipment	−5.6	80.8	80.3

(b) Turkey domestic resource costs (TL per dollar)

	Mean	Variance		Mean	Variance
Food & Beverages	14.11	46.06	Glass & Ceramics	10.80	28.35
Textiles	13.48	43.77	Iron & Steel	13.68	29.70
Forest Products	10.44	n.a.	Iron & Steel Products	93.87	43,737.12
Leather Products	10.24	n.a.	Other Metal Products	14.17	22.89
Paper Products	23.69	67.40	Machinery & Parts	21.81	139.31
Rubber Products	45.59	890.49	Transport Equipment	27.78	278.88
Plastic Products	37.05	843.90			
Chemicals	14.56	16.92			
Cement	14.80	6.26			

Sources: (a) Frank, Kim and Westphal (1975, table 10-3). Subsidies were computed under the Corden treatment of home goods; (b) Krueger (1974, table VIII-1).

facilitate private economic activity – the opposite of the incentive system in many import substitution regimes, including that of the Turkish.

No measure of the biases of the two regimes can capture the difference between them, largely because the commitment of the Korean government provided a degree of assurance to exporters that was probably more valuable than some of the incentives that are measurable. None the less, for the study on *Foreign Trade Regimes and Economic Development* (Krueger, 1974; Frank et al., 1975), the bias of the Turkish and Korean regimes was estimated as of the early 1960s: for Korea, it was estimated that in 1966 the relative price of import-competing goods to exportables in the domestic market was 0.94 times that in the international; in Turkey in 1969, it was about 3.01 times as great.

Moreover, the variation in effective exchange rates and effective rates of protection was much greater in Korea than in Turkey. Table 13.6 gives some estimates. Although both means and variances are affected by the degree of disaggregation and the coverage of the estimates, the data in the table give an idea of the difference between the Turkish and Korean regime. In many sectors, the incentive for exporting in Korea was greater than the incentive for selling in the domestic market; the opposite was the case only when there were very few exports. Moreover, there was only one sector where the average rate of protection exceeded 80 per cent; the next highest was 20 per cent, and the range was from a negative 20 per cent to a positive 20 per cent. In Turkey, by contrast, almost all incentives were for production in the internal market; there was probably no sector in which the incentive to export even equalled the incentive to sell domestically. And, as between activities, the range of incentives varied ten-fold, or by 1000 per cent, with variances commensurately great.

There can be little doubt, based not only on the data in table 13.6 but also on other evidence, that the Korean incentive structure was much more uniform across activities than was the Turkish, and that the average incentive to export was probably at least as great as that to produce for the domestic market. This contrasts sharply with Turkey's inner-oriented policies.

Response to the Oil Price Increase

As was mentioned in section 1 above, neither Turkey nor Korea has any significant amount of oil. Consequently, the terms of trade of both countries were seriously affected by the oil price increase of 1973–4, although the prices of Turkey's primary commodity exports rose as a partial offset to the oil price increase. Relative to 1972, Korea experienced a 23 per cent deterioration in her terms of trade by 1974 (based on export and import unit values) contrasted with Turkey's 20 per cent drop. Because trade was much more important in Korean GNP, the total impact on Korea was much greater than on Turkey.

The policy response of the two countries was quite different. In part because reserves were high and the response to the 1970 devaluation was still improving the balance of payments, the Turkish government did virtually nothing in the short run. By comparison, the Korean reaction was immediate and sharp. In Turkey the nominal exchange rate was adjusted only with significant lags, despite the rapid inflation; in 1976 the nominal exchange rate was TL16.67 per dollar as compared with TL14.93 at the end of 1970, although the price level was almost triple its 1970 level. Even after adjusting for inflation in dollar prices, the real price of foreign goods had fallen 40 per cent relative to domestic output in the six-year period.

As inflation was seen to be a major policy problem, the domestic price of energy was restrained. No significant alterations were made in the key parameters confronting the private sector, and public expenditures and the tax structure were not altered. In the absence of any marked policy response to the oil price increase, the initial impact was, therefore, a significant increase in the current account deficit: after a current account surplus of $660 million in 1973, there were deficits of $561 million, $1648 million and $2029 million in the ensuing three years.

The Korean policy response was substantially more complex. The nominal effective exchange rate for exports was increased from 310 won per dollar in 1970 to 398 in 1973 and 484 in 1975. This adjustment more than compensated for the differential between domestic and foreign inflation, so that the purchasing–power–parity, price–level–deflated effective exchange rate (PPD PLD EER) for exports was increased from 308 won per dollar in 1970 to 396 won at the end of 1973; even at the end of 1975 it still stood at 231 won per dollar, a higher real rate than had prevailed at any time in the 1960s.[9] On the import side, the adjustment was even greater; the PPP PLD EER had been 260 in 1970, rose to 332 in 1973 but then fell back to 287 by 1975.

In addition to raising the real exchange rate, the domestic price of energy was adjusted promptly, with some adjustments in domestic tax rates undertaken to offset the impact on low-income groups. Also, systematic efforts were begun to find new sources of foreign exchange earnings, and the government actively encouraged Korean efforts to develop a market, especially in the Middle East, in construction activities.

Despite these adjustment measures, a large jump in the current account deficit and a sharp increase in inflation were both triggered by the oil price increase. However, the government was able to increase borrowing in the international private capital market to cover the current account deficit; with that, growth promptly resumed.

The Korean economy suffered a year of relatively slow growth in 1974, but then resumed rapid growth in 1975. Gaining confidence from the country's ability to withstand the oil price increase, but recognizing that the increase would strengthen the need for earning and saving foreign exchange, policy-makers concluded that Korea was ready to enter the 'next stage' of development, and undertook measures to start development of 'heavy industries,' including machine tools, shipbuilding and an array of other engineering industries.

For Turkey, the period 1976–9 was one of increasing short-term macroeconomic imbalance, as expansionary demand policies resulted in an acceleration of inflation, the balance of payments situation worsened and the rate of growth diminished, so that per capita income began falling by 1978. Even without the oil price increase of 1979, the Turkish government would have been unable to sustain its macroeconomic policy stance (including exchange rate policies and the trade regimes as well as fiscal, monetary and domestic credit policies). There were simultaneously mounting political difficulties, as domestic violence increased, and the government was unable to come to grips with either the political or the economic problem.

In January 1980 the Turkish government announced a series of far-reaching reforms, starting with a massive devaluation and an announcement that henceforth there would be frequent adjustments in the exchange rate to keep pace with differentials between domestic and foreign inflation. In addition, prices of outputs of public sector enterprises were increased sufficiently to reduce their deficits and thus sharply cut the size of the public sector deficit.

This general stance of reform, begun under the Demirel government, was continued under the military government headed by General Evren which took power in September 1980. In 1983, however, after some abrupt bankruptcies in the financial markets following very high nominal and real interest rates, the leadership of economic policy was changed, and with it the fiscal–monetary stance was eased. With the election of late 1983, however, Prime Minister Ozal, who had earlier led the reform effort, resumed the reform program. Quantitative restrictions on imports were virtually eliminated; efforts were made to rationalize, and perhaps even privatize, some of the State Economic Enterprises; and a variety of moves to increase currency convertibility, liberalize the credit market and banking system and open up the economy were gradually undertaken.

In Korea, the strains placed upon the economy by the expansionary policies pursued to develop the heavy engineering and chemical industries were already becoming apparent in 1977 and 1978. The demand for some types of technically trained personnel rose so rapidly that real wages and salaries for skilled labor tripled within a three-year period and the differential between wages of skilled and unskilled workers rose substantially. Furthermore, the investment and import costs of the new factories were extremely high. Partly for that reason, and partly for concern about the financial implications to domestic producers who were indebted in foreign currency, the won was not revalued to maintain purchasing power parity with major competitors; and, with a few exceptions (most notably shipbuilding), the new enterprises tended to incur large losses and to operate at small fractions of their intended capacity. Difficulties were compounded by the oil price increase of 1979, and then by the political uncertainties that followed the assassination of President Park Chung Hee. By late 1980 the economy was in severe macro-imbalance – real GNP growth in that year was −6.4 per cent. The wholesale price index increased 40 per cent from December 1979 to December 1980, the current account deficit jumped to 9 per cent of GNP, and the rate of gross investment was virtually zero for the last half of the year.

Policies were set in place to address these issues. These included an exchange rate realignment, and also a concerted effort to restore macroeconomic balance. Monetary growth, which had been 27 per cent in 1980, fell to 15 per cent in 1983 and 8 per cent in 1984; the fiscal deficit simultaneously fell to 1 per cent of GNP by 1983. The GNP growth rate returned to the 7 per cent range, the deficit on current account had been reduced to 1.7 per cent of GNP by 1984, and inflation was down to 2 per cent at an annual rate.

Thus, both Korea and Turkey entered the early 1980s with economic problems resulting from past policies as well as the effects of worldwide recession and 1979 oil price increase. In the Korean case, the source of the difficulty was the attempted shift of the industrial base toward heavy chemical and engineering industries and the other policies, especially exchange rate, that had been adopted in support of that stance. In Turkey the problems

Table 13.7 Indicators of economic performance in Korea and Turkey, 1960–1984

	Real GNP		Per capita income		Exports	
	Korea	Turkey	Korea	Turkey	Korea	Turkey
	(1960 = 100)		(1960 = 100)		($b)	
1961	105.6	102.0	102.6	99.4	0.041	0.347
1962	107.9	108.3	101.9	102.9	0.055	0.381
1963	117.7	118.8	108.1	110.2	0.087	0.368
1964	129.0	123.6	115.1	111.9	0.119	0.411
1965	136.5	127.5	119.0	111.8	0.175	0.464
1966	153.9	142.8	131.2	122.7	0.250	0.491
1967	164.1	148.8	134.5	125.3	0.320	0.522
1968	182.6	158.7	146.2	130.0	0.455	0.496
1969	207.7	167.3	162.7	133.7	0.622	0.537
1970	223.6	177.0	171.3	137.9	0.835	0.588
1971	243.1	194.9	182.7	148.1	1.068	0.677
1972	257.0	209.5	189.5	155.2	1.624	0.885
1973	293.4	220.8	212.5	159.5	3.225	1.317
1974	315.9	237.1	224.9	167.1	4.460	1.532
1975	337.8	255.9	236.5	175.6	5.081	1.401
1976	385.5	275.6	265.6	185.3	7.715	1.960
1977	434.5	294.9	294.8	194.3	10.047	1.753
1978	476.7	286.5	318.5	184.9	12.711	2.288
1979	507.7	293.9	321.0	185.8	15.055	2.261
1980	481.3	290.9	311.9	180.0	17.505	2.910
1981	511.1	302.8	326.0	181.8	21.254	4.703
1982	539.9	316.5	339.1	188.0	21.873	5.746
1983	592.2	327.2	365.7	190.0	24.445	5.728
1984	636.2	346.7	387.6	201.3	29.244	7.134

Source: International Monetary Fund, 'International Financial Statistics', 1985 *Yearbook*.

essentially had their origins in the inner-oriented policies that had been pursued for several decades; the oil price increases and other events of the 1970s had exacerbated the underlying inefficiencies of the economy, but adjustments to those phenomena could not be undertaken independently of addressing the underlying issues.

3 CONTRASTS IN PERFORMANCE

Table 13.7 provides data on overall economic performance. As can be seen, real GNP in Korea increased six-fold between 1960 and 1984, whereas Turkish

Table 13.8 Indices of agricultural and manufacturing production, 1960–1984 (1960 = 100)

	Agricultural production		Industrial production	
	Korea	Turkey	Korea	Turkey
1961	110	102	105	105
1962	102	106	139	106
1963	112	110	158	122
1964	132	117	170	159
1965	134	110	180	176
1966	144	125	226	215
1967	136	127	292	238
1968	138	134	397	266
1969	158	134	479	298
1970	156	139	535	305
1971	160	149	623	337
1972	166	153	724	373
1973	170	142	982	434
1974	178	158	1268	468
1975	202	169	1515	506
1976	220	181	1997	556
1977	236	183	2405	601
1978	252	186	2976	616
1979	258	190	3335	584
1980	210	192	3271	554
1981	232	195	3709	599
1982	238	203	3882	628
1983	240	203	4500	662
1984	250	208	n.a.	n.a.

Sources: World Bank EPD databank. For Korea, statistics from Bank of Korea *National Income*, supplemented by IBRD Economic Report, various issues; for Turkey, data from State Planning Organization.

GNP rose at about half that rate. Turkish growth in the 1960s had been somewhat less rapid than Korea's, but the differences became much more pronounced in the 1970s, and especially the late 1970s.

The differential in per capita incomes rose even more sharply than that of GNP. Although both countries had rates of population growth of around 2.9 per cent in the late 1950s, the Turkish rate fell only to 2.5 per cent in the late 1960s and to 2.1 per cent in more recent years. By contrast, the Korean population's growth rate had already fallen to around 2 per cent by 1970 and to 1.6 per cent by the late 1970s and early 1980s. Whereas Korea and

Turkey each had populations of just over 20 million in the early 1950s, the Turkish population is estimated to have been 48.27 million in 1984, while Korea's was 40.58 million. It will be recalled that estimated per capita incomes (in 1955 prices) were $70 and $210 for Korea and Turkey, respectively, in the first half of the 1950s, a differential which increased during that decade. By 1983, however per capita incomes in 1983 dollars were estimated to be $1240 for Turkey and $2010 for Korea: whereas Turkey's estimated per capita income was about three times Korea's in the early 1950s, in was only about 60 per cent of Korea's by the early 1980s. While international comparisons of living standards are always subject to difficulty, there is little question that Korea was the poorer country in the 1950s and the more affluent in the 1980s.

This fundamental transformation affected all sectors of the economy. As can be seen from table 13.8, agricultural production as well as industrial production rose more rapidly in Korea than in Turkey, although manufacturing was unquestionably the leading growth sector. Interestingly, in both Korea and Turkey, agriculture's share in GNP fell sharply: from 36.5 to 13.9 per cent between 1960 and 1984 for Korea, and from 37.5 to 18.4 per cent over the same years for Turkey. But despite the sharper fall in Korea, agricultural production was almost 2.5 times as great in 1985 as in 1960, whereas in Turkey agricultural production rose a still respectable, but none the less substantially smaller, 62 per cent. For manufacturing, the structural shift was sharper in Korea; whereas 13.7 per cent of GNP originated in manufacturing in 1960, the 1984 figure was 29.2 per cent (with an estimated increase in manufacturing output of 1255 per cent). In Turkey the manufacturing share increased from 11.6 to 23.0 per cent of GNP, for a total increase of 548 per cent. Thus, it was not that manufacturing growth led in one country while agricultural growth led in another: manufacturing rose more rapidly in both countries, but the dominant phenomenon was Korea's faster overall growth.

This faster growth implied, among other things, a much more rapid increase in real wages and urban employment in Korea than in Turkey. Table 13.9 provides some estimates of the orders of magnitude of the increase. For Korea, real wages had been virtually stagnant in the late 1950s, and remained so in the early 1960s, although nonfarm employment rose rapidly, from 2.15 million in 1960 to 3.14 million in 1965. After 1965 nonfarm employment continued to grow at rates of almost 10 per cent annually, but real wages also began rising. By 1970 real wages had risen about 45 per cent over their 1960 level. Thereafter, as labor became scarcer, more of the increase in demand for labor was reflected in a rising real wage – which more than doubled between 1970 and 1980 – while nonfarm employment grew more slowly, although it almost doubled over the decade.

Data for Turkey are incomplete, but over the entire two decades after 1960, nonfarm employment is estimated to have risen only from 2.8 million to about 5.7 million (compared to 2.1 million to 8.59 million in Korea), and real wages at most rose by about 60 per cent. Even then, real-wage increases had been

Table 13.9 *Real wages and employment, 1957–1984*

	Korea		Turkey	
	Real wages[a] 1970 = 100	Nonfarm employment[b] (millions)	Real wages[c] 1970 = 100	Non-agricultural employment[d] (millions)
1957	54.8	2.01	n.a.	n.a.
1958	61.3	1.95	n.a.	n.a.
1959	62.5	1.94	n.a.	n.a.
1960	57.3	2.15	72.2	n.a.
1961	60.5	2.55		
1962	60.8	2.58	77.6	2.90
1963	57.9	2.72	78.9	n.a.
1964	54.9	2.81	85.2	n.a.
1965	56.8	3.14	90.7	n.a.
1966	59.0	3.30	91.3	n.a.
1967	65.5	3.65	87.8	3.68
1968	72.8	4.00	90.4	3.68
1969	89.7	4.26	98.1	n.a.
1970	100.0	4.63	100.0	n.a.
1971	109.2	5.05	93.5	n.a.
1972	111.4	5.22	90.7	4.61
1973	119.5	5.51	98.3	4.82
1974	133.9	5.88	99.7	5.02
1975	133.5	6.23	103.4	5.20
1976	151.8	6.70	118.2	5.43
1977	175.8	7.28	125.2	5.63
1978	206.3	7.95	105.9	5.64
1979	226.4	8.31	95.1	5.72
1980	213.3	8.59	71.1	5.79
1981	206.0	8.89	65.7	n.a.
1982	225.8	9.61	63.0	n.a.
1983	245.1	10.20	66.6	n.a.
1984	259.1	10.51	68.1	n.a.

[a] *Source:* Kim and Roemer (1979) for 1957–75.
[b] *Source:* Kim and Park (1985), p. 13 for 1963–82.
[c,d] *Source: IBRD Policies & Prospects for Growth*, 1980, p. 145.
Real-wage data updated from Vgur Korum, 'Turkish Export Structure and Foreign Trading Companies in Outer Oriented Framework,' mimeo, October 1985.

caused in part by the political impasses and the power of unions in Turkey to obtain wage increases independently of conditions in the labor market; such increases as there were were at the expense of expanded employment. There is considerable evidence that much of the effort of employers in the late 1970s was to find ways to automate their factories and reduce their vulnerability to strikes and labor agitation. One of the unfortunate but probably essential parts of the Turkish reforms of the early 1980s was the decline in real wages that took place.

Rapid growth in Korea was reflected not only in rising real wages and employment opportunities, but also in rising real incomes for all segments of society. Indeed, except for the early 1960s, when the evidence is ambiguous, and the period of 'heavy industry emphasis' in the late 1970s, the evidence would suggest that the Korean income distribution, which was relatively egalitarian at the beginning of the period, became more so. By contrast, the available evidence would suggest that Turkish income distribution was more unequal in the 1950s, and became even more so with growth.[10]

The biggest contrast is in export performance of the two countries. Data are given in table 13.7. In 1960 Korea's exports were on $33 million, compared to Turkey's exports of over $300 million. By 1984 Korea's exports were $29.2 billion, and Turkey's were $7.13 billion. In both cases, the composition of exports had changed; by 1984 almost 94 per cent of Korean exports were manufactures, whereas for Turkey the figure was 54 per cent. And, whereas export represented only 2.4 per cent of Korean GNP in 1960, they were 38.4 per cent of Korean GNP in 1984. By contrast, Turkish exports were about 4 per cent of GNP in 1960, 6 per cent of GNP in 1978 and 10 per cent of GNP in 1984. To be sure, the relative importance of imports to the domestic economy had also increased in the Korean case.

Of course, the expansion of manufactured exports in Korea was the main stimulus to industrial growth. Korean industrial production rose 45-fold over the 23 years after 1960; Turkish industrial production in 1983 was 6.6 times what it had been 23 years earlier. The data in table 13.8 show vividly the difference in performance.

Along with Korea's export performance came creditworthiness and her ability to access international capital markets. As table 13.10 shows, a major part of the structural transformation in Korea was the rapid rise in the domestic savings rate – from only 0.8 per cent of GNP in 1960 to well over 20 per cent in the late 1970s and around 20 per cent in the early 1980s. It will be recalled that real interest rates had been negative in the late 1950s; financial reforms in the mid-1960s assured savers of positive real returns on their savings, and the savings rate began rising dramatically.

Even so, it proved highly profitable to attract foreign capital, especially in the late 1960s and early 1970s. As can be seen from table 13.10, Korea's capital inflows were much more important relative to GNP than were the Turkish – and Korea's were mostly private inflows, whereas much of Turkey's was official financing which was negotiated to cover balance of payments difficulties. For Korea, foreign capital augmented domestic savings by as

Table 13.10 Savings, investment, capital flows and inflation, 1960–1984 (as % of GNP)

	Domestic gross savings		Gross investment		Capital inflow		Inflation rate	
	Korea	Turkey	Korea	Turkey	Korea	Turkey	Korea	Turkey
1960	0.8	13.7	10.9	16.1	8.6	0.5	10.7	5.3
1961	2.9	12.9	13.2	15.8	8.6	0.4	13.2	2.9
1962	3.3	11.6	12.8	15.3	10.7	2.0	9.4	5.7
1963	8.7	11.1	18.1	15.4	10.4	1.6	20.6	4.2
1964	8.7	13.6	14.0	15.3	6.9	1.6	34.6	4.4
1965	7.4	13.4	15.0	14.9	6.4	1.3	10.0	8.9
1966	11.8	15.8	21.6	17.6	8.4	1.1	8.9	4.4
1967	11.4	16.5	21.9	17.3	8.8	1.0	6.4	5.1
1968	15.1	16.0	25.9	18.0	11.2	1.4	8.1	3.4
1969	18.8	15.9	28.8	17.5	10.6	1.8	6.8	6.0
1970	17.3	16.8	26.8	19.5	9.3	2.3	9.2	5.6
1971	15.4	13.6	25.2	17.3	10.7	2.1	8.6	17.0
1972	15.7	16.4	21.7	20.1	5.2	4.3	13.8	18.4
1973	23.5	15.7	25.6	18.1	3.8	1.1	6.9	19.8
1974	20.5	14.4	31.0	20.7	12.4	0.6	42.1	29.7
1975	18.6	14.3	29.4	22.5	10.4	3.7	26.6	11.0
1976	23.1	17.7	25.5	24.7	2.4	6.3	12.1	16.0
1977	25.1	16.9	27.3	25.0	0.6	7.0	9.0	23.5
1978	26.4	14.6	31.1	18.5	3.3	4.0	11.6	50.1
1979	26.6	14.2	35.4	18.3	7.6	0.9	18.8	64.8
1980	19.9	13.5	31.5	21.4	10.2	3.5	38.9	107.9
1981	19.6	15.8	28.4	21.5	7.9	2.0	20.4	37.5
1982	21.5	16.9	26.2	20.3	4.8	2.2	4.7	25.8
1983	26.9	16.4	27.8	20.7	3.1	2.7	0.2	30.4
1984	30.1	11.0	30.0	20.1	3.5	2.4	0.7	51.6

Sources: Korean savings, investment and capital inflow: Kim and Park (1985, table 2-7); Korean and Turkish prices: International Monetary Fund, *International Financial Statistics Yearbook*, 1985, pp. 100–1; Turkey gross domestic investment and savings: State Planning Organization, Turkey; Capital Inflow: International Monetary Fund, *International Financial Statistics Yearbook*, 1985, pp. 628–9.

much as 60 per cent in the late 1960s – permitting an investment rate well in excess of 25 per cent of GNP while domestic savings rates were still below 20. For Turkey, by contrast, capital flows have remained 2–3 per cent of GNP, and Turkish investment, which was initially a much higher fraction of GNP than Korean, has not exceeded 20 per cent.

It should be noted, however, that the difference in savings performance has been far smaller than the difference in growth rates – the greater difference has been the efficiency with which investment was allocated and employed.

There is also an interesting contrast on the macroeconomic front. As the last two columns of table 13.10 show, until the 1970s Korea's inflation rate generally exceeded the Turkish. Both countries experienced accelerating inflation right after the 1973 and 1979 oil price increases, although Turkey was in any event undergoing a period of accelerating inflation during the latter part of the 1970s. After 1980 it was a major objection of policy in both countries to bring inflation under control, although in the Turkish case this objective was combined with that of opening up the economy. As the figures in table 13.10 show, Turkey continued to experience double-digit inflation rates, with rates of around 50 per cent in 1984 and 1985; by contrast, in Korea the rate of inflation is estimated to have fallen to less than 1 per cent annually in 1984 and 1985.

4 CONCLUSIONS AND POSTSCRIPT

There are too many factors at work influencing economic performance in any given country, or any pair of countries, for analysis to permit iron-clad conclusions. None the less, the contrast between Korea and Turkey is striking. By almost any measure, Turkey was the more affluent country in the 1950s, and was better positioned for economic development: her natural resources were far superior; her initial savings rate and level of per capita income was higher; and her record of growth during the 1950s appeared exceptionally good.

Korea in the 1950s was unable to grow rapidly despite the opportunities for above-average growth that usually arise in the aftermath of a war. Her savings rate was exceptionally low, and her export performance was very bad. The country's per capita endowment of natural resources was also poor.

In so far as there are either economic advantages or economic disadvantages to a military alliance with the United States, both countries had them. And, in so far as proximity to a rapidly growing region of the world affects growth, Turkey and Korea had Europe and Japan, respectively.

Both countries in the 1950s were subject to macroeconomic imbalances and rates of inflation that were then regarded as very high by world standards. Both adopted reforms in the late 1950s and early 1960s. In the Korean reforms the trade regime was central, and shifting its orientation was the lasting achievement of the period. Inflation did decelerate, and shifts in the government budget and rising real interest rates encouraged domestic savings. These were significant shifts, but the centerpiece was the move toward an outer-oriented trade regime. Korean analysts suggest that there was a fair degree of unanimity in the view that Korea could no longer depend on aid and that there was no choice but to make the outer-orientation work. While US aid officials and others participated in the discussions and decisions (and may have been instrumental in convincing policy-makers that there was a feasible alternative), the decisions of the late 1950s appear from all accounts to have been Korean decisions.

By contrast, by mid-1958 the Turkish government recognized that the economic situation was unsustainable, but only in the sense that economic activity was severely disrupted because import flows had virtually ceased. Reforms were adopted only reluctantly, and only because there appeared to be no other way to reschedule debt and provide for a resumed flow of imports that were deemed essential to halt the decline in economic activity. While rationalization of the chaotic trade regime that had preceeded the August 1958 program was clearly an objective of policy, there was no intention whatsoever to open up the economy, or to abandon the traditional suspicion of private economic activity. Partly because there was little faith in the efficiency of incentives, and partly because of the belief in indirect controls, the aims were purely for macroeconomic balance. There was no intention to alter the balance of incentives between exportable and import-competing production. While Turkey was, during the 1960s, probably more successful in maintaining price stability than was Korea, the degree of protection accorded to domestic firms increased, and Turkey became, if anything, more inner-oriented with the passage of time.

If there are any central lessons from the contrast of Korea and Turkey, they are probably two. First, the prevailing economic structure of a country can never be taken as a given; it must be seen in light of the economic incentives that arise from the policy environment and condition people's behavior. Second, there is an important difference between 'liberalization' efforts where the sole intent is to remove some of the bias against exports that existed in the last phase of a balance of payments crisis, and a reform effort aimed at fundamentally altering the bias of the trade regime.

In this regard, it is important to note that there were significant mistakes made by Korean policy-makers. It is not that economic policy in one country was 'right' and the other 'wrong.' If there was a difference in policy formulation itself, it rather lay in the speed with which policy-makers recognized their mistakes and dealt with them. By the early 1980s, all members of the Korean economics community were agreed that the effort to promote heavy industry had been a mistake; there were incipient debt-servicing difficulties in 1969 and on several later occasions. The problems were rapidly identified in each instance, and efforts were then made to insure that the same mistakes would not be repeated. Likewise, Korean performance has not been without its drawbacks: import liberalization has proceeded only slowly and reluctantly, and financial liberalization is still far from completed.

Turkey's economic difficulties were clearly apparent to all observers in 1957, in 1969 and by 1976. Yet in each instance, the fact that the economy was inner-oriented permitted policy-makers to persist in 'patch-up' efforts rather than to address their fundamental problems. In one sense, the outer-orientation of the Korean trade regime must be given the fundamental credit for the more satisfactory Korean performance compared with the Turkish. At a deeper level, however, it might be argued that it was the Korean policy-makers' willingness to confront their problems and to recognize difficulties early which, on one hand, led to the decision for an outer-oriented trade strategy, and on the other hand led them to address perceived difficulties more quickly, and (perhaps more importantly) more fundamentally, than did the Turkish policy-makers.

Turkey's effort at a shift toward a more outward orientation began in the winter of 1980. Even then, quantitative restrictions were not removed, and the major shift was through the guarantee to maintain a more realistic exchange rate. Although those in authority clearly recognized the need for a fundamental change in economic policy, there were many influential Turks, in and out of government, who did not accept the changes.

None the less, the commitment to an outer-oriented regime has continued to the time of writing. Against the background of worldwide recession, Turkey has liberalized quantitative restrictions substantially, and maintained real incentives for exporters. Export performance in consequence has been impressive, with exports which stood at only $2.9 billion in 1980, rising to $7.1 billion in 1984. Performance has been impressive enough to persuade many Turks that the earlier suspicion of private economic activity may have been overdone.

While the commitment to an outer-oriented regime has been much less firm than was the Korean commitment two decades earlier, there has been enough success to provide some momentum for its continuation. Whether initial successes with the shift will have resulted in enough of a shift in Turkish thinking, or whether the next shift in political power will reverse the liberalization achieved so far, remains to be seen.

The centrality of trade policy in both Korea and Turkey is beyond dispute. The experience of these two countries vividly demonstrates the central importance of trade policy, and the importance of analyses of the sort pioneered by Max Corden, in affecting countries' economic wellbeing.

NOTES

1 See Lewis (1968) for a history.

2 It is doubtful if the conversion of land from forests and grazing land to wheat was economic in the long run; see Hirsch and Hirsch (1963).

3 Frank, Kim, and Westphal (1975, p. 9).

4 It is unclear how military expenditures and military imports enter into the national income accounts in either country. Korea has continued, throughout the period of rapid development, to devote sizable resources to military expenditures. However, Turkey as a member of NATO has also had a large military budget and has received military aid. It seems likely that the drain of resources into military expenditures in the two countries was fairly comparable, and that this constitutes a similarity, rather than a difference, between them.

5 Data from International Monetary Fund, *International Financial Statistics*, supplement to 1966/67 issues, Korea page.

6 This result was not unintended. The object of the Rhee government had been to maximize aid inflows, and 'balance of payments needs' were used as a lever in aid negotiations; see Cole and Lyman (1971).

7 Despite the measures, a sizable black market developed, and trade statistics of that period undoubtedly understate the actual value of trade.

8 Once the export drive was under way, exporters were permitted to import any item used in production for export duty-free. The percentage of imports subject to any quantitative restriction fell sharply in the early 1960s, but in 1967 still stood at 39.6 per cent, although these restrictions did not apply to exporters. The ratio fell gradually thereafter, reaching 15.2 per cent by 1984 (see Nam, 1985, table 3).

9 Source: Hong, (1981, table 8.6). All PPP PLD EER estimates are in constant 1965 won prices.

10 All estimates of income distribution are fraught with difficulty. For 1973 it is estimated that the bottom 20 per cent of the Turkish income distribution received 3.5 per cent of all income, while the top 20 per cent received 56.5 per cent. For Korea, the corresponding 1976 estimates are 5.7 and 45.3 per cent (see World Bank, *World Development Report*, 1985, table 28).

REFERENCES

Cole, David C. and Lyman, Princeton (1971). *Korean Development, The Interplay of Politics and Economics.* Cambridge, Mass.: Harvard University Press.

Frank, Charles R. Jr, Kim, Kwang Suk and Westphal, Larry E. (1975). *Foreign Trade Regimes and Economic Development: South Korea.* New York: Columbia University Press for the National Bureau of Economic Research.

Hale, William (1981). *The Political and Economic Development of Modern Turkey.* New York: St Martin's Press.

Hirsch, Eva and Hirsch, Abraham (1963). Changes in agricultural output per capita of rural population in Turkey, 1927–60. *Economic Development and Cultural Change*, 14, 4, 440–57.

Hong, Wontack (1976). *Factor Supply and Factor Intensity of Trade in Korea.* Seoul: Korean Development Press.

Hong, Wontack (1981). Export promotion and employment growth in South Korea. In Krueger et al. *Trade and Employment in Developing Countries*.

Kim, Kihwan (1985). *The Korean Economy.* Seoul: Korea Development Institute.

Kim, Kwang-suk and Park, Joon-Kyung (1985). *Source of Economic Growth in Korea: 1963–1982.* Seoul: Korea Development Institute.

Kim, Kwang-suk and Roemer, Michael (1979). *Growth and Structural Transformation.* Cambridge, Mass.: Harvard University Press.

Krueger, Anne O. (1974). *Foreign Trade Regimes and Economic Development: Turkey.* New York: Columbia University Press for the National Bureau of Economic Research.

Krueger, Anne O., Lary, Hal B., Monson, Terry and Akrasanee, Naronschai (eds) (1981). *Trade and Employment in Developing Countries*, vol. 1: *Individual Studies.* Chicago: University of Chicago Press.

Lewis, Bernard (1968). *The Emergence of Modern Turkey.* London: Oxford University Press.

Mason, Edward S., Kim, Mahn Je, Perkins, Dwight H., Kim, Swang Suk and Cole, David C. (1980). *The Economic and Social Modernization of the Republic of Korea.* Cambridge, Mass.: Harvard University Press.

Mitchell, Clyde (1952). *Land Reforms in Asia, A Case Study*, Washington, DC: National Planning Association, Pamphlet no. 78.

Nam, Chong Hyun (1985). Trade policy and economic development in Korea. Discussion Paper no. 9, Korea University, Seoul.

14

GATT Reform: Selected Issues

Robert E. Baldwin

1 INTRODUCTION

There is general dissatisfaction in both developed and developing countries with the operation of the global trading regime. In particular, there is much criticism of the international organization that was established in 1948 to provide a set of rules of 'good' international trading behavior, to sponsor multilateral trade-liberalizing negotiations, and to help resolve disputes among its members, namely, the General Agreement on Tariffs and Trade (GATT).

Not only has this institutional mechanism been unable to prevent a significant increase in the use of non-tariff trade-distorting measures in recent years, but more and more trade policy actions are being take outside of the GATT framework. Nogues, Olechowski and Winters (1985) estimate that 27.1 per cent of the total imports of the industrial countries are now covered by non-tariff barriers (36.1 per cent for agricultural products and 16.1 per cent for manufactured goods). Moreover, of the 20.8 per cent of total imports covered by quantitative restrictions, only 7.6 per cent were reported by members as coming under GATT rules (Winters, 1985). Another manifestation of the dissatisfaction with the GATT framework is the frequent criticism of its existing rules and the call for changes in and extensions of these rules.

This paper reviews the major areas of dissatisfaction with existing GATT rules and mechanisms and examines the pros and cons of various proposals for changing them. There are four general areas of dissatisfaction.

1 The unconditional most-favored-nation (MFN) principle, the cornerstone of the GATT, is being honored more in the breach than in the observance and should either be changed or be reasserted.
2 Existing GATT rules, especially those covering 'fair' trading practices, agriculture and textiles, are not stringent enough.
3 There is a need for the GATT rules and agreements to be extended to cover such matters as services trade, trade-related investment requirements, and the protection of intellectual property rights.

4 Existing GATT mechanisms for settling disputes, reaching decisions, and dealing with the developing countries are ineffective and unfair and should be revised.

2 THE MOST-FAVORED-NATION PRINCIPLE

Discussions about the appropriateness of the MFN principle and the permitted derogations under current GATT rules arise in considering such diverse matters as the safeguard provisions of article XIX, the comparative openness of different country markets, customs unions and free trade areas, and the generalized system of preferences. Those who believe that the GATT should be modified to permit the greater use of selectivity and the conditional MFN principle base their case on the perceived unfairness of the unconditional form of the principle and the regime-weakening actions that occur outside of the GATT framework because of this perception.

It is argued, for example, that when increased imports from one or a few countries cause serious injury to a domestic industry, it is unfair to impose tariffs or quotas on other suppliers of the product whose exports have not increased in an injury-causing manner. This view, according to the proponents of GATT changes in the principle, has led to the widespread use by governments of voluntary export restraints and orderly marketing agreements – measures that are taken outside of the GATT framework and that tend to weaken respect for other GATT rules. As Alan Wolff (1985) has argued, permitting the selective application of import restraints in safeguard cases is necessary if the GATT is to continue to play a central role in maintaining an open trading framework. The unequal treatment among countries that already occurs under GATT-sanctioned customs union and free trade arrangements and under the Generalized System of Preferences (GSP) is also cited as a reason why a shift to the selectivity principle in safeguard cases should not be regarded as too radical.

A similar argument for shifting to the conditional form of MFN is that the present GATT principle is tending to retard the pace of liberalization (Hufbauer, 1984). Countries now are reluctant to reduce trade barriers because of the free-rider problem associated with the unconditional MFN principle. Reciprocal bargaining works best, it is said, when free rides can be controlled, as under the conditional MFN approach. The claim that US markets are far more open than foreign markets is another frequently heard argument for shifting to this approach (Cline, 1983). According to this view, it is necessary to pursue an aggressive policy of selective retaliation in order to force other countries to open their markets to a comparable degree. Still another argument for conditional MFN that has come out of the recent literature on trade policy under imperfectly competitive conditions is that a country can secure a larger share of the international monopoly profits by varying the degree of trade restrictiveness (or export subsidization) among foreign suppliers (or export markets).

Those who favor the maintenance of the unconditional MFN principle and, in some cases, a tightening of its application so as to curtail the spread of preferential arrangements give the following reasons for their views. First, discrimination of the type that will increase under selectivity and the new notion of reciprocity will worsen international political relations. Second, conditional MFN and the bilateralism to which it leads result in a more inefficient use of world resources and a consequent reduction in world income and growth rates as low-cost producers are replaced by high-cost suppliers. Third, discrimination is often ineffective in achieving its intended purposes owing to shifts in supply sources. Fourth, acceptance of conditional MFN will open the way for the introduction of more trade restrictions, both directly and through retaliatory actions, and will further undermine the GATT. Finally, the administration of a conditional MFN system is cumbersome and costly because of the need to renegotiate all previous agreements when a new agreement is concluded that changes the old balance of concessions.

There must clearly be a subjective element in one's views about the relative merits of conditional versus unconditional MFN. If the international trading order will disintegrate even more unless the traditional MFN principle is given up, and if the trading world is so highly imperfect in a competitive sense that an active, aggressive trade policy position is needed to prevent exploitation, then the case for conditional MFN has merit. Unfortunately, we do not have enough historical experience on the first point or enough empirical evidence on the second to reach a firm judgement on this interpretation of the nature of the international trading regime. However, the potential political and economic costs appear to be so large, and the uncertainty about the policy's effectiveness so great, that it seems prudent to explore less radical changes in GATT rules before abandoning this cornerstone principle of the organization.

Since it is often said that the requirement to provide compensatory duty reductions (or else risk retaliation) has been an important reason why countries adopt safeguard measures outside of the GATT framework, dropping the compensation requirement (subject to a time-limited, degressive protective arrangement) seems a reasonable alternative to try first. Moreover, most of the instances where unfairness is a major issue can be handled under existing GATT rules on fair trade which permit discriminatory protective responses.

3 REVISING EXISTING GATT RULES

One aspect of the current international trading regime about which public and private leaders in the United States often express great dissatisfaction is the manner in which existing GATT rules covering 'fair trade' operate. They point to the greater openness of markets in the United States compared with markets in Japan and the European Community and the greater assistance provided by the governments of these and most other countries to their domestic industries. Because of these conditions, many government and industry officials believe that, unless current GATT rules are somehow changed to provide 'a level playing field,' the United States should vigorously enforce its own fair trade laws or introduce subsidies itself.

US views on the fairness issue differ considerably from those of most other countries. In many European countries, for example, some traditionally export-oriented industries have suffered rapid losses in their foreign market shares as other countries have developed modern industrial capacity in these sectors. Since import restrictions are not an effective means of assisting an export industry, the governments of these countries feel justified in providing subsidies to these sectors to ease their adjustment problems.

Similarly, most developed countries other than the United States believe on infant industry grounds that the state should assist the establishment of high technology industries – not just with tariffs and other import barriers, but also by providing capital at below commercial market rates of interest. They maintain that their capital markets are not as large or do not function as well as those in the United States and thus there is a need for the government to step in. Furthermore, they point to the technological benefits received by US industries from the large defense and space expenditures of the US government. The developing countries also justify the use of government subsidies to speed up their industrial development on infant industry grounds and because of imperfectly operating private domestic markets.

In justifying government subsidies, other countries point to such statements in the subsidies code as: 'Signatories recognize that subsidies other than export subsidies are widely used as important instruments for the promotion of social and economic policy objectives and do not intend to restrict the right of signatories to use such subsidies to achieve these and other important policy objectives which they consider desirable.' In contrast, US officials point to another part of the code in which signatories agree to seek to avoid the use of subsidies that 'may cause or threaten to cause injury to a domestic industry of another signatory or seriously prejudice the interests of another signatory or may nullify or impair benefits accruing to another signatory under the General Agreement.' They believe other countries' subsidies are in fact causing material injury to many US industries.

Some movement toward reconciling these two divergent viewpoints is needed to avoid a potentially serious breakdown of international discipline on the fair trade issue. One step in this direction might be to try to distinguish better between domestic subsidies of the beggar-thy-neighbor type and those that either can be justified on the same adjustment grounds as protection introduced under article XIX or that contribute to the efficient growth of the world economy. In particular, temporary and degressive subsidies could be permitted for export-oriented industries that are seriously injured by export competition in third markets. Delineating between subsidies that are justifiable from an economic viewpoint on infant industry grounds and those that are aimed simply at shifting market shares at the expense of collective income in the trading community is more difficult, but a key feature of permissible subsidies is that they would be temporary, degressive, and carefully monitored by a GATT committee.

In addition to changes in the GATT rules on subsidies, a comprehensive subsidies negotiation is needed which would be conducted in a manner similar to the item-by-item tariff-negotiating technique, and to the way in which items to be covered by the government procurement code are determined. The objective would be to phase out particular subsidies gradually, to bind their levels for specified periods of time, or perhaps to introduce export taxes (where permitted) to offset the export-subsidizing element in domestic subsidies. The incentives for another country to engage in such negotiations would be not only the willingness to reduce one's own subsidies but the threat of carrying out the countervailing duty actions permitted under GATT rules.

Each country would undertake a comprehensive evaluation of all the subsidizing practices of other countries that it believes are causing material injury to one or more of its industries, seriously prejudicing its interests or nullifying or impairing its GATT benefits. Each country would then make specific requests of other countries concerning the reduction or offset of injury-causing subsidies. At the same time, each country would announce the countervailing duty actions it was prepared to initiate domestically if bilateral or multilateral negotiations were not successful. If past experience is any guide, most countries would be willing to enter into serious negotiations aimed at preventing the imposition of countervailing duties against their exports. Countries which believe their subsidies do not violate GATT rules could announce that they would either request the formation of GATT panels of experts to make decisions on their contention or would take appropriate unilateral action. With a large number of panels, significant progress could be made in establishing precedents and procedures in the panel decision-making process.

The agreements reached in such negotiations, which could cover other NTBs besides subsidies, would be submitted to Congress by the President for approval and would include the necessary domestic implementing legislation. Industries covered by the agreements would be precluded from seeking countervailing duties during the time period covered by the agreements, just as industries covered by the reciprocal tariff agreements negotiated in the 1930s were not subject to the provisions of the 1930 Tariff Act requiring the President to set tariffs that equalized the cost of production of US and foreign producers. However, the escape clause provisions of article XIX would still apply.

The possible danger of a comprehensive negotiation on unfair trading practices is that the entire liberal international trading order might unravel if the participants failed to reach mutually acceptable agreements. However, this is just what is happening under the piecemeal approach now being followed on the subsidies issue.

As noted earlier, a number of governments want the provisions of GATT covering agricultural products changed to prevent export subsidization in this sector. Likewise, a number of governments want to terminate the Multifiber Arrangement and make the textile and apparel sectors subject to the usual GATT rules. These are important issues, but they will not be considered further here.

4 EXTENDING GATT RULES

In recent years the United States has pressed for the adoption of new rules to cover certain forms of trade not currently subject to the international discipline of the GATT. These include trade in services, trade-related investment requirements, counterfeiting, and intellectual property rights. Most industrial countries have joined the United States in calling for negotiations on new codes covering services, counterfeiting and intellectual property rights, but a number of key developing countries have actively opposed bringing these issues before that body. Support for efforts to limit investment-related performance requirements is lacking even among some major developed countries.

The effort to bring traded services within the GATT framework indicates a recognition that this form of trade is becoming increasingly important. Total recorded world receipts from exports of private business services were $366 billion in 1983, compared with only $91 billion in 1971 (US Department of Commerce, 1985). In both years these sums equaled about one-fifth of world merchandise exports.

The classification of services into four categories by Sampson and Snape (1985) is useful in bringing out the various issues that arise in attempts to liberalize this type of trade. They divide traded services into: (1) transactions that occur without the international movement of either the factors producing the service or the receivers of the service; (2) transactions that take place as a consequence of the international movement of productive factors but not of the receivers of the service; (3) transactions that occur with the international movement of the receiver of the service but not the provider of the service; and (4) transactions involving the movement of both productive factors and the receivers of the service.

Such services as consulting, insurance, banking, and the provision of technological information, which are supplied through correspondence and other standard means of communication by productive factors located in the exporting country, are examples of the first category. The provision of insurance, banking, transportation and construction services involving the movement of productive factors to the importing country illustrates the second category. Tourist and education services, in which the consumer of the service moves to the country where the service is produced, fit the third grouping. Transactions such as one country's ships or planes transporting people from another country to a third country belong in the last category.

As Sampson and Snape point out, with their classification all policies restricting international trade in services can be divided conveniently into restrictions on services transactions *per se*, restrictions on the movement of factors producing services, and restrictions on the movement of the receivers of services.

Services trade that fits in the first category is in principle no different from trade in goods. However, it may be more difficult for officials in the importing country to know when such transactions have occurred, and thus to regulate them, than trade in goods. But this problem also arises with regard to some commodity trade. As Sampson and Snape note, freedom of trade in these services requires no barriers on international contracting and on the transmission of information by mail, telegraph and electronic means.

It is the second category of services trade that seems to pose the most difficult problems for liberalization, since the provision of the service usually involves direct investment in the consuming country and/or movement of labor into the country. Most governments are ambivalent about direct investment and movements of labor into their countries. They welcome the employment opportunities provided by direct investment, but they are concerned about the control it gives foreigners over domestic economic activity. Many governments are, for example, reluctant to allow foreign firms to determine the rate at which exhaustible natural resources are exploited. Similarly, in such activities as banking and insurance, governments are concerned about protecting consumers from undue risk, preventing monopoly practices, and controlling monetary and exchange-rate policy. These concerns also prompt them to regulate domestic firms in these activities. In other fields, such as telecommunications, a desire to provide services to most citizens has brought about government ownership, involving the subsidization of some activities and monopoly pricing of others. Significant liberalization in this field will require deregulation and the ending of preferential domestic relationships. Obviously, the key issue in this category is the right of foreigners to establish affiliates in a country and to receive nondiscriminatory national treatment, once established.

Most governments are also ambivalent toward the movement of foreign labor into their countries to help provide services consumed there. When there is a shortage of the type of labor required to produce the service, inflows of labor are welcomed, especially if the stay of workers is only temporary. But governments typically want local labor to be trained to fill all but a small proportion of the jobs generated by foreign firms, since increasing employment for their own citizens is a prime government objective.

The desire of governments to generate employment at home is also a reason why there are barriers to services trade in which the receiver of the service moves to the country producing the service. Limits are often imposed on the amount of funds that students and tourists can take out of a country to save foreign exchange and encourage domestic activity in the services they consume. In addition, there is concern that those educated abroad may not return to their home country to help in its development. The same factors influence governments when they impose barriers to the movement of their citizens to another country to consume services provided by a third country.

All observers agree that negotiations in the services area will be difficult, especially in fields such as banking, insurance, and telecommunications, where there is extensive government control. Some writers, for example, Neu (1985), believe that the effort involved in negotiating in such fields as banking is not worth the disappointing results likely to emerge from such negotiations. Others are concerned that the time and resources required for negotiations in the services area will diminish the effort devoted to strengthening existing GATT rules, such as safeguards and subsidies, which in their view should be the prime concern of the next negotiation.

It is difficult, however, to justify leaving services trade outside of an international framework of 'good' behavior such as the GATT. The rapid growth of this trade is another manifestation of the increasing interdependence of nations, and the problems related to this development are best dealt with as they arise. It may well be that it will be possible to frame only very general codes of good behavior, such as the subsidies and government procurement codes agreed upon in the Tokyo Round. But this framework can retard the growth of barriers to trade in services and serve as a basis for subsequent detailed negotiations, such as were advocated earlier in the subsidy areas.

There is less international support for bringing trade-related investment requirements under GATT discipline than for traded services. However, because of the upsurge in recent years of trade-related performance requirements tied to direct investment in a country (Bale, 1984), trade officials are increasingly concerned that such requirements will seriously undermine the existing liberally oriented trading order. One survey found, for example, that local-content requirements are commonly imposed by governments of advanced developing countries such as Brazil, Mexico and India on companies investing in these countries (Bale, 1984). In about half of the cases, these local-content requirements raised significantly the cost of doing business in these countries. Requirements obliging investing firms to export a certain quantity or proportion of their output are also common. The Mexican government requires foreign companies investing in the auto industry to offset imports and other payments abroad by an equivalent value of exports. In addition, the minimum local-content requirement in this industry is 50 per cent.

In return for accepting trade-related performance requirements (as well as other requirements dealing with such matters as technology transfer, local equity participation and employment of host-country labor), foreign companies usually receive such benefits as tax holidays, rebates of duties on imported goods, infrastructure development and the exclusive right to produce a particular product. While these benefits may be sufficient to enable the foreign firm to earn a profit, the net effect of the various trade-related requirements and benefits is to restrict imports, artificially promote exports, and generally distort the use of world economic resources. Countries that impose performance requirements may reap short-run economic gains, but there is an abundance of development experience indicating that such distorting policies retard the growth process over the long run.

Existing GATT rules cover some trade-related investment requirements, but they have been ineffective in preventing the increased use of these measures. For example, in 1982 the United States initiated a GATT action against Canada's use of local-content and export requirements under its Foreign Investment Review Act on the grounds that they violated articles III and XVII of the General Agreement. Article III states that imported products must be accorded treatment no less favorable than that accorded to like products of national origin in respect of all laws affecting their sale, purchase or use, while article XVII requires GATT signatories to act solely in accordance with commercial considerations in imposing measures affecting imports or exports by private traders. The GATT panel appointed to consider the case agreed that Canada's local-content requirements were inconsistent with its obligations under articles III and XVII but decided that GATT rules did not cover its export requirements.

A specific GATT code dealing with trade-related performance requirements imposed on foreign investors is very much needed to halt the spread of these trade-distorting regulations and to begin eliminating the existing ones. It would be desirable to link it with a general code on investment flows, but the strong disagreement among nations on the extent to which governments should interfere with inward or outward investment flows makes it unlikely that an investment code can be negotiated at this time. While not as strong, there is also considerable opposition, especially among the developing countries, to more explicit GATT rules aimed at preventing the imposition of trade-related performance requirements on the foreign firms that are permitted to invest in a country. Until a greater consensus can be reached, probably the best way to proceed is to continue to file GATT actions against these requirements (perhaps citing the 'unfair trade' provisions of the Agreement in the case of export requirements) and at the same time to attempt to negotiate bilateral agreements covering performance requirements. Unilateral actions are also likely to be needed to bring some countries to the bargaining table.

Providing greater protection for intellectual property rights and preventing the counterfeiting of trademarked commercial goods are other areas needing an extension of GATT rules. It has been estimated that in the United States alone the value of counterfeit imports is $6 billion annually (Aho and Aronson, 1985). The rapid expansion of trade in such items as computer software has increased the pressures from most of the technologically advanced countries for such rules. A code to prevent counterfeit trade in trademarked merchandise was tentatively agreed on in the Tokyo Round by the major trading nations, but it has not been put into effect owing to the opposition of the developing countries. These countries still argue that the matter should be considered in the World Intellectual Property Organization rather than in the GATT. However, no matter what organization deals with the issue, the case for strengthening the rules against counterfeiting and the use of intellectual property without some payment to the owners is very strong and justifies the use of discriminatory unilateral actions against offending countries.

5 DISPUTE SETTLEMENT PROCEDURES

Another area of general dissatisfaction with the present trading order is the dispute settlement system of the GATT. It is alleged that the panels of experts appointed to render non-binding decisions in a dispute are influenced by political pressures from the disputants (particularly the major trading powers) and thus are not objective enough. Some countries have also blocked the adoption by the Contracting Parties as a whole of a panel's decision when this decision was unfavorable to them. Even when a decision has been adopted by the group, some countries have ignored it and continued the condemned practice.

An obvious drawback to current procedures is the appointment to dispute settlement panels of officials representing the GATT governments that may later be involved in a dispute. There is a natural tendency for current decisions, or even the question of whether to bring an action against another country, to be influenced by possible decisions and actions on unrelated disputes in the future (Hudec, 1978). It is frequently suggested that the decision-making process would be improved by the establishment of a permanent roster of experts who are not currently representing any government and in whom members have confidence. In addition, it is sometimes proposed that the GATT Secretariat be permitted to initiate inquiries.

The 1982 ministerial agreement that no single nation would veto the dispute settlement process may help to improve the manner in which panel decisions are handled, but more experience with this is needed before a firm conclusion can be drawn. It must be recognized, however, that, unless there is general acceptance of GATT rules, there is little chance of compliance with these rules, particularly by the large trading nations. The only way to make the dispute settlement process effective is to restore confidence that the rules work to the advantage of all countries in the long term.

6 CONCLUSIONS

Although there is general dissatisfaction with the manner in which the international trading regime is operating, there seems to be no practical alternative but to try to improve upon the existing institutional framework. Attempts to replace the GATT with a new organization are at best likely to result in an even broader set of rules with a greater number of permitted exceptions than we now have, and most likely in no agreement at all. In attempting to modify the GATT to achieve greater conformity with a set of international rules of 'good' behavior, the greatest danger may be yielding to short-run pressures for agreement at the long-run cost of harmonious international political relations and world economic growth. Rule changes must not be made that go against political and economic principles that have proved their worth over many years of historical experience.

Much of the current dissatisfaction in the United States with the international trading order can be traced to US macroeconomic policies that have resulted in a very strong dollar and have put severe competitive pressures on both import-competing and export-oriented industries. No GATT rule changes will alleviate this problem; only changes in macroeconomic policies will do this. As the United States tries to adapt to the ending of its hegemonic position in the world economy, there is also a natural tendency to blame the unfair practices of others as the cause of the relative decline in the US competitive position. But GATT rule changes are likely to have only a marginal effect on the US competitive position. Some changes can and should be made that will give the United States more time to adjust to its new role. However, we must be careful not to create a set of international trading rules that appear to help in the short term but works against the long-run interests of the United States and the rest of the trading world.

REFERENCES

Aho, C. Michael and Aronson, Jonathan D. (1985). *Trade Talks: America Better Listen!* New York: Council on Foreign Relations.

Bale, Harvey E., Jr. (1984). Trade policy aspects of international direct investment policies. In R. E. Baldwin (ed.), *Recent Issues and Initiatives in US Trade Policy*. Cambridge, Mass.: National Bureau of Economic Research.

Cline, William R. (1983). 'Reciprocity': a new approach to world trade policy? In William R. Cline (ed.), *Trade Policy in the 1980s*. Washington, DC: Institute for International Economics.

Hudec, Robert E. (1978). *Adjudication of International Trade Disputes*, Thames Essay no. 13. London: Trade Policy Research Centre.

Neu, C. Richard (1986). International Trade in Banking Services. Paper presented at the Centre for European Policy Studies/National Bureau of Economic Research Conference on Europe – United States Trade Relations, Brussels, June 12–14, 1986.

Nogues, Julio J., Olechowski, Andrzej and Winters, L. Alan (1985). The extent of non-tariff barriers to industrial countries' imports. Washington, DC: World Bank.

Sampson, Gary P. and Snape, Richard H. (1985). Identifying the issues in trade in services. *The World Economy*, 8, 171–81.

US Department of Commerce (1985). *United States Trade Performance in 1984 and Outlook*. Washington, DC: US Department of Commerce, International Trade Administration.

Winters, L. Alan (1985). Negotiating the removal of non-tariff barriers. Washington, DC: World Bank

Wolff, Alan W. (1985). The need for new GATT rules to govern safeguard actions. In William R. Cline (ed.), *Trade Policy in the 1980s*. Washington, DC: Institute for International Economics.

15
The Importance of Frontier Barriers

Richard H. Snape

1 INTRODUCTION

This paper focuses on the distinctions between frontier and non-frontier interventions by government, and between measures that stimulate and reduce international trade. It does so from a number of aspects: first, the effects of policies on the countries adopting them; second, the impact of policies on trading partners; and third, the negotiation of international trade 'law'. The argument is as follows.

1. Frontier barriers are frequently a vital element in causing or supporting the inefficient allocation of resources in the countries imposing the barriers – open frontiers severely constrain inefficiencies, whether they arise from private or government actions.
2. Frontier barriers are generally more harmful to trading partners (and potential partners) than other policies that affect international trade – in part directly, but also by supporting other policies that harm foreigners.
3. Policies that are aimed at expanding international trade are less harmful in practice than those that tend to contract it.
4. International trade negotiations and law cannot be successful unless they focus on what is definable.
5. There is no agreement as to what constitutes fair trade and as to which non-frontier policies distort international trade.
6. Therefore, frontier barriers should be a primary focus of domestic policy concern and, particularly, of negotiations of international trade policies.

It follows, then, that much of the international negotiation in recent years that has concentrated on subsidies that promote exports has been barking up the wrong tree. Much of this barking has been due to a search for fair trade, or a level playing field, as it is frequently called.

The paper develops a proposal put forward by Max Corden at a conference of the Institute for International Economics. Looking at international

I am much indebted to Peter Lloyd and Gary Sampson for comments.

negotiations, he outlined the choice between complex rules, decentralized complex negotiations, and simple rules, and leaned to a simple-rules approach. In short, his preferred simple rules are:

> - Abolish quantitative restrictions and tariffs;
> - Permit subsidies – especially employment subsidies and adjustment assistance;
> - Possibly allow for temporary, transparent safeguard arrangements.
>
> (Corden, 1983, p. 746)

2 FRONTIER AND NON-FRONTIER MEASURES

To a significant extent, the distinction between policies that affect international trade and those that do not is blurred: all economic policies can be expected to have a greater or lesser impact, however indirect, on international trade. Furthermore, policies that affect international trade directly can be simulated by combinations of other policies. Thus, the incentive and trade-restricting effects of a 10 per cent import tariff can be replicated by a 10 per cent consumption tax combined with a 10 per cent production subsidy. Nevertheless, for many purposes it is useful to distinguish between those policies that directly impact on international trade and those that do so only indirectly. Those that do so directly I shall term 'frontier measures'.

Frontier measures, then, are those policies which discriminate between national and foreign sources of supplies or between national and foreign destinations. Included (*inter alia*) are import and export taxes and subsidies; quantitative restrictions on imports and exports, including voluntary export restraints, orderly marketing arrangements and domestic content schemes; government procurement that favours domestic suppliers; and countervailing and anti-dumping duties. Non-frontier policies do not discriminate between sources or destination. Thus, a production subsidy is not 'frontier' because it does not discriminate according to destination of the produce and applies whether or not there are imports; a consumption tax is not 'frontier' because it applies equally to products from all sources; similarly, taxes or subsidies or factors of production without reference to nationality are not frontier policies. Of course, these non-frontier policies may affect international trade – both production subsidies and consumption taxes may reduce imports and/or promote exports.

A production subsidy for a commodity for which domestic demand is unimportant may appear little different from an export subsidy, while a consumption tax on a commodity which is not produced at home may appear similar to an import tariff. But in general, the distinctions are clear in terms of incentives. A production subsidy does not discourage domestic consumption whereas an export subsidy does; similarly, an import tariff encourages domestic production whereas a consumption tax does not.

'Free international trade' is commonly taken to mean the absence of frontier measures relating to trade in goods and services. Usually the focus is on the movement of the commodities or services themselves, but as some services can only be (or are best) traded when the producers and receivers of services are in physical proximity, frontier measures which discriminate between factors of production or receivers of services according to nationality are also relevant to the concept of 'free trade' (see Sampson and Snape, 1985). Nevertheless, the focus of this paper is on trade in products rather than factors. The arguments advanced would be much stronger if free trade in factors were being countenanced as well as trade in products.

3 THE IMPACT OF POLICIES ON THE COUNTRIES IMPOSING THEM

Optimum Policies

The Haberler–Meade–Bhagwati/Ramaswami–Johnson–Corden literature on distortions has a clear message: the correction of domestic distortions leads logically to the use of domestic policy measures, while international distortions lead to trade (i.e. frontier) measures. The closer the impact of the policy weapon to the source of the trouble, the more likely it is to be successful in curing it. This analysis tends to reinforce the general case for free international trade; for, terms-of-trade effects apart, it is rare for arguments for government intervention to be based on propositions that are strictly of an international economic nature.

The simplicity of this message is modified when there are more objectives than policy instruments, when there is uncertainty, and when one takes into account the cost of implementing policies (e.g. the costs of raising revenue to finance lump-sum subsidies). Nevertheless, it provides a sensible starting point for policy-makers (Corden, 1974, ch. 2 and 3). Thus there is a presumption that frontier policies, even when used in an attempt to offset a market inefficiency, would perform less adequately in meeting the objective than other policies, and may very well make things worse. To have frontier policies removed from the toolkit would be no great loss in the pursuit of economic efficiency for most countries – even granted the terms of trade argument for intervention, which is, of course, one country's gain at the expense of others.

Outward- v. Inward-looking Regimes

The efficacy of outward-looking policies in promoting growth and resilience appears to be well established by the work on developing countries of Little, Scitovsky and Scott, Krueger, Bhagwati, Balassa and others, though the lesson is not confined to these countries. Of course, 'outward-looking' regimes often employ trade-promoting measures which may lead to the inefficient expansion of some industries. However, it appears that such policies usually do little more on balance than counteract the effects of trade barriers on other products. Statistical measurements of 'trade bias' across countries show relatively small biases for export-promoting countries but some major biases for import-replacing countries (Krueger, 1978, p. 260; 1983, ch. 3). The dispersion of incentives across industries – the essence of an inefficient set of incentives – has been substantially greater under import replacement regimes. In part this is because trade barriers, particularly when they are in non-tariff forms, tend to breed more and more barriers (Krueger, 1983, pp. 38–9; Bhagwati, 1978). Having embarked upon a course of assistance against import competition, it becomes increasingly difficult to refuse new applications, particularly when the competition comes by way of loopholes in existing regulations. In contrast, 'a genuine export promotion policy must be accompanied by the maintenance of a fairly open and liberalized trade regime, which tends to be self-reinforcing' (Krueger, 1983, p. 33).

Limiting Distortions

While frontiers that are relatively free from barriers may not on their own guarantee an environment for growth, they create a binding constraint on the extent to which non-frontier policies and other domestic distortions can generate sets of incentives that breed inefficiency. If one really wishes to create an environment to develop a highly inefficient economy in a country that might in other ways be suited to growth (if, say, it has stable internal and external political relations), frontier barriers appear to be an essential ingredient. And it seems that the objective will be achieved most effectively if the barriers are in non-tariff forms, for these inevitably bring wasteful rent-seeking, uncertainty of implementation and other bureaucratic inefficiencies.

Open frontiers thus not only provide the possibility of the conventional 'gains from trade' through production according to comparative advantage, economies of scale, transmission of knowledge and so on: they may also result in countries producing closer to their own production possibility frontiers, and at efficient points on these frontiers. They can constrain many market inefficiencies, in particular those related to monopolistic powers in both product and factor markets; and, perhaps more important still, they can constrain governments in the distortions which they can produce.

Market distortions

Product markets There is abundant literature and evidence regarding the constraints that open frontiers place on monopoly power in product markets (Corden, 1974, ch. 8). In part, there is the basic point that monopoly power depends not on the number of producers in a market, but on the number of independent sources of supply. But also important is the industry structure and the impact on this of open frontiers. The connection between trade policy and industry structure has attracted a good deal of attention in some Canadian and Australian literature. More recently, the arguments have been formalized in a general equilibrium context by Harris and others (Harris, 1984). Estimates of the 'cost of protection' have been increased greatly by allowing for the impact of the additional foreign competition on industry structure brought by reduced barriers to trade (Parmenter, 1984).

Product market distortions in the form of monopolies or cartels are often encouraged or created by governments and are frequently implemented or buttressed by frontier barriers. Adam Smith had much to say in this regard. In more recent times, Jan Tumlir in particular has reminded us of governments' contributions to cartelization:

> The distinguishing feature of the new protectionism is that it infringes on competition in more, and more drastic, ways than the old varieties. . . . In some industries and countries or regions, protectionism assumes the form of defensive cartels in which the organized self-interest of an industry is backed by the coercive power of public authority, which enforces discipline among firms and grants the protection without which higher prices could not be maintained at home. In other situations, a public authority seeks protection for industries under its jurisdiction through agreements that, whether negotiated directly with the foreign export industry or with its public authority, almost inevitably imply cartelization of the foreign suppliers.
>
> (Tumlir, 1979, pp. 250–1)

He (and Smith) have emphasized the inefficiencies of such arrangements.[1]

The arguments here may appear somewhat at variance with the success of the so-called 'Japanese model'. There is, of course, some dispute as to the extent to which Japan has actually adopted what is termed the Japanese model (Council of Economic Advisers, 1984, ch. 3). But, leaving this aside, the thrust of the argument is *not* that some countries may not be able to secure an efficient allocation of resources and constrain monopolistic and oligopolistic inefficiencies even in the presence of frontier barriers – particularly if they have the determination to integate into the world economy through exports in the manner implicit in the Japanese model. (And, of course, exports imply imports, so that export success implies that frontier barriers cannot be restraining imports to the extent that is often suggested in descriptions of the Japanese model.) Rather, the point is that relatively open frontiers impose constraints, which otherwise might not exist, on inefficiencies.

Factor markets Sources of factor market inefficiencies include immobility of factors of production, rigidity (usually downwards) of factor prices, and a whole variety of regulations, taxes and subsidies which may cause the ratio of the marginal productivities of various factors of production to be different across industries. Will these distortions, and the loss of output they cause, be greater or less when there are low barriers to trade? In the presence of such distortions, it is possible that lower barriers (or free trade) may result in reduced real output (Johnson, 1965; Brecher, 1974). But it is not sufficient to examine the effects of low barriers *given* the factor market distortions: attention should also be given to the effects of open frontiers on the distortions themselves.

With regard to factor price rigidity, immobility of factors of production, restrictive work practices and so on, to the extent that they impose real output costs on the economy in the presence of open frontiers, a significant part of the cost is likely to accrue to the group imposing the distortion, though not to all members of the group. For example, if downward rigidity of real wages brings reduced output and increased unemployment when frontiers are opened, the unemployment will hit the workers in the industries which are adversely affected. There is a trade-off, among the workers themselves, of wages for employment. This being so, and in the absence of government support for those imposing the distortions, the opening of frontiers may very well lead to a reduction of the distortions. The obverse of this is illustrated in a number of developed countries in which minimum wage legislation, and/or immobility of factors of production, appear to have led to barriers to the imports of labour-intensive products – 'trade policy is labour market policy' is a simplified summary of the interconnection.

In relation to those factor market distortions which are more directly a consequence of government policy, some are intimately linked to frontier barriers and thus would yield to open frontiers. Some developing countries provide significant examples of these trade-related factor market distortions (Krueger, 1983, ch. 7). One such example is the subsidies that accrue to the users of capital goods because of the relatively favourable treatment that imports of these goods usually receive when there are extensive quantitative restrictions on imports, or when imports are restricted by means of exchange control. Another is the more or less arbitrary manner in which imports of capital goods are often determined and allocated when imports are severely restricted. In many countries such distortions are major sources of inefficiency. Open frontiers would directly remove the distortions.

Government distortions

As already noted, the distortions introduced by governments may be in product or factor markets. The contribution of governments to some factor market distortions has just been described. Government distortions may be divided into those that involve expenditure and those that do not, and into those that are at the frontier and those that are non-frontier. Thus, import and export barriers have two characteristics: they are at the frontier, and they do not require government expenditure, apart from the cost of an administrative machinery – indeed, some forms of frontier barrier raise revenue for Treasuries. In contrast, export (or import) subsidies generally require expenditure.[2]

Assistance to industries which is 'off-budget' appears in general to be greater and more durable than on-budget assistance, and among off-budget forms, assistance through frontier barriers in prone to be relatively unrestrained in extent and duration, particularly when it is in non-tariff forms. Therefore, such barriers tend to be essential ingredients in major government-related distortions in markets for tradable products. This is so even though direct subsidies tend to be less costly in terms of real national income (at least in the economist's conception of real national income) than import barriers. Subsidies which do not involve expenditure (e.g. tax concessions) also appear to give limited assistance as compared with frontier barriers. In part this is because the taxes themselves limit the extent of tax exemptions.

Import tariffs and non-tariff barriers on most manufactured goods are restricted by GATT obligations, but many other forms of industry assistance (e.g. domestic subsidies) can be used with impunity as far as GATT is concerned. However, so strong is the preference for trade barriers over other forms of assistance that countries choose to negotiate GATT-evading voluntary export restraints or organized marketing arrangements, thereby worsening their own terms of trade, rather than provide assistance to favoured industries through non-frontier policies which do not worsen their terms of trade.

Just why there is such a bias towards trade barriers as a means of assistance does not appear to be fully explained. One popular explanation is the separation of powers and functions within the bureaucracy and the ease of 'capture' by industry interests of Departments of Trade as compared with Treasuries; a second is that a tax on imports is often perceived to be a tax on foreigners; another is the relative concealment of assistance through means such as tariffs as compared with on-budget subsidies (Corden, 1974, pp. 54–7). But to many these explanations, though having substance, are not completely satisfying. Perhaps the most important element in the choice is the distinction between assistance which requires government expenditure and that which does not.

Be that as it may, it appears that in all tradable commodities barriers to imports are a necessary ingredient of substantial sectoral protection and distortions that persist over an extended period. This applies not only to developing countries but also to developed countries in those sectors in which assistance has been running at high levels in recent years – agriculture, clothing, textiles, footwear, steel, automobiles and some electronic products. As tariffs have been lowered on these products (with the exception of agriculture), the tariff assistance has been replaced not by non-frontier measures, but by non-tariff frontier barriers. It is significant that shipbuilding, in which on-budget expenditure in some countries has been substantial, has seen rather more rapid reduction of assistance than some other sectors. And it is only when support for European agriculture stated to have major budgetary implications (which it did not when it was simply import-replacing) that opposition to the Common Agricultural Policy within Europe started to gain strength.

To suggest that governments could distort their economies less if they did not impose barriers at the frontier carries little operational content unless there is a will by governments to distort less. Why, if governments wish to distort less, don't they do just that? The conflict between general and particular interests is of importance here. It is quite common, if not universal, for governments to set themselves general constraints to restrict their own actions on particular issues. Their perception of the general interest, and commitments to it, can be used to provide the backing to say 'no' to particular pressure groups. (The lesson of Ulysses and the sirens lives on.) Thus, the acquisition of international commitments in the context of a consideration of the general good is a means by which governments may buttress themselves against special interest pressure. The arguments above suggest that commitments regarding the containment of frontier barriers have a special value for governments that desire to preserve efficient production structures; if special interests are not able to secure barriers to trade, the amount of harm they can do to the common weal will be relatively limited. The arguments bring out the importance, to the country imposing them, of frontier barriers. It is not being suggested that a country with closed frontiers *may* not be able to function efficiently – subject, of course, to the constraint that it is a closed economy. Rather, it is that open frontiers constrain the extent to which inefficiencies can develop and persist in market structures.

4 EFFECTS ON OTHER COUNTRIES

Subsidies and Import Barriers

Are frontier barriers of more harm to trading partners than other policies? To answer this question it is necessary to specify the objective of the policies, the structure of the industry in which the policies are implemented, and whether an importing or exporting country is imposing the policy (Snape, 1986). Of course, if the objective is to reduce imports (or expand exports) of particular commodities by a certain amount and this objective is achieved, frontier and non-frontier measures imposed in the same country will have the same effects on other countries, at least in the short run.

If competitive conditions prevail, and if the policy objective is assistance to a domestic industry (rather than contraction of imports *per se*), then policies that assist domestic producers without decreasing domestic demand will generally be less harmful to foreign exporters. Thus production subsidies would be better than barriers to imports from the point of view of foreign producers, for, with the same degree of assistance, the level of imports will be greater. While it is possible that, in raising revenue to pay such subsidies, total import demand in general may be more restricted than it would by a barrier to the relevant import, this appears to be rather unlikely in practice.

For exportables, and when production subsidies are being compared with export subsidies, the position is less clear-cut. For any given degree of assistance to producers, exports will tend to be greater with export subsidies than with production subsidies, for the former raise the price to domestic consumers as well as to producers and thereby discourage domestic demand. All export-promoting subsidies tend to improve the terms of trade of the rest of the world considered as a whole – and thereby give a potential gain to the rest of the world. (Note that we are focusing on export-promoting subsidies as such. As already noted, export promotion is often combined with import barriers on the same product in the same country, and the combination of these two policies together does not necessarily improve the terms of trade of the rest of the world.) So export subsidies, in tending to produce more exports for the same amount of domestic protection, and by the criterion of terms-of-trade effects, give more benefit to the rest of the world than do production subsidies. But such is the power of producer relative to consumer interests, together with the fact that export-promoting subsidies are so frequently combined with import barriers on the same product in the same country, that there is general hostility to export-promoting subsidies. (The different interests of grain and meat exporters on the one hand, and importers on the other, to the European Common Agricultural Policy is well demonstrated by Anderson and Tyers, 1986.)

Moving back to import barriers, when there are elements of monopoly in production or importing, things can become more complicated than when competition prevails. If a government is trying to secure a particular price for producers when domestic production is monopolized, it will be possible for quotas allocated to importers to yield a higher level of imports than even a production subsidy (or an import tariff), and thus for the import quota to be of more benefit to foreign exporters.[3] But this rather paradoxical case does not carry over to where the domestic objective is a target level of production: here the objective will be achieved with a higher level of imports when assistance is by means of a production subsidy than if a trade barrier is used.

If there is monopolistic importing (but competitive production), again production subsidies tend to imply higher levels of imports than do trade barriers when protectionist objectives are pursued. A similar conclusion holds when a particular enterprise (or group of enterprises) has a monopoly in both production and importing.

In summary, then, in most circumstances frontier barriers in importing countries do more harm to other countries than do production subsidies that yield the same degree of protection. And, for an exporting country, export subsidies tend to give better terms of trade to the rest of the world than do production subsidies, again for the same degree of protection.

It is sometimes argued that import barriers may be less harmful to foreign producers than production subsidies, for while trade barriers will not normally turn importers into exporters, subsidies to production may do so. This argument has some substance in that a country's trade barrier is only likely to generate exports of the relevant product: (1) if it is accompanied by a subsidy on exports or production, or (2) if there are economies of scale and the trade barrier permits a higher price on the domestic market which then cross-subsidizes sales on the export market (Pursell and Snape, 1973). But against this, the costs to Treasuries of subsidies are generally reduced very greatly if the subsidies are accompanied by trade barriers to imports of similar products. Because of this, export-promoting production subsidies *unaccompanied by import barriers* are in most cases of little threat to producers in other countries.

Voluntary Export Restraints

There is a presumption from the above that production (or export) subsidies will be less harmful to foreigners than import barriers in pursuing protective objectives. But how will restraints by foreign exporters compare? It is fairly clear that they will be preferred by foreign exporters if import barriers are the alternative. Such a choice leads to 'voluntary' export restraints. For any given quantity of trade, exporters are likely to secure for themselves the economic rent attached to restriction if they impose the controls, whereas the importing country is likely to secure this rent if it is the country that is restraining the trade. But the comparison of an export restraint with a production subsidy is less clear-cut. Suppose competitive production and trading conditions prevail and the government in the importing country wishes to assist producers, either by a production subsidy or by securing a restraint on exports by foreign exporters. With a production subsidy there will be more trade than with the voluntary export restraint but the price received by exporters will be less. It is not clear in general which policy would be better for exporters.

If they are able to affect the terms of trade, exporters as a whole will be better off with some (though not any) restriction of trade than with free trade. In facilitating this restriction by encouraging 'voluntary' export restraints, importing countries assist the exporters. But of course, the degree of restraint that would meet the objectives of the importing countries is unlikely to be the restraint that would maximize income for the exporters, and it may not even increase this income. Thus, while voluntary export restraints may assist exporting enterprises, they are not necessarily better for exporters – or for potential exporters – than open frontiers.

A great deal has been written about voluntary export restraints in recent years (e.g. Hamilton, 1984; Hindley, 1980; Greenaway and Hindley, 1985). It is important not only to a compare these with other forms of industry assistance at a given moment, but to consider how they evolve over time. The prime example is the Multifibre Arrangement (MFA) and how the extraordinary complex set of export restraints that has been established under the MFA unbrella has evolved from a relatively simple short-term textile arrangement of 1961. The MFA appears to have developed its own dynamic of complexity; while it may be preferable to other forms of frontier barrier yielding equal protection, and while developing country exports of clothing and textiles have, in general, continued to grow under the MFA (Hughes and Krueger, 1984), it appears most unlikely that non-frontier protection measures in developed countries could have imposed anywhere near the same restraint of imports or the same cost on exporters and potential exporters of clothing and textiles. Furthermore, the MFA and other voluntary export restraint arrangements have induced the cartelization of exporters, and the protection of existing exporters from new entrants, thereby inhibiting the efficient development of production in exporting countries.

Other Export Barriers

Export barriers are not only erected at the behest of trading partners, as they have in the case of voluntary export restraints. They are also erected explicitly to improve the exporters' terms of trade (OPEC is the prime example), or to stimulate domestic processing (Malaysian restrictions on the export of unprocessed tin is a case in point). The protective objective could generally be achieved at lesser cost to trading partners by production subsidies; the terms of trade objective of course leads to the use of a trade restriction as the logical weapon, but, as noted earlier, it is a gain at the expense of other countries, lowering world income in the process, and thus can be regarded as a rather noxious form of intervention from an international perspective.

In summary, then, frontier barriers generally have more harmful effects on other countries than non-frontier measures addressing the same objectives. Voluntary export restraints may, in some circumstances and in the short run, provide an exception to this, but not, generally, in the longer term. Depressed and unstable world prices of many primary products, for example, are a direct consequence of frontier barriers – the export subsidies of the European Economic Community, on which much attention is currently focused, would be of little concern but for the European frontier barriers that support them (Sampson and Snape, 1980; Valdes and Zietz, 1980).

5 INTERNATIONAL NEGOTIATIONS

It has been argued above that frontier barriers are of crucial importance in sustaining domestic inefficiencies and that, in their effects on other countries, non-frontier policies and trade-promoting policies that are unsupported by frontier barriers on the same products will generally be of little consequence, at least in the longer term. Therefore, to get to the heart of the cause or sustainer of distortions associated with international trade, one needs to focus on frontier barriers. Attempting to contain export-promoting subsidies while tolerating the barriers to trade which buttress them is akin to swatting mosquitoes while being eaten by crocodiles. Furthermore, there is difficulty in principle in defining and measuring a non-frontier subsidy and the extent to which it may promote exports, and considerable differences of opinion exist between various governments in this area. Thus it is argued that international negotiations are best focused on frontier policies and, among these, on frontier barriers.

Where GATT Started

The basic principles underlying the GATT as first negotiated were:

1 non-discrimination with regard to both source and destination of trade: non-discrimination is enshrined in article 1, and is encapsulated by the 'unconditional most-favoured-nation' rule – that is, any benefit that is given to any member of GATT must be extended, unconditionally, to all other members;
2 concentration on measures that have direct impacts on international trade, that is, that are applied at the frontier;
3 proscription of those frontier measures that do not operate through the price mechanism. Thus, article XI of GATT is entitled 'General Elimination of Quantitative Restrictions'. (The restrictions to be eliminated were those on exports as well as imports, although the application to exports is often overlooked.)

There were exceptions to all these principles. Grandfather provisions were relevant in many areas, for example in relation to trade preferences which already existed. Customs unions were allowed as exceptions to the MFN rule. Quantitative restrictions on imports were permitted in balance of payments crises (particularly for developing countries) and, in some circumstances, for agricultural products. Temporary escape from obligations was provided where serious injury to domestic producers was caused or threatened, though such 'safeguard' action was to be non-discriminatory and could require compensation to the exporting country. But despite these qualifications, the general theme of the GATT was non-discrimination, transparency and, largely though the 'binding' of negotiated concessions, predictability. With the exception of the legitimization of countervailing and anti-dumping duties, the emphasis was on containing and reducing frontier barriers, particularly non-tariff forms. And even with regard to countervailing and dumping duties, by defining the circumstances in which they could be used, the GATT restricted their use.

Developments of GATT

Two major developments of GATT since 1947 have been the effective removal of some commodities from the provisions of its 'general' rules (and an evasion of the rules in the case of some other products), and a concerted attempt to eliminate subsidies that promote exports. The more commodities that have been extracted from GATT coverage – and these extractions have permitted the growth of non-tariff barriers – the greater has been the pressure, in some quarters, to control subsidies.

Agriculture was a problem right from the start, being the Achilles' heel of the US opposition to British support for the limited use of quantitative import barriers. Special provisions for agriculture were written into the original GATT to cope with problems associated with US farm price support; these were then ignored by the US Congress (Gardner, 1980, p. 375). In 1955 a 'waiver' was granted by the Contracting Parties which legitimized the US actions. Other countries then applied for, and received, waivers from their

GATT obligations with respect to their agricultural products. In more recent times, the inability of GATT procedures to constrain the actions of the EEC with respect to sugar exports following successful complaints by Brazil and Australia in the late 1970s indicated a further shrinkage of the applicability of the GATT rules to agriculture (Teese, 1982).

Clothing and textiles emerged as a developing country 'problem' as Japan and then other countries started on the path of industrialization. A short-term cotton textiles arrangement in 1961 led to a long-term arrangement in 1962 and then to the first Multifibre Arrangement in 1973 (encompassing man-made fibre and wool products as well as cotton), and subsequently to MFA II, III, and now IV. The export restraint arrangements of the MFA effectively remove the specified products from coverage by the articles of GATT. As these trade barriers have not been erected under terms of the safeguard article XIX of GATT, compensation for exporters is not required and the restraints can be, and indeed are, discriminatory – that is, they are not negotiated equally with all exporters. Voluntary export restraints of course now apply to many products other than clothing and textiles.

The attempt to prohibit export subsidies came with the GATT review of the mid-1950s, which amended the articles so as to prohibit subsidies which resulted in a lower price for goods (other than primary products) on the export market than on the home market (article XVI: 4).[4] A note to this new section explains that the intention is to 'reach agreement to abolish all remaining subsidies', presumably meaning all subsidies that promote exports of manufactured goods.

Subsidies, and their control, occupied a great deal of time in the Tokyo Round of multilateral trade negotiations. The outcome was a Subsidies 'Code', which is an 'agreement on interpretation and application' of the relevant GATT articles. The Code continues the trend started in the GATT review in attempting to distinguish between export subsidies and other subsidies, and in prohibiting export subsidies (except on agricultural products and by developing countries). The prohibition is enforceable through the multilateral machinery of GATT, but the main remedy in practice against export subsidies and other export-promoting subsidies is still through countervailing duties. The Code provides an illustrative list of export subsidies. (Despite article XVI:4, no mention is made of dual pricing as a criterion in defining an export subsidy.) Subsidies other than export subsidies are not prohibited, but signatories to the Code agree to seek to avoid damaging, by means of subsidies, industries located in other signatories. More importantly with respect to these subsidies, the legalistic procedures of the United States are highly tuned in their 'search-out and countervail' mission against all subsidies that are deemed to promote exports, and this sense of mission appears to have increased in recent years. However,

> the uncertainties and ambiguities surrounding the distinction between export subsidies and other subsidies having export implications or effects have had anomalous consequences. While the Subsidies Code may be of some benefit to

contracting parties especially vulnerable to countervailing action, the confused and contradictory nature of their provisions has reduced their regulatory and surveillance functions to almost farcical proportions.

(Farran, 1986, p. 206)

The Search for the Level Playing Field

The legalism that has developed around the distinctions between unfair (i.e. subsidies, dumping) and fair trading practices and the various degrees of injury to domestic injury that can lead to countervailing or anti-dumping duties on the one hand, or article XIX safeguard action on the other, is itself a barrier to trade. A new form of scholasticism, concerned with the distinction between fair and unfair trade, a distinction which is not too far from the just and unjust price, has arisen. It is much concerned with such questions as whether the training of horticulturalists by a government is to be regarded as a subsidy on the export of roses. If it is, then the exports can have countervailing import duties levied upon them if there is *material* injury (or threat thereof) to the flower industry in the importing country. On the other hand, if it isn't an export-promoting subsidy, there has to be *serious* injury (or threat thereof) before remedial action can be taken, and the action cannot then discriminate specifically against the offending source of supplies.[5]

Protection which is available provided certain degrees of injury are experienced by industries, the required degrees depending on the cause of the injurious competition, has been termed 'contingent' protection (Grey, 1986). This contingent protection is reminiscent of the concept of 'made to measure' protection, a term coined by Corden[6] (1967, pp. 147–9; 1974, pp. 220–3) – protection that will preserve an industry in its current form, without yielding 'excessive' profits. He has, furthermore, emphasized the disincentive effects of such protection on *X*-type efficiency (Corden, 1974, p. 223). Its costs are increased by the uncertainty of application – the vagueness of 'injury' and the various avenues through which injury-based assistance may be sought imposes costs on the country with the 'injury' as well as on exporters.

Political pressure for international trade negotiations within the United States in recent years has arisen almost entirely from feelings of unfairness – the 'unfairness' of foreign governments in blocking US exports while the United States appears to many to have relatively open markets, and in providing advantages to their exporters which are not available to US exporters. (It should be noted, however, that the statistics of 'openness', with respect to non-tariff barriers, do not support this view that the United States has more open frontier than other countries – see Nogues et al., 1985.)[7] President Reagan expresses it thus:

> To make the international trading system work, all must abide by the rules – all must work to guarantee open markets. Above all else, free trade is, by definition, fair trade. When domestic markets are closed to the exports of others, it is no longer free trade. When governments subsidize their manufacturers and farmers

> so that they can dump goods in other markets, it is no longer free trade. When governments permit counterfeiting or copying of American products, it is stealing our future, and it is no longer free trade. When governments assist their exporters in ways that violate international laws, then the playing field is no longer level – and there is no longer free trade. When governments subsidize industries for commercial advantage and underwrite costs, placing an unfair burden on competitors, that is not free trade. . . . I believe that if trade is not fair for all, then trade is 'free' in name only.
>
> (Statement on US trade policy, September 23, 1985)

Clayton Yeutter, the US Trade Representative, added:

> Other nations must understand that the political support in the United States for maintaining and building a more open trading system will be impossible to maintain if progress is achieving more open and fair trade abroad is not made soon.
>
> (Administration statement on international trade policy, September 23, 1985)

Economists need no reminding of the futility of pursuing 'fair' trade or the just price. They are also conscious of the impossibility of measuring in practice, or even of defining, what is a non-frontier export-promoting subsidy. There is no agreement between governments as to what is a legitimate government field of action in industry (e.g., provision of infrastructure) and hence no hope of defining a level playing field. The countervailing of non-frontier subsidies therefore risks irritation of trading partners.

Fairness is a potent political force: the question is how to channel it into fruitful paths. While fair trade rhetoric may cloak the pressures for countervailing and anti-dumping actions, the basic motivation is, after all, protectionist. Anti-dumping, countervailing, article XIX safeguard action and 'voluntary' export restraints are all designed to limit injury to particular industries. There is a great deal to be said for getting them all on one track and thereby dispensing with the fair/unfair distinction. One way that appeals to many economists, and some lawyers (e.g. Barcelo, 1980, 1984), is to concentrate on the consequence of trade actions rather than the causes – that is, to use safeguard procedures that are currently available with respect to 'fair' trade to deal with 'unfair' trade also. There are problems with this, for it could increase the safeguard barriers to fair trade. Such an extension of safeguards could see the compromise of the non-discriminatory application of safeguard actions (an important constraint on their use, despite circumvention by the negotiation of voluntary export restraints), and a weakening of the degree of injury to industries that would justify their use. But provided the safeguard valve can be limited in application and duration, and provided it is non-discriminatory,[8] it appears to have much in its favour.

The other way of handling the 'fair trade' momentum is to focus it on trade barriers by *all* countries rather than on subsidies. I argued earlier that most of the trade-promoting subsidies would be of minor influence if they were not buttressed by trade barriers on the same products. Similarly, most dumping would not be feasible without frontier barriers in the dumping country which enable its producers to segment markets. We come again to frontier barriers as the desirable focus of attention and to where GATT, despite all the exceptions, has had most of its success.

6 CONCLUSION

It has been argued above that barriers to international trade frequently have a crucial role in the maintenance and development of inefficiencies, whether they are in the market itself, or are the consequences of government policies. Trade barriers are also, in general, a notably harmful policy instrument from the point of view of other countries. Thus governments have a particular stake in constraining their own frontier barriers, as well as those of others countries. Subsidies, on the other hand, whether on production or exports, tend to have rather limited effects *unless* they are supported by trade barriers. Furthermore, there is little agreement on the definition and measurement of the export-promoting effects of non-frontier subsidies. Attempts to negotiate in this area are unlikely to be fruitful, and the countervailing of such subsidies generates friction. For all these reasons, it appears wise to concentrate international negotiations on frontier barriers – which for developed countries largely means non-tariff barriers, since tariffs imposed by most OECD countries are low – rather than on subsidies.

NOTES

1 For a recent illustration of Tumlir's point, see 'A cartel to stop America's chip makers feeling dumped upon' (*The Economist*, March 22, 1986, p. 65).

2 One form of export subsidy that does not require government expenditure is a 'home-price' scheme under which dual pricing by producers, with a higher price on the domestic than on the export markets, is aided by an import barrier.

3 The logic is as follows. The additional monopolistic pricing power that is conferred on domestic producers when there are quantitative restrictions of imports leads to reduced production and a higher price than would occur with an equal level of imports under an import tariff. Thus a target price for the producer will be achieved with a higher level of imports under import quotas than with an import tariff, and there may even be a higher level of imports with an import quota than with a production subsidy (see Snape, 1986, pp. 205–11).

4 Article 26 of the charter for the International Trade Organization contained a provision that in part defined export subsidies by such a dual pricing criterion, and encouraged the elimination of export subsidies.

5 Those who enjoy such exercises of the mind could see Mundheim and Ehrenhaft (1984).

6 Gary Sampson drew the similarity of the concepts to my attention.

7 Even excluding fuels, for major categories of which import restrictions have not been binding in recent years, the United States does not measure up particularly

well in terms of restrictiveness of its non-tariff barriers. For manufacturing as a whole, measures of restrictiveness show it to be about average among major industrial countries, and above average in textiles, iron and steel and vehicles (see Nogues et al., 1985, tables 1C and 1D; also tables 8, 9 and 10 for comparisons with other authors).

REFERENCES

Anderson, Kym, and Tyers, Rodney (1986). International effects of agricultural policies. Chapter 5 of R. H. Snape (ed.), *Issues in World Trade Policy: GATT at the Crossroads*. London: Macmillan.

Barcelo, John J. III (1980). Subsidies, countervailing duties and antidumping after the Tokyo Round. *Cornell International Law Journal*, 13, 257–87.

Barcelo, John J. III (1984). An 'Injury-only' regime (for imports) and actionable subsidies. In Don Wallace, Jr et al. (eds), *Interface Three: Legal Treatment of Domestic Subsidies*. Washington DC: International Law Institute.

Bhagwati, Jagdish (1978). *Foreign Trade Regimes and Economic Development: Anatomy and Consequences of Exchange Control Regimes*. Vol. XI of a Special Conference Series on *Foreign Trade Regimes and Economic Development*. Cambridge, Mass.: Ballinger Press for the National Bureau of Economic Research.

Brecher, Richard A. (1974). Optimal commercial policy for a minimum-wage economy. *Journal of International Economics*, 4, 139–49.

Corden, W. M. (1967). Australian tariff policy. *Australian Economic Papers*, 6, 131–54.

Corden, W. M. (1974). *Trade Policy and Economic Welfare*. Oxford: Clarendon Press.

Corden, W. M. (1983). Toward a policy synthesis: panel discussion, 3. In William R. Cline (ed.), *Trade Policy in the 1980s*. Washington, DC: Institute for International Economics.

Council of Economic Advisers (1984). *Annual Report of the Council of Economic Advisers*. Washington, DC: US Government Printing Office.

Farran, Andrew (1986). The interplay of law and economics in international trade regulation. Chapter 10 of R. H. Snape (ed.), *Issues in World Trade Policy: GATT at the Crossroads*. London: Macmillan.

Gardner, Richard N. (1980). *Sterling–Dollar Diplomacy in Current Perspective* (expanded edn). New York: Columbia University Press.

GATT (1984). *International Trade 1983/84*. Geneva: GATT.

Greenaway, David and Hindley, Brian (1985). *What Britain Pays for Voluntary Export Restraints*. Thames Essay no. 43. London: Trade Policy Research Centre.

Grey, Rodney de C. (1986). The decay of the trade relations system. Chapter 2 of R. H. Snape (ed.), *Issues in World Trade Policy: GATT at the Crossroads*. London: Macmillan.

Hamilton, Carl (1984). Economic aspects of 'voluntary' export restraints. Seminar Paper no. 290 (August), Institute for International Economic Studies.

Harris, Richard (1984). Applied general equilibrium analysis of small open economies with scale economies and imperfect competition. *American Economic Review*, 74, 1016–32.

Hindley, Brian (1980). Voluntary export restraints and the GATT's main escape clause. *The World Economy*, 3, 313–41.

Hughes, Helen and Krueger, Anne O. (1984). Effects of protection in developed countries on developing countries' exports of manufacturers. Chapter 11 of Robert E. Baldwin and Anne O. Krueger (eds), *The Structure and Evolution of Recent US Trade Policy*. Chicago: University of Chicago Press for the National Bureau of Economic Research.

Johnson, Harry G. (1965). Optimal trade intervention in the presence of domestic distortions. In Robert E. Baldwin et al., *Trade, Growth and the Balance of Payments*. Chicago: Rand-McNally.

Krueger, Anne O. (1978). *Foreign Trade Regimes and Economic Development: Liberalization Attempts and Consequences*. Vol. X of a Special Conference Series on *Foreign Trade Regime and Economic Development*. Cambridge, Mass.: Ballinger Press for the National Bureau of Economic Research.

Krueger, Anne O. (1983). *Trade and Employment in Developing Countries*. Vol. 3: *Synthesis and Conclusions*. Chicago: University of Chicago Press for the National Bureau of Economic Research.

Mundheim, Robert H. and Ehrenhaft, Peter D. (1984). What is a 'subsidy'? a discussion paper. In Don Wallace Jr et al. (eds), *Interface Three: Legal Treatment of Domestic Studies*. Washington, DC: International Law Institute.

Nogues, Julio J., Olechowski, Andrzej and Winters, L. Alan (1985). The extent of non-tariff barriers to industrial countries' imports. World Bank Discussion Paper no. DRD115, January.

Parmenter, B. R. (1984). Major themes in the results of papers presented to the 1984 Conference on Trade Policy Modelling. Paper presented to the Conference on General Equilibrium Trade Policy Modelling, Columbia University, April 1984; IMPACT Project Preliminary Working Paper IP-21, University of Melbourne.

Pursell, G. and Snape, R. H. (1973). Economies of scale, price discrimination and exporting. *Journal of International Economics*, 3, 85–92.

Sampson, Gary P. and Snape, Richard H. (1980). Effects of the EEC's variable import levies. *Journal of Political Economy*, 88, 1026–40.

Sampson, Gary P. and Snape, Richard H. (1985). Identifying the issues in trade in services. *The World Economy*, 8, 171–81.

Snape, R. H. (1986). The impact on exporters of import restrictions. Chapter 9 of K. Tucker and C. Baden Fuller (eds), *Firms and Markets: Essays in Honour of Basil Yamey*. London: Croom Helm.

Teese, C. F. (1982). A view from the dress circle in the theatre of trade disputes. *The World Economy*, 5, 43–59.

Tumlir, Jan (1979). The new protectionism, cartels, and the international order. In Ryan C. Amacher et al. (eds), *Challenges to a Liberal International Economic Order*. Washington DC: American Enterprise Institute for Public Policy Research.

Valdes, Alberto and Zietz, Joachim (1980). *Agricultural Protection in OECD: Its Costs to Less-Developed countries*. New York: International Food Policy Research Institute, Research Report 21.

Index

Abernathy, William J. *et al.* 119–20
access, market 38, 205, 206–07, 228–9
  for high-technology industries 128–41
adjustment
  assistance 216
  industrial 15, 24, 75–6, 78
  and resource boom 87
advantage, comparative
  concept of 23, 94, 151, 158, 218
agriculture
  development of 176, 180–1, 182, 195–6
  and fair trade 208–09
  and GATT 204, 226–7
  support for 184, 221
aid, overseas, *see* United States, overseas development
Anderson, Kym & Tyers, Rodney 223
antitrust policies 112, 114–17, 124
Armington, Paul S. 159
assignment rules 4, 8–9, 15
  optimal 7–14, 15–16
Ataturk, Kemal 174, 177
Australia, effects of tariffs 74, 227
automobile industry, US 211
  costs 118–20, 121, 122–6
  oligopoly in 113–17
  prices 118, 120–1, 122–4, 126
  protectionism in 129, 221

balance of payments
  and factor prices 59–60, 64
  and GATT 226
  Korea 182–3, 201
  Turkey 185, 187–8, 191, 192, 198, 201
Baldwin, R. E. 16, 69n., 71
barter, policy 79–80
Benvignati, Anita M. 73n.
Bergsten, C. Fred 41n.
Bertrand, Trent J. 54, 57, 73, 78, 121–2
Bhagwati, Jagdish N. 8, 36n., 38n., 41–3, 145
Bhagwati, Jagdish N.; Brecher, Richard A. and Hatta, Tasuo 47
Bhagwati, Jagdish N. and Srinivasan, T. N. 8–10, 32, 41n., 42, 47, 50n.
Bhagwati, Jagdish N.; Srinivasan, T. N. & Wan, Henry Jr. 54, 64
Bhagwati, Jagdish N. and Wan, Henry Jr. 54–5, 61
bilateralism, trade 206
Blackorby, Charles; Boyce, Richard and Russell, R. Robert 147n.
boom
  resource-based 86–96
  traded resource 93–4
  see also 'Dutch Disease'
border protection, *see* frontier barriers; protection
Boston Consulting Group 135
Brander, James A. 132, 143n.
Brander, James A. and Krugman, Paul R. 132, 139
Brander, James A. and Spencer, Barbara J. 73n., 79, 137
Brecher, Richard A. and Bhagwati, Jagdish N. 47
Brecher, Richard A. and Diaz Alejandro, Carlos F. 54, 64
Breton, Albert 78
Britain
  and GATT 226
Burgess, D. F. 5

Cairnes, J. E. 25
Canada
  effects of tariffs 74
  and GATT 212
  resource booms 94
capital
  allocation 75
  costs 118, 126
  inflow 92–3, 189, 198–9
  market 72, 155–7

capital *(continued)*
mobility of 75–6, 86–97
bundled 99
internationally mobile 91–3, 99–100
nationally trapped 87–91
outflow 93–4
shadow price 55, 65
see also factor price, shadow as
substitutable for resources 89–91, 93, 95, 97
see also demand; investment; labor; specific factor models; subsidy
cartelization
and industrial subsidy 115
and trade barriers 219, 224
Carus-Wilson, E. M. 168
Cassing, J. 13, 18n.
Cave, Richard E. and Jones, Ronald W. 41n.
Chamberlin, E. H. 144
choice, practical
models of 76–8
Chun, Doo-Hwan 178
'closed-loop' analysis 133, 140
clothing industry 16, 221, 224, 227
Turkey 174
Cole, David C. and Lyman, Princeton 183n.
Common Agricultural Policy 221, 223
see also agriculture; European Economic Community
compensation
for import injury 24, 36, 206
in international market 79, 81–2, 226
and VERs 41, 227
competition
in high-technology industries 128–9, 136–40
international 73–5, 76n., 77, 80–1
monopolistic 144, 151, 159
perfect 144–8
and VERs 42, 113–16
competition, imperfect 38, 112, 128–9, 141, 206
and intra-industry trade 143–4, 150
and VERs 133, 115–16
conjectural variations model 113–17
Conservative Social Welfare Function (CSWF) 22, 36–7
modelling 23–8
in small country with certainty 25–8, 31
in small country with uncertainty 28–31
as temporary protection 23, 24, 37
three countries with uncertainty 33–6
two countries with certainty 31–3
see also welfare
consumption
contraction in 69
in developing economies 183–4
of final goods 169–71
in resource boom 94
taxation of 216
Cooper, Richard 2
Corden, Dorothy 163
Corden, W. Max 126
academic career 2–3
on Conservative Social Welfare Function 22, 24
education 1
on factor mobility 86 & n., 99
on learning by doing 72
at LSE 1–2
on protection policy 8–9, 69n., 74n., 143, 162–3, 173, 228
on ranking policies 8
on trade policy 202, 215–16
Corden, W. Max and Findlay, Ronald 64–6
Corden, W. Max and Neary, J. P. 86n.
cost-benefit analysis 54, 60–2, 64–5
Council of Mutual Economic Assistance (CMEA) 181
counterfeiting, opposition to 209, 212
country-of-origin requirements 37
Cournot model 74, 79–80, 115–16, 121–2
in high technology industries 132, 134, 140
credit
creation of 183–4
and economic development 185–6, 187, 189, 193
customs unions 205, 226

Dasgupta, Partha and Stiglitz, Joseph 72n.
Deardorff, Alan V. 28, 145n., 149n.
deficits, budget
Korea 183
Turkey 184
demand
in automobile industry 113–15, 118–19, 120–1, 123, 126
for capital 89, 147
and economic development 176, 183, 187–8, 192
for exports 79, 132, 134, 151
for imports 73, 222

for labor 89, 147, 196
and price levels 130
for raw materials 166–7, 169–70
and trade barriers 222
and trade volumes 144–5, 146–7, 156, 158
development
economic policy in 172–202
trade policy in 209, 211–12, 217, 227
see also Korea; Turkey
Diamond, Peter and Mirrlees, James 54, 63–4
Diaz Alejandro, Carlos 162–3
Diewert, W. Erwin and Woodland, Alan D. 54, 61
distribution, costs of 135
Dixit, A. 129
Dixit, A. and Grossman, A. 129
Dixit, A. and Norman, Victor 143n.
Dixit-Stiglitz model 144
domestic content control 211–12, 216
Drèze, Jean and Stern, Nicholas 62
'dumping, reciprocal' 132, 136, 139
'Dutch Disease' 86–8, 90–5
duties
anti-dumping 216, 226, 228–9
countervailing 208, 216, 226–9

Eaton, Jonathan and Grossman, Gene M. 24, 28, 112, 123, 129, 140–1
Economides, Nicholas 152
employment
in developing economies 196–8
full, and factor prices 57–9, 89
full, and product differentiation 146
preservation of 77–8
public-sector 66
and services trade 210
as target variable 10–11
endowment, effective 151–3, 158
differences, effects of 143, 145–6, 148, 155–6
Turkey 182
entry deterrence
theory of 74
see also access, market equilibrium, free-trade 145, 148–50, 153
equilibrium analysis, general 218
and VERs 41, 42, 43–7
equilibrium analysis, partial
and industrial policies 68n.
and VERs 41–2, 43, 46
escape clause mechanisms 36n.
'Etatism' in Turkey 174
European Economic Community
access to markets 206
industrial policy 77
and trade safeguards 36–7, 225, 227
see also Common Agricultural Policy
exchange rate
and foreign investment 210
Korea 182–3, 186, 189–90, 192–3
purchasing-power-parity, price-level-deflated 192
Turkey 184, 185, 188, 190, 191, 192–3, 202
expenditure, government
of developing countries 180–1
and frontier barriers 220–1
exports
costs of 132
developing economies 176, 180–1, 183–9, 198, 200–02, 224
elasticity pessimism 172
monopoly in 73
of raw materials 163, 166–9
subsidies 74, 79, 113, 128–9, 173, 185–6, 188–9, 207–8, 215–16, 220–30
tax on 46–50, 112, 162, 168–71, 208
and trade volumes 152
exports, voluntary restraint (VER) 28, 38, 41–51, 78, 113, 205
as benefiting foreign exporter 42–7, 49–50
as benefiting home welfare 47–8
compared with import restrictions 42–6, 50
costs of 35
and frontier barriers 216, 218, 221, 224–5, 227, 229
and higher-quality exports 41
Japanese 41, 47, 123
see also competition, perfect; competition, imperfect; equilibrium analysis, general; equilibrium analysis, partial

factor mobility
bundled 99–110
composite bundling 100, 110
and frontier barriers 217, 219–20
international 88, 99–110
limitations on 99
modelling 5–7, 11, 25
national 86–8
reverse bundling 99–100, 108–09
see also capital; 'Dutch Disease'; labor; specific factor models; welfare
factor price, shadow 54–66
applications 64–6

factor price, shadow *(continued)*
derivation 58–62, 64–6
equalization 61
foreign-exchange-equivalent 55, 58
indeterminacy 59
Falvey, Rodney E. 41, 143n.
Falvey, Rodney E. and Lloyd, P. J. 24
Farran, Andrew 227–8
Feenstra, Robert C. 41, 112n., 145n.
Findlay, Ronald 162n.
Findlay, Ronald and Wellisz, Stanislaw 54–5, 60, 62–3
first-best, theory of 69–71, 73
fixed target models 10
footwear industry 16, 221
Turkey 174
Foster, Edward 65
Frank, Charles R., Kim, Kwang-suk and Westphal, Larry E. 176n., 183, 190
frontier barriers to trade 14, 16, 215–31
impact on imposing countries 217–22
impact on other countries 222–5
and non-frontier measures 216–17
see also GATT
Fudenberg, D. and Tirole, J. 133

GATT
development of 226–8
dispute settlement 213
extension of 209–12
and frontier barriers 221, 230
and industrial policy 79, 80–1
proposed changes 41, 204–09, 213–14
reform of 204–14
Safeguards Code 22, 25, 36–8, 228
and trade policy 23, 25n., 204, 225–6
Generalized System of Preferences (GSP) 205
Gomez-Ibanez, Jose A. *et al.* 113
goods, intermediate 162, 168, 171, 184, 185–6, 188
Gorman Polar Form 147n.
Grossman, Gene M.and Eaton, Jonathan 78n.
Group of Thirty 3

Harris, Richard 218
Harrod, Roy 2
Heckscher-Ohlin model 6, 11, 13, 18n., 25n., 65
and factor mobility 103–5
and trade flows 143, 145–6, 148, 151, 158
Helpman, Elhanen 143n., 144n., 145n.
Helpman, Elhanen and Krugman, Paul R. 99
Herander, Mark G. and Thomas, Christopher R. 100
Hirsch, Eva and Hirsch, Abraham 176n.
Hong, Wontack 145n., 192
Hosios, A. J. 5–6, 14
Houseman, Susan N. 76n., 77
Hufbauer, Gary Clyde and Rosen, Howard F. 36n.

immigration policies 99, 100–01, 103–05, 110
see also labor: mobility imports
automobile 114–15, 123
costs/benefits of 23
and economic development 180–1, 182–6, 188–9, 192–3, 198, 201
of final goods 167, 170
and government intervention 77, 79
home, fixed volume 44–5, 47–8, 226
increase in 154–5, 157
licences 36, 184
monopoly 73, 223
non-tariff barriers 204, 208, 216, 221–4, 226
prices 43, 45–9
certain 25–8, 31–3
uncertain 28–31
as protection constraint 16n., 23, 42–3, 72, 137, 205
raw materials 162, 169, 171
substitution 168, 174, 183, 186–8, 190, 218
taxes 45–50, 216, 221
see also quotas; safeguards; tariffs
income
changes in 11–14, 22, 154, 167
in developing economies 198, 200
diversification of sources 14
national 74–5, 167
redistribution 22, 27–8, 29–31, 58, 62–3
on foreign exporting countries 35, 37
in trade models 144–5, 146–7, 149–50
and trade volumes 150–9
see also prices; utility function, indirect; wage level
industrialization: and economic development 184, 187–8, 193, 201
resource-based 168, 171
industry, high technology 73, 207
effects of protection on 128–41
tariff protection 71
see also competition
industry, high-wage/high-skill 70, 78
industry, infant 15, 16, 72, 172, 174, 207

industry, policies for 68-84
  definition 69
  and indicative planning 76
  and international relations 78-82
  political economy of 76-8
  and public choice 68
  and trade policy 69-70, 71-5
  see also competition: international; knowledge, industrial
inflation
  Korea 176, 182-3, 185, 186-7, 189, 192-3, 200
  Turkey 175, 176, 184, 187-9, 191, 192, 200
information, failure of 15, 75, 76
interest groups: and industrial policy 77
  and trade policy 222
interest rates, Korea 183, 186, 189, 193, 198, 200
International Monetary Fund (IMF), and Turkish economic reforms 185, 187
intervention, government 10, 14, 215
  automobile industry 114-15
  and industrial policy 73, 74-6, 77-8, 79
  justifications 8, 217
  optimal *see* second-best, theory of
  and shadow prices 54, 57-8, 62-3
  and structural adjustment 15
  and trade policy 22-3, 112-13, 204, 218-22, 229-30
investment, national Korea 184, 193, 199
investment, private
  bundled mobility 99-100
  foreign 189, 210
  and government intervention 76, 81
  in industrial knowledge 70-1, 72
  and oligopoly competition 74
  trade related, and GATT 209, 211-12

Jackson, John H. 22n.
Japan
  access to markets in 128, 206
  exports 41, 47
  and GATT 227
  and oligopoly competition 75n., 113-15, 116-17, 119-25
  relations with Korea 174-5, 177, 180-1
'Japanese model' 219
JBH model 5-7, 8-9
  Long Run version 11, 12, 13, 18
  Short Run version 11-12, 13
  Very Short Run Version 14
Johnson, Harry G. 2, 8, 16n., 32, 69, 74
Jones, R. W. 4-5, 13, 18-19, 25n., 86n., 94n.
Jones, R. W. and Easton, S. T. 88n.
Jones, R. W.; Neary, J. Peter and Ruane, Frances P. 94n.
Jones, R. W. and Scheinkman, J. A. 4, 11-12, 13

Katz, Abraham 119-20
Kemp, M. C. and Ohyama, M. 162n.
Khang, C. 5
Kierzkowski, Henryk 143n., 144n.
Kim, Kwang-suk and Park, Joon-Kyung 197n.
Kim, Kwang-suk and Roemer, Michael 197n.
knowledge, industrial 16, 70-3, 74, 81, 218
Korea
  economic policies 182-4, 186-7, 189-200
  economic reforms 182-3, 184-5, 186-7, 189-91, 193, 200-02
  economic structure 179-82, 194-6
  historical background 174-6
  political background 177, 178-9, 182
  trade policies 173-4, 200, 201-02
  see also balance of payments; deficits budget; exchange rate; inflation; interest rates; investment, national; Japan; shipbuilding industry; textile industry
Korum, Vgur 197n.
Krishna, Kala 113
Krugman, Paul, R. 72, 129, 137, 143n., 144, 145n., 151n.

labor
  costs 126
  inflow 1, 210
  input 163-5
  mobility 14, 75-6, 86-9, 91, 210
    reverse bundled 99-100
  shadow price 65-6, *see also* factor price
  social opportunity cost 75
  as substitutable for capital 75, 92-3, 95, 96, 146, 148
  as substitutable for resources 89-91, 92-3, 95, 96-7
  supply 91, 93, 96, 163
  see also demand; factor mobility
Lancaster, Kelvin 2, 143n., 144
learning-by-doing 72-3, 81, 128, 132-5

Leidy, Michael 31n.
Lewis, Bernard 174n.
Lieberman, Marvin B. 72
Linder, Staffan B. 151, 159
Lipsey, Richard 2
Little, Ian M. D. and Mirrlees, James A. 54
Little, Ian M. D.; Scitovsky, Tibor and Scott, Maurice 217
Lizondo, Jose Saul 44n.
local content requirement, *see* domestic content control
London School of Economics 1–2
Lucas, Robert 113

McCulloch, Rachel and Johnson, Harry G. 43n.
McFetridge, Donald 77n.
McKenzie, Lionel 162
Magee, Stephen P. 25
market
  disruption, and protection policy 10, 15, 32, 112, 123, 218–20,
    and VERs 41 & n.
  entry to 134, 135–9, 144
  and industrial knowledge 70, 72
  and international oligopoly 73–5
  and reallocation of resources 75–6
  segmentation 132, 138
  see also access, market
Marshall Plan 176, 184
Mason, Edward S. *et al.* 178–9
Mayer, Wolfgang 25n., 144n.
Meade, James E. 41n., 44
Menderes, Adnan 177, 185, 187
Metzler output paradox 50n.
Metzler paradox 46, 50n.
middle class, and industrial policy 78
migration policies 1, 100–01, 105–08
military expenditure, developing countries 181, 182
monopoly 81, 118, 122, 124–5
  exports 73
  imports 73, 223
  subsidies to 115
  and trade barriers 218–19, 223
most-favoured nation (MFN) tariff 37, 114, 116, 122–4, 126
  conditional 205–06
  unconditional 204, 206, 226
  see also tariffs
Motzkin's theorem 61, 63
Multifiber Arrangement (MFA) 50–1, 209, 224–5, 227
Mundell, Robert 2
Mundheim, Robert H. and Ehrenhaft, Peter D. 228n.
Mussa, Michael 15, 25n., 37, 75n.

'natural friend/natural enemy' theory 11–14
Neary, J. Peter 15, 75, 86n.
Neary, J. Peter and Ruane, Frances P. 54
Neary, J. Peter and van Wijnbergen, S. 86n.
Neu, C. Richard 211
Nogues, Julio J.; Olechowski, Andrzej and Winters, L. Alan 204, 228

objectives, non-economic
  protection policies 8, 9–11, 15, 16n.
  and shadow prices 58
oil price, effect of increase in 191–4, 200
oligopoly, international 73–5, 80–1
  in high-technology industries 139
  tariffs and subsidies under 112–26
OPEC 225
'open-loop' analysis 133–4, 140
output
  and economic development 176, 187, 195–6
  of finished goods 162, 163–4, 166–8, 171
  insufficient 72
  and market forces 69
  as policy variable 10–11, 74
  and production costs 131
  protection 16, 79
  in resource boom 89, 91–4, 96
  and trade restriction 139, 219–20
Ozal, Turgut 178, 193

Park Chung Hee 178–9, 185, 189, 193
patent grant and industrial knowledge 70–1, 81–2
Pelcovits, Michael D. 43n.
Point Four Program 176, 184
Postan, M. M. 168–9
Power, Eileen 162, 168–9
preference
  consumer 146–7, 149–50
  electoral 77–8
premium-seeking 50–1
price
  autarky 133, 148–9
  booms 87
  commodity, and income 11–14
  control 184

distortions 8–9, 15–16, 69
and effects of protection 138, 139–140
factor, equalization 101–8, 110, 145, 151–2
fixing 115
resource, changes in 86, 88–9, 92
rigidity 15–16, 219–20
world 54–5, 58–61, 63, 225,
uncertainty over 29–30, 31–4
see also factor price, shadow; imports; prices; inflation; raw materials
price, shadow 79, 118
determination of 63, 133–4
see also factor price, shadow
product, marginal, of factors of production 219
of labor 90–1, 97, 164, 166, 168
of land 167
of raw materials 164, 166
product differentiation 143–4, 150–3, 158–9
horizontal 144, 158
vertical 144–8, 158–9
product homogeneity 35, 145, 146, 148–9, 152–3
production
costs 118–21, 130–4, 137, 144, 149
diversification 59
expansion 69, 198
location 102, 158–9
see also subsidy
production, factors, ownership of 64, 151
production, public sector
shadow prices 64, 65–6
social costs 54–6, 58, 61–3, 66
profit
of foreign firms 112, 122–4
in high-technology industries 131, 136–9
maximization 164
shifting 74–5, 112
of US firms 119
'profit-seeking, directly unproductive' (DUP), theory of 42, 47
property, intellectual, protection of 204, 209, 212
protection policy 4–19, 37, 70, 162
as assignment problem 4, 7–8, 15
contingent 228
costs of 16, 113, 217–19, 228
demand for 4–5, 113
in developing economies 183–4, 185–90, 200–01
effectiveness of 4, 162–3, 168–9, 171, 172–3
effects of 128–9, 138–40
of home market 129, 136–7, 139–40
ineffectiveness 15–16, 172
JBH model 5–7, 8–9, 11–14
justification 4, 8
'made-to-measure' 228
non-economic objectives 8, 9–11, 15, 16n.
rules 4
sectoral 221
temporary 23, 24, 37–8, 207–08, 216
'true enemies' 12–13, 14
'true friends' 12–13, 14, 18
see also quotas; retaliation; tariffs

quotas 113
and developing economies 185–6
externally allocated 25, 28, 30, 32–3, 35, 36–8
on first- and second-period trade 10
as globally marketable 37, 38
internally allocated 27–8, 30, 32, 34
preference over tariff 22, 24
and trade barriers 223

Ramaswami, V. K., Johnson, Harry G. and Corden, W. Max 217
rational expectations theory 75, 78n.
raw materials 162, 163–71
in developing economies 184, 185–6, 188
price 165–7, 168–71
see also wool trade
Reagan, Ronald 228–9
re-industrialization, as protection policy 8, 11
rent-seeking 81
and trade barriers 218
universal opposition to 13–14
universal incentive for 11, 13–14, 15
rents
restriction-included 41 & n.
shifting of 75, 137, 140
resource, *see* boom, resource-based; industrialization; resource-based
resources
allocation of 68, 81, 164
failures in 75–6
and frontier barriers 215, 219
immiserizing 75
and industrial knowledge 71, 73
see also prices
retaliation against protection 10, 24, 32, 36, 114
and changes in GATT 205–6
high-technology industries 129, 139–40

revenue, government
  factor prices 60
  and tariffs 123
revenue-seeking 42, 47–50
Rhee, Seungman 178, 183
Ricardo, David 94, 143, 145n., 146, 148, 155
Rodriguez, Carlos Alfredo 41
Rodrik, Dani 100
Roemer, M. 171
Ruffin, R. and Jones, R. W. 13n.
Rybczynski, Ted 2, 64
Rybczynski line 48–50

safeguards
  for foreign residents 35–7
  against import damage 22, 23–5, 28, 31n., 36
  see also GATT: Safeguards Code
Sampson, Gary P. 228n.
Sampson, Gary P. and Snape, Richard H. 209–10
Samuelson, Paul A. 29, 86n.
  on factor mobility 103–5
Sanyal, K. and Jones R. W. 162n.
savings, domestic, in developing economies 198–9, 200
scale, economies of
  and trade barriers 218, 223
  trade flows 144, 151, 158
second-best, theory of 15–16, 69–70, 73, 75–6, 79
sensitivity analysis 114, 124–5
services, trade in
  and frontier barriers 217
  and GATT 204, 209–11
Shaked, Avner and Sutton, John 144n.
shipbuilding industry 221
  Korea 193
Smith, Adam 219
Smith, Alasdair 54
specific factor models 4–11, 15, 25, 101–02
  international capital mobility 91–3
  nationally trapped capital 87–91
  and resource boom 86–7, 94–5
  and vertical product differentiation 146–8
Spence, A. M. 131, 133
Spencer, Barbara J. and Brander, James A. 76n.
Srinivasan, T. N. and Bhagwati, Jagdish N. 54–5, 60, 62
Stackelberg model 74
standard optimum tariff thesis 112
State Economic Enterprises (SEEs)
  Turkey 174, 184–5, 187, 193
steel industry 16, 221
Stolper, W. and Samuelson, P. A. 11–12, 25n., 168
Stone-Geary function 147
subsidy 9–10, 15–16, 69, 79, 207
  to capital 15
  Code 227
  costs of 223
  employment 216
  and GATT 207–08, 210, 227
  import 46
  and industrial knowledge 71, 72, 73
  and monopoly imports 73
  and oligopoly industries 74, 75n., 112, 115, 122–6
  to production 79, 116, 117, 123–4, 216, 221–5, 230
  and resource boom 95
  and shadow prices 57–8, 62
  see also exports; protection policies
supply
  modelling 144–5, 151
  of raw materials 166–7, 170
surcharge on imports 183, 185

Takacs, Wendy E. 41
Tan, A. H. H. 9
Tarr, David G. and Morkre, Morris E. 120
Tariff Act 1930 208
tariffs 24
  distribution of proceeds 10n., 27–8, 29–30
  and domestic production 69, 72, 73–4, 79
  and economic development 172–4, 183–4, 189
  and frontier barriers 221
  and high-technology industries 71–2, 73, 138
  and immiserizing imports 64
  and monopoly industries 73, 75
  and oligopoly 113–17, 122–6
  as optimal policy 16n., 27–8, 32–4, 169
  and political economy 76, 77
  ad valorem 30, 42, 122
  see also most-favoured-nation tariff; quota; standard optimum tariff; terms-of-trade argument
taxation
  on consumption 216
  on factor mobility 99

and income redistribution 27, 58
industrial policy 62, 71, 75n., 79, 112
reduction 81-1
and resource boom 95
as subsidy 15-16, 57-8, 186, 189, 221
see also exports; imports
technology
change in, and trade 22-3
and intermediate goods 164, 166-7
international differences in 105-06, 108
in trade flows 145-6, 148-9, 151-3, 156-9
see also industry: high-technology
terms-of-trade argument 15, 16, 69-70, 217, 222-5
see also tariffs
textile industry 16, 204, 221, 227
Korea 175
Turkey 174
see also Multifiber Arrangement; wool trade
Toder, Eric J. 119-20
trade
barriers, non-tariff 69n., 215-31
and economic development 172-3, 183-6, 189, 191-2, 200-2, 209, 211-12, 217, 227
and high-technology industries 22-3, 128-9
and industry structure 218-19, 222
international, and resource boom 93-4, 95
and labor market policy 220
policies 68-70, 114, 117-18, 122, 124-6, 173
restriction 10, 27, 42-3, 75-6, 173, 204
see also quota; tariffs
see also Conservative Social Welfare Function; free trade; trade flows; volume, trade
trade, 'fair' 204, 206-09, 215, 228-30
trade, free
areas 205
and bundled factor mobility 101-03
and Conservative Social Welfare Function 27, 29, 31-4
and economic development 172
and frontier barriers 216-19
and high-technology industries 129, 135-40
industrial policy 78n.
trade, free
and oligopoly industries 117, 139
and Pareto efficiency 8
and trade volumes 151, 171
trade flows
inter-industry 143, 151, 152, 155-8
intra-industry 143-8, 15 2, 155-9
trade unions, and developing economies 198
trade war, *see* retaliation
transportation, costs of 132, 135, 138-9, 145n., 152n.
Tumlir, Jan 219
Turkey
economic policies 182, 184-200
economic reforms 182, 185-6, 187-8, 190-2, 194, 198, 200-02
economic structure 179-82, 194-8
historical background 174-6
political background 177-8, 182, 192
see also balance of payments; clothing industry; deficits, budgets; endowment, effective; exchange rate; footwear industry; inflation; International Monetary Fund; State Economic Enterprises; textile industry

unemployment
benefits 24
Harris-Todaro model 64-5
international levels 82
and shadow prices 64-6
and trade barriers 220
United States
automobile industry 112-26
and GATT 23, 205-7, 209, 212, 214, 226-7, 228-9
high-technology industries 128
import safeguards 37
and industrial knowledge 72
industrial policy 77, 79
market access 205, 206-7, 228-9
and overseas development 175-6, 177, 181, 182, 183n., 184-5, 187, 189, 200
utility function, indirect 12-13

Vandendorpe, A. L. 9, 16n.
Venables, A. 138
volume, trade 143-58
and relative incomes 150-8

wage level
and bundled factor mobility 108-09
and developing economies 193, 196-8
and final output levels 168, 171
inflexibility 75
in resource boom 88-93, 95, 97
and shadow price 66

wage level *(continued)*
and trade barriers 220
and trade volumes 149, 157
see also income
welfare
and bundled factor mobility 109–10
consumer 25, 58, 60–2, 66, 137–40, 144, 146, 149–50
foreign 42–7, 49–50, 138
global 68, 70–3, 75, 79–80, 139
national 47–9, 68, 71–5, 76, 80, 116–17, 123–6, 140–1, 169–70
see also Conservative Social Welfare Function
Wolff, Alan W. 25n., 36n., 205
wool trade, British medieval 162–3, 168–71
World Intellectual Property Organization 212

Yeutter, Clayton 229
Young, Leslie and Anderson, James E. 24

M. Davies